Also by Marcus Luttrell

LONE SURVIVOR

"Every bit as thrilling as *Black Hawk Down* and, unexpectedly, quite moving."
—Edward Nawotka, *Dallas Morning News*

"One of the most gripping and heartbreaking descriptions of heroism in combat to come out of the wars in Afghanistan and Iraq.... An astonishing survival tale."
—Fritz Lanham, *Houston Chronicle*

"In the face of huge odds, in a foreign land, a Navy SEAL survived to tell his story. It's inspirational, dynamic, and we should all feel proud to be a part of his team. Thank goodness America's Marcus Luttrells are always out there." —David Scott, Commander, *Apollo 15*

"A true story that showcases both American heroism and Afghani humanity."
—Dennis Drabelle, *Washington Post Book World*

SERVICE

A Navy SEAL at War

MARCUS LUTTRELL

WITH JAMES D. HORNFISCHER

LITTLE, BROWN AND COMPANY
NEW YORK   BOSTON   LONDON

Little, Brown and Company
Hachette Book Group
237 Park Avenue
New York, NY 10017
littlebrown.com

The publisher is not responsible for websites (or their content) that are not owned by the publisher.

Printed in the United States of America

Originally published in hardcover by Little, Brown and Company, May 2012
First Back Bay Books trade paperback edition, May 2013
First Little, Brown and Company mass market edition, May 2014

Map by Jeffrey L. Ward

10 9 8 7 6 5 4 3 2 1

I dedicate this book to my brother, for walking through hell with me, and to my wife, for pulling me out of the shadows.

FTWTTT.

Contents

The true soldier fights not because he hates what is in front of him, but because he loves what is behind him.

—G. K. CHESTERTON

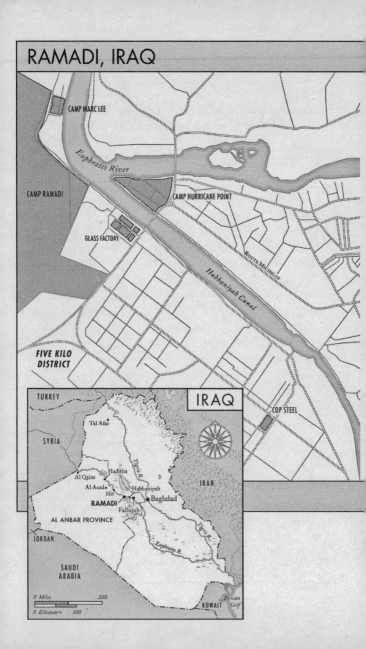

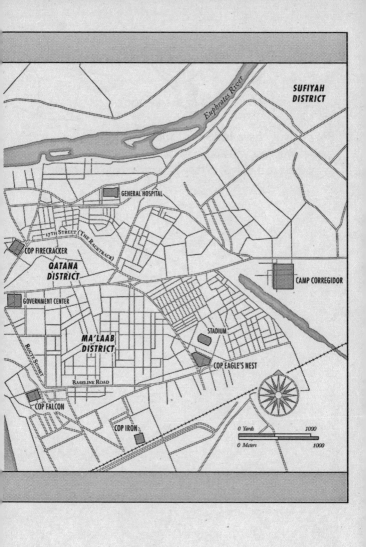

SUFIYAH DISTRICT

Euphrates River

GENERAL HOSPITAL

17TH STREET (THE RACETRACK)

COP FIRECRACKER

QATANA DISTRICT

CAMP CORREGIDOR

GOVERNMENT CENTER

STADIUM

MA'LAAB DISTRICT

COP EAGLE'S NEST

ROUTE SYDNEY

Baseline Road

COP FALCON

COP IRON

0 Yards   1000

0 Meters   1000

A Note to the Reader

Pseudonyms have been used for special operations personnel who are still active. Retired operators are referred to by their real names if they have given their consent.

Preface

I've written this book to honor the skill, courage, and sacrifice of the exceptional people I know who serve not only in the SEAL teams but in all the other service branches who I've served with along the way. Really this is a book for all who serve. It's for anyone who wears the uniform; who, when the shooting starts, move toward the gunfire instead of away from it. It's for a brave breed of individuals, the warfighters, who put everything on the line because it is expected of them, because they stand up for the United States and sometimes die for the privilege.

There are a lot of things in life that matter. But nothing matters as much as who or what you decide to serve.

The people I write about in this book devoted themselves to something larger than themselves. Driven by a fire that burns within them to defend their brothers, their sisters, their neighbors, and their nation, they volunteered to stand in a dangerous place in the world and offer themselves as expendable.

In my years in uniform, I was one of the lucky ones. My pride in serving in the SEAL teams has enabled me to look at myself in the mirror every morning, after everything that's happened.

I decided to write *Service* when I thought about all the selfless, brave souls I knew whose work "downrange" crossed paths with mine. In these pages, you'll get a glimpse of our elite special operations warriors who occasionally make headlines but strongly prefer to remain anonymous, quiet professionals. And you'll hear about warriors from other branches of the military whose service means something to me. By the end of the book, you'll see that we all share at least one trait in common: an ability to get back up and keep pushing forward, through war, through pain, and back into civilian life, where our service to our families and our communities is just as important as anything we did in uniform.

I was one of those quiet professionals. It was my fate to come out of the shadows. I wrote *Lone Survivor* to honor three of my brothers who went into battle with me one afternoon in Kunar Province, Afghanistan, and didn't come home, and sixteen of America's best who died on a helicopter, flying into hell to save us. Since then, sadly, that mission can no longer lay claim to being the darkest day in the history of the special operations world. The bad days keep coming. On August 6, 2011, we lost thirty of our most elite. None of us will ever forget our losses.

On the afternoon on June 28, 2005, I awoke to find myself alone, hidden in a crevice near the peak of the mountain known as Sawtalo Sar, after three of my teammates had been killed in action and the helicopter carrying the rescue team, unbeknownst to me, had been lost in action as well. I lost a little bit of myself out there. In failing in a task, in meeting a serious setback or a defeat on a mission or in our careers, we come out the other side changed. If we don't, we've failed again. But long before that doomed operation, I had learned that part of my strength came from never letting a single experience in my life define me. I believe that there is a reason for everything. The situations I've found myself in are stepping-stones on a path to a larger and unknowable destination. I now have a wife and a son, so many glorious blessings. But this remains the same: after every step, even the missed ones, I'll pack up, push through, and soldier on. I can only hope to do this because I have a family who loves me. Some are family by blood. Others are family *in* blood, men who won the honor of wearing the Trident, and who as teammates proved the truth of the saying, "The only easy day was yesterday." Many members of my family live, breathe, and work in dangerous, undisclosed locations all around the world. Some of them are no longer with us, having paid the ultimate price while doing their work, and in death still stand watch over us. They pledged themselves to that job and gave their last full measure to fulfill the pledge. Our family stays together not by training, courage, or skill but by the forces that bind us: love, honor, commitment, and loyalty.

This book is a salute to everyone who's worn Old Glory on his shoulder, carried a rifle for this nation, and guarded the front line or been deployed behind it, into the enemy's backyard—whether in today's wars or in others. Too many heroes never get the recognition they deserve from the public. I am proud to be able to share a few of their stories from my own perspective. Since I wrote *Lone Survivor,* my personal story has become very public and I have felt strongly ever since that many others out there deserve to have their own service recognized. Service in wartime pushed them to the limit. They gave their all—and got something back that no one else can claim:

collectively, they form a single thread woven into the fabric of this country's history, part of something larger than themselves. There are other things in life that matter. But to me, nothing matters as much.

—February 2012

SERVICE

Prologue

Brotherhood

October 2009
Pensacola, Florida

It was about four in the morning when my cell phone started buzzing. I sat up, grabbed it off the nightstand, and looked at the display. The caller was one of my closest teammates, JT.

At that hour, I knew what the score was. Sliding my finger over the glass to answer the ring, I asked him, "What's wrong with my brother?"

It had to be about Morgan, and it was.

"He's stable, bro, but he's really jacked up."

My body went weak as I replied, "I'm on my way." As I hung up, my stomach lurched. I ran to the bathroom and started throwing up.

JT was calling from the Naval Medical Center in Portsmouth, Virginia. That night, twenty-three miles off Virginia Beach, my brother and his platoon were on a training op. The skies were clear and the seas were rolling easily when their Black Hawk helicopter approached a U.S. ship. The helo descended from her port side and entered a hover over the upper superstructure. As the pilot eased closer to the ship, USNS *Arctic,* the crew let out the ropes. As they dropped to the deck—basically a limp fireman's pole running from the bird to the deck—Morgan and his squad sat at the ready, legs dangling down from the open right-side door.

With America's effort to stop international piracy ramping up, search-and-seizure exercises like this one were a regular part of the training schedule. Six months earlier, after pirates took over the containership *Maersk Alabama,* one of our sniper teams set up on the fantail of a U.S. warship and killed the trio of criminals who were holding the American captain hostage.

But as my brother and his teammates were preparing to fast-rope down to the *Arctic,* their aircraft's main rotor clipped a heavy guyline supporting one of the ship's huge exhaust stacks. The blades gathered in the thick cable, reeling it in around the shaft. As the Black Hawk jerked downward, the guys perched in the door were thrown back into the crew compartment. They tumbled across the deck of the helo and piled into the left side of the fuselage. Then the helicopter crashed into the ship, steel on heavier steel, and rocked over onto its side.

Morgan was knocked dizzy by the impact, but cleared his head in time to see flames rushing at him as if they were shot from a giant flamethrower. Blinded by the smoke and with a fractured back, he struggled away from the inferno. Crawling out of the wreckage, he fell about fifteen feet down to the next deck of the ship. The impact was shattering, and it knocked him out cold.

As shipboard firefighters went to work, a hazmat crew was called out and all hands took care of the wounded. When they finished triage, they found that one man, the

Black Hawk's crew chief, had been killed, and eight more, including Morgan, badly injured. Quickly, another helo landed on the ship, took the casualties aboard, and flew them to the hospital in Portsmouth. From there, the news traveled fast.

When JT called me, I was in Florida doing physical rehabilitation following back surgery. After my last two combat deployments, my spine was a constant project for the docs, but nothing was going to keep me from flying to Portsmouth to see my brother. Morgan and I always drop whatever we're doing to cover each other's backs—and "always" means *always*. I called a generous friend who had a private plane and prevailed upon him to help me. As he routed the plane to the Pensacola airport to pick me up, I packed a three-day bag, jumped into my rental car, and sped to the general aviation hangar. Within a few short hours the Gulf of Mexico was disappearing behind us.

The flight north seemed to take forever, and the nearer we got to the Norfolk airport, near Portsmouth, the slower time seemed to move. I reached the hospital to learn that Morgan was in the MRI lab waiting on a scan. When the elevator doors opened, he lifted his head and cut his eyes in my direction, and I sprinted as fast as I could to him. He was strapped down to a gurney, suffering from a bad case of the hiccups. Each one of those little spasms in his diaphragm whipped through his busted-up core and racked him with pain. Our eyes locked, and the sight of him lying there injured brought a wash of acid into my throat. My stomach flipped again, but there was nothing down there left to throw up.

"Hey, *mijo*," he said, using his nickname for me—meaning "baby boy" in Spanish. The sound of his voice brought me back to reality. I took Morgan by the hand, gave him a careful hug, and said, "I'm here, bro. We'll get through this."

The hospital tech, hunched over his computer, was busy with something and didn't seem to notice what was going on. Apparently, the MRI couldn't be performed while the patient was convulsing with hiccups, but nothing was being done about the situation. I lit into the tech forcefully about focusing on what should have mattered most: "Get your lazy ass away from that computer and get my brother some help before I jerk your arms off and beat you half to death with them!" That promptly got Morgan medicated, and when the contractions finally stopped, the techs slid him into the tube.

Seeing my brother laid up and helpless in traction tore my guts out. He's one of the toughest men I've ever known. He isn't just pain-tolerant or pain-resistant—he's pain-*defiant*. When he snapped an ankle in college and didn't have the money for treatment, he just hopped around on that busted hoof for weeks because he had to go to class and keep working. During his career he's broken plenty of bones and had plenty of bloody scrapes, but those were nothing like this: the MRI showed that his back was fractured in six places, and that his pelvis was broken, too.

In the waiting room, I linked up with JT and another close teammate of ours, Boss. During the five days Morgan was in the hospital, the three of us set up a cot in his room and didn't leave him for a minute. We kept a rotating watch, twenty-four hours a day. Morgan doesn't take painkillers unless the pain prevents him from sleeping or otherwise gets in the way of his healing, so we did our best to keep him diverted. We made sure he had visitors when he wanted them. We brought in a DVD player and reading material and tried to keep things lively and upbeat. Most important, we let him rest.

When he had to relieve himself, we ran the nurses out and did the work ourselves. One of us took his head, the other his feet, and the third one took his midsection, and we rolled him over nice and easy and let him do his business. With all those meds and liquids flowing into him through that IV, it was usually a mess. (I remember it being like a scene from *The Exorcist,* but out of the other end.) You could always tell who the lowest-ranking guy in the room was, because he had cleanup. Whatever he needed, we helped the best we could. That's what brothers do.

But you can't keep Morgan down for long. When his appetite returned, we knew he was on his way. And when JT started hitting on the nurses, I knew we had turned another corner; it was clear that Morgan's situation had settled down enough to let us start thinking about ourselves a little again. That was when we started laying the tough love on him.

"Your back's broken—welcome to *my* world, bro. But what took you so long to get here?"

"You're not feeling sorry for yourself, are you?"

"If you man up, you know this'll be over soon."

"If you don't get it done, your team's going downrange without you."

That last one burned him most.

When the docs came in, we asked them if they could relocate the big scar on his forehead down to about mid-cheek, because most chicks dig scars.

Once in a while we gave it a rest long enough to give him a sponge bath, but mostly we made sure he knew that his team would expect him back as soon as surgery and rehab were done. Just for posterity's sake, we took some hilarious photos of him whacked out and lying in his own misery. We figured the day would come when we'd need to whip out those pictures just to keep him humble.

After a surgical procedure and several more days of hospital life, Morgan finally said, "Bro, I've got to get the hell out of here." This wasn't because he'd tired of our unofficial treatment program—he'd simply reached the point where he had to escape from captivity. That was when we drew up the evac plan.

It was quick and dirty, and with an operator like JT on point, we thought it just might work. Come nighttime, JT went down the hall and started hitting on one of the nurses. When we heard the laughter start, Boss took advantage of the diversion to throw on some borrowed lab coats, heave Morgan into his wheelchair, and roll him right out of his room. It was as simple as a walk to the elevators. Against medical advice, we wheeled him out the door and carried him to freedom. Operation Homebound was a success.

After the dust settled from all that, Morgan ended up with me in Pensacola, right back where I was when JT called me with the news. He joined me at a state-of-the-art facility, Athletes' Performance, that has a special rehab program for getting guys like us back to speed. Believe me, after working out there for a while, I knew what it would take for Morgan to get healed up again. But I also knew he would do whatever it took. Quitting is impossible when a brotherhood like ours circles up around you and focuses on getting you right again. They'd done it for me after I came home from Operation Redwing in July of 2005. Now it was Morgan's turn.

Serving in uniform during wartime, you find that the urgency of the situations you're in makes your relationships with your brothers tight, permanent, and unlike any others in your life. Relationships with those outside your closest fraternity seem fleeting, temporary, and disposable. But all of us are brothers. That's something I realize every time I run into a combat veteran in civilian life.

There aren't many degrees of separation between any of the 2.4 million men and women who've served in Iraq or Afghanistan. We've smelled the shitty air in Iraq and felt our lungs burn in the Hindu Kush. We've squeezed ourselves into Humvees and Black Hawks and been shot at. We've been stuck in slowly moving convoys, more than a little worried about what the next bump in the road will trigger. I think of the soldiers and U.S. Marines we fought side by side with, the point men and breachers, the bomb techs, the JTACs, intel guys, pilots and other augmentees, the doctors and medics, support platoons, and all the others. More than anyone else, of course, I think of my teammates. Many of them are still in the teams today, still writing their stories, visiting hell upon America's enemies. Just thinking of them takes me back to the good ol' days. I know I wouldn't be here without them.

The only way out of hell is to walk right through it. When you do, it always helps to have your brothers by your side.

Part I

How We Fight

1

One More Round

In any team environment, and especially in a group of highly driven people dedicated to a difficult mission, you'll always find smaller crews that stick together tightly and lean on each other, no matter how hard things may get. That's the way it's always been with the men who are the core of my world. Naval Amphibious Base Coronado, the home of our odd-numbered SEAL teams, is right on the beach, just steps away from the Pacific's swells. At Coronado, where SEALs are born, we were drawn together by a force that was part personality and part sensibility. We snapped together like magnets.

JT is one of them. He's an Iowa kid, tough as a cornstalk, and stands about six foot four, as fit and strong as God meant any man to be. He's a champion triathlete, not to mention one of the finest enlisted warriors in the SEAL community. Reckless with his wit and shockingly effective in any kind of fight, he's the kind of guy you're glad to have on your side, whether on deployment to a combat zone or in a small-town bar when there's some stupid trouble brewing. With his big personality, he's our point man in most situations. Outgoing and upbeat, he's always ready for whatever his impulsive hilarity may bring us. He's been that way forever.

Boss is an integral part of the circle, too. Originally from Arizona, he was in my boat crew in BUD/S, the training course where frogs are born, and until he finally proposed to his bride-to-be, he was JT's roommate as well. A loyal friend and teammate, he and JT developed a bond so strong that JT joked to Amy, then Boss's fiancée, that their wedding wouldn't go through until the two SEALs were officially divorced. Boss is a true free spirit. His spirit is so free that I can imagine it flying all the way back to ancient Greece and inhabiting the body of a Spartan hoplite surrounded at Thermopylae. A master parachutist and hell on wheels in a gunfight, he was born in the wrong century, I sometimes think.

Josh, six foot six and all power and smarts, is one of us, too. After finishing at the Naval Academy, the redneck from Louisiana went on to BUD/S. Graduating with Class 232, right between Morgan and me, he served in several platoons before taking a break to pick up a graduate degree from Columbia University. After that, he returned to the fold and ran with our best. There's something kinetic about the dynamic between us, and there's no one other than my twin brother, Morgan, who I'd rather have watching my back.

JJ, one of relatively few African Americans in the SEAL teams, hails from Oklahoma but calls Texas home now. He started his career with my original unit, SEAL Delivery Vehicle Team 1 (SDVT-1), the ultimate deepwater frogmen. His call sign was Underwater Brother, and he's one bad mofo. A solid operator and a hellacious gunfighter, he's been at my side through nearly my entire career. I've come close to losing my life more than once. I'm still here only because of things JJ has done.

Then there's Morgan, my twin brother—seven minutes my senior. He and I are simply inseparable. When I lay wounded on that mountain, with media reports suggesting I was dead, Morgan knew otherwise just from the feeling that filled his heart. He walked among the crowd of friends and strangers that had gathered at our family's ranch outside Huntsville, Texas, assuring one and all in no uncertain terms that I was alive. He kept saying, "If they haven't found his body yet, then he is *not* dead." He just seemed to know. It was a twin thing. We often say we'll be together "from the womb to the tomb"—FTWTTT for short.

The SEAL community is one big circle, but these men are the core of my world. When I came home from Operation Redwing, all I really needed to get right again was to spend time in their presence. We've bled together, sweated together, and shed tears together. We've shared the same quarters and run through the same cycles of training and deployment. No matter what direction I might have been facing, I knew one of these guys always had my back. The longer we knew each other, the more we were aware of the fact that hung heavily in the air every time we got together: this day together might be our last. So we lived our lives as such.

It was never good form to say it too often, but Morgan and I spent every day of our lives up to that point sure that we would never reach age forty. Something, somewhere, was bound to happen. We'd flame out in a blaze of glory, uncelebrated except within the brotherhood.

I had nearly done that, over in Afghanistan. I was lucky to have made it home alive. Still, in a heartbeat, I would have traded my homecoming for the chance to bring any one of the teammates we lost that day home to his family.

On June 27, 2005, near a mountain peak in the Hindu Kush, almost two miles above sea level, our four-man recon team had gone out on a mission to kill or capture a senior Taliban leader. The next day we were compromised when some goatherds came upon us with their flock. We discussed what to do with them—kill them or free them—and mercy won out. Soon after we let them go, they betrayed us to the enemy. In short order, we were fighting a group of heavily armed Taliban insurgents, primed for battle and pissed off by our appearance on top of their rock. Surrounded and outnumbered, we followed our training, moving together and fighting with discipline, retreating (and mostly falling) down a steep cliff face. Ripping off measured bursts from our rifles, we claimed dozens of enemy lives, but the incoming hail of fire was too much for us to handle.

Danny Dietz, our comms guy and a damn good SEAL, was shot many times and ended up dying in my arms. Our officer in charge, Lieutenant Michael Murphy, stepped out of his cover to make a radio call requesting rescue, knowing it would cost him his life. Matt Axelson, our lead sniper, fought like a lion even after being shot in the head. He and I parted company when an RPG flew in and blasted us in different directions. I tried to find Axe—I didn't want to be alone—but he was gone forever.

These men fought with everything they had and then some. They never quit. They will never be forgotten. God bless them.

Early that afternoon, having scrambled into the cover of a rocky crevice, I regained consciousness to find myself nearly buried between the steep slopes. As I tended to my wounds and took refuge from the enemy, who was scouring the hills in search of us, a Chinook helicopter, unbeknownst to me, was inbound to our rescue. Carrying a sixteen-man team, the aircraft met its end when a young Taliban fighter shot an RPG through the open rear ramp as the bird was hovering to land, dropping it to the ground and killing all the men on board.

Laid up in the middle of nowhere, badly wounded, and slowly dying from blood loss, exposure, and dehydration, I called out to God. There came, at last, an unlikely group of saviors: a posse of Pashtun tribesmen—not loyal to the Taliban—who found me and showed me mercy. They took me into their care, fended off my pursuers, led me to their village, and protected me as one of their own.

As it turned out, God heard everything I had to say. He put my life in the hands of a doctor from that tribe, Sarawa, and the village elder's son, Gulab, who guarded and sheltered me for four days until my brothers in arms came for me, as they always do for one of their own.

After all the headlines about the losses we suffered that day—unprecedented at the time—my homecoming was making news of its own. Just before I touched down in San Antonio, JJ took a call from a reporter for a national cable TV news network. Insisting that she be the first to interview me and demanding an exclusive, she told JJ, "The people want this." JJ replied in his easy but firm frogman way, "Just tell the people to say thanks. That's pretty much all the interview you need." She was offering him money as he hung up the phone, and she promptly went on the air anyway, making up a few things for her story.

About thirty minutes later my plane rolled up to the terminal and I was limping down the stairs to the tarmac to rejoin my brothers. In their company, I started my second lease on life. But on the four-hour drive home from the airport, the emotions were still too raw and I wasn't able to talk much. The simple presence of these men was what I needed; just seeing them reminded me how I was supposed to be. I felt an overpowering urge to *get right,* to return to being *like them* again. When my body was ready, I'd be ready to say good-bye to the docs, get back on the horse, rejoin another SEAL team, have a wild laugh with my brothers, and do what every team guy is bred to do: find his way to the closest war.

I'd hardly been home three weeks when Morgan got orders to rejoin SDVT-1 in Hawaii. That's how we always rolled: whenever I'd catch up to him he was ready to head somewhere else—and vice versa. This happened wherever we found each other, from Afghanistan to Texas, Iraq to Hawaii, and everywhere in between.

I followed him a few weeks later, rejoining our team at Pearl Harbor in August. I loved the SDV teams. They're the hardest-working bunch of webfoots in the Navy. But every time I was with them, it felt like there was an empty hole without the guys from Redwing there. SDVT-1* had taken a devastating blow on June 28, 2005. Make no mis-

---

* During Redwing, I and others from SDVT-1 were assigned to serve as extra muscle for Team 10. In the SEAL teams, guys who augment a unit in that way are known as straphangers.

take about it: my lost teammates are still part of me. They reside in my soul. Not a day goes by when I don't think about them and miss them terribly. I just needed to focus on work—but that wasn't always easy.

My twin brother is a great soul and twice the SEAL operator I ever was, no doubt about it. But we're both stronger, more whole, in each other's company. We've fought as a team all our lives—and we grew up fighting, from grade school through college. Bar fights. Martial-arts tournaments. Street fights. We were and always have been a damn good team. Fighting side by side, we're one person. If I go in low, he goes in high.

FTWTTT.

We've leaned on each other in good times and in bad. Dad made sure of that. If we ever came home from a night out and one of us had gotten into a scrape and the other was untouched, that meant trouble for the unscathed one, because Dad knew that one of us hadn't stepped up. The few times Morgan and I got into it between us, Dad would size up the results and whip the winner for beating up his brother, then raise a hand to the other for losing. Having been brought up this way, it was natural for us to put on the uniform and go off to war together. More than ever, when I came home, I wanted it to be like old times in East Texas; I wanted to stand back-to-back with my brother again and take on the world.

So I decided I wouldn't spend another day in the teams without him by my side. With help from higher command, we both received orders to join Team 5—the next team in the hopper to go overseas. Because of the physical therapy required by my injuries, I was delayed getting into the training cycle, but I linked up with Morgan and my new teammates in Team 5 soon enough.

On a beautiful stretch of beach in Coronado known as the Silver Strand, the screams and cries of the BUD/S students fighting to earn their Tridents and the hard cadences of the instructors dealing out hell reminded me what it had cost to become a SEAL. The smell of the mighty Pacific—freezing in December and merely cold as hell every other month—boosted my spirit and filled me with motivation to get back what I had lost.

But climbing up on that horse again—that was going to be tough.

Several of my spinal disks had been fractured and were grinding around like rods in a ruptured crankcase. My shooting hand was busted up so bad that the finest handiwork of the Navy surgeons who had pieced it together with metal bars and transplanted tendons hadn't restored its full range of motion—and it hasn't come back to this day. A strange parasite is still twisting up my guts and won't go away. Nonetheless, I was charging hard with the boys of Team 5.

My favorite book, *The Count of Monte Cristo,* is all about revenge. So is one of my favorite movies, *The Boondock Saints,* the story of two Irish brothers who take on the Russian mob in Boston. (The film has a cult following in the teams.) It's an article of faith in our community: when you get hit, you get up and hit back. SEALs never quit and we never forgive or forget. Ever.

We're going to make them pay for Mikey.

Pay for Danny.

Pay for Axe.

And pay for the sixteen warriors on that helo who flew in to save us that day, all of them in the prime of life, ages twenty-one to forty. There were the SEALs—Lieutenant

Commander Erik S. Kristensen, Jacques J. Fontan, Daniel R. Healy, Jeffrey A. Lucas, Michael M. McGreevy Jr., Shane E. Patton, James E. Suh, and Jeffrey S. Taylor—and the aviators from the Army's 160th Special Operations Aviation Regiment, the Night Stalkers: Shamus O. Goare, Corey J. Goodnature, Kip A. Jacoby, Marcus V. Muralles, James W. Ponder III, Stephen C. Reich, Michael L. Russell, and Chris J. Scherkenbach.

No forgetting, no forgiveness.

Working in the austere, all-business environment of the NSW (Naval Special Warfare) compound at Coronado, Team 5 had a heavy workload in preparing for deployment. When the training cycle was done, we'd be bound for Iraq, the trash can of the Middle East, teetering on the brink not only of civil war but of total existential breakdown. We understood that our mission there would be far larger than the agenda of retribution that I was harboring. But maybe, I thought, by going back to war I could keep the privilege, at least in my own mind, of wearing the Trident on my chest. We have a saying in the teams: "Earn your Trident every day." It's harder to stay a SEAL than it is to become a SEAL.

Morgan always set me straight whenever I had doubts. Knowing my heart and soul, he asked, "Does a firefighter quit after going into a burning house? Does a cowboy stop riding if he gets thrown off a horse? No, he doesn't. And you've got to get back on that horse and ride back into the fire." I think he knew that this was exactly what I needed to hear.

Every team has its own reputation. Team 1, a West Coast outfit, has been called Stalag 1 for its tradition of severe discipline. Team 2, from the East Coast, is known as BUD/S Team 2 for the tough physical training its commanders always insist on. Those two teams have glorious battle histories going back more than fifty years, to the founding days of the teams during Vietnam. Guys in the East Coast teams like to kid West Coast teams that Southern California is easy duty—beach detachments, complete with volleyball nets. But I've found that each team develops its own unique way based on the character of the guys who run things. At Team 5, the incoming skipper, Commander Leonard, put a powerful positive stamp on the way we'd do business.

Morgan and I were immediately impressed with him. A veteran of the teams since 1979, he had come up through the enlisted ranks before taking his commission. The Navy term for an officer who follows that route is "mustang." He had an approachable, blue-collar style. But he understood, too, that it was important for an officer to remain at a distance from the everyday life of his platoons. He was the kind of officer who looked around, saw what needed to happen, and made hard calls that no one could bitch about because of the way he commanded our respect. Hell, Skipper, as we called him, was leading SEAL teams in action all around the world when many of us were still in grade school.

Commander Leonard didn't seem to mind that Morgan and I were together in his squadron—a no-no in the risk-averse, post–*Saving Private Ryan* Navy. I think he realized we had a lot to contribute while together, and that the risk of something happening to one of us would be double if we were apart.

The Skipper's right-hand man was every bit as important and influential—his command master chief. Lean, scrubbed, fit, cool, and smart, Master Chief had a big job as Skipper's senior enlisted adviser. A nineteen-year veteran of the teams at the time, and as skilled as SEAL operators come, he was a hard man who was also known for having a formidable intellect. It was his intelligence, clarity of mind, and smooth but direct way with people, both senior and subordinate, that put him in a class by himself, at least in my eyes. His presence was a constant reminder that brawn without brains is powerless.

Based on his recent experience with another team, Master Chief gave Skipper a breakdown on the situation in western Iraq's insurgent hotbeds. It was a full-on crisis in cities like Ramadi and Habbaniyah. He told him what was working and what wasn't in the struggle to rid the area of Al Qaeda's murder squads. The Skipper and Master Chief steered our training mind-set based on what he'd seen in the Sandbox.

It felt good to get back into the mix with a bunch of running and gunning frogmen. Men like Skipper and Master Chief did me the greatest favor possible: they put me in a platoon as a regular frontline operator and demanded that I be treated as anyone else would be. Sometimes that wasn't easy, and I hated it. Visiting dignitaries often wanted to meet the "lone survivor" of Operation Redwing and have me tell them the story personally. The calls came so frequently to my cell phone that the Skipper and Master Chief finally had to step in and ask people to direct all inquiries through them. They were always deferential and respectful. They heard the requests (usually made by an aide of some kind) and made a polite request in return: "Sir, if your boss can call me directly and tell me that Marcus needs to be pulled out of training for combat in Iraq, that it's okay to interrupt preparations that will help him save lives and affect his platoon's combat effectiveness, if your superior will call me and say that this is more important than the lives of our sailors, then I'll bring Marcus to see him right now. But he does have to call me and tell me that first." That next phone call never came.

The guys never said anything out loud, but I'm sure that all the outside attention affected the platoon as a whole. Once our leadership put the brakes on that, though, things went back to normal: team first, personal issues later. That's what good leaders do for their men—they keep them free of distractions, their front sights zeroed on their most important work.

By the time you become a master chief in the teams, you've gone places far past the back of beyond, and you've gained a whole encyclopedia of secret knowledge from firsthand experience. For instance, having served in the SDV teams, where a frogman spends more than half his waking hours under water, Morgan and I believed that the darkest place in the world was underneath an aircraft carrier at night. That was until we met Master Chief. He told us a story about a training dive he had done in the muddy waters of the Persian Gulf. He and his teammate found their compasses going haywire because they had swum about twenty meters into a large underwater sewage pipe. Just goes to show you that in the SEAL teams you're always going to run into guys who've swum through far nastier shit than you have.

In the teams, you're an old man at thirty-five. I was thirty, but with my multiple injuries I was worried that I couldn't keep up with the younger guys anymore. I remember Master Chief fixing me with a knowing look and saying that if, during predeployment workup, things ever reached the point where either he or I didn't think I could deploy, he would quietly arrange for me to go somewhere else. He promised to make that call early and move on.

During workup, we spent several weeks at a military and police marksmanship school. The facility had professionally designed assault courses and more than thirty target ranges, and our instructors tested us in almost every combat scenario imaginable. We shot targets in a variety of settings and practiced house runs, the techniques of assault, and clearing small buildings. Over and over we rehearsed our urban fieldcraft. Thanks to this constant practice, we had a way of getting it done.

Workups often last longer than actual deployments do. The platoons need that time to sharpen their skill sets and allow that all-important chemistry to develop. A dedicated group of instructors known as the training detachment, or TraDet, is in charge. They keep a constant watch on what other special ops units are seeing downrange and draw the lessons into our training. There's plenty of fieldwork and intensive classroom study, too. It's the kind of thing you don't see on many campuses: Blowing Things Up, Stalking Targets in the Night, Bashing Down Doors, and Dragging Bad Guys Away in the Dark. And we do a good bit of traveling around the country for various kinds of specialized training. It's state of the art, informed by the experiences of the battle-wise SEAL operators who were most recently in harm's way.

The first phase of workup focuses on individual skills. I arrived in time for one of my favorite training blocks: the couple of weeks we spent at an automobile racetrack in the Southwest learning tactical driving drills. This was easily the most fun I've had in the teams. Fun wasn't on the agenda for our instructors, though: they were dead serious about testing and sharpening our high-speed vehicular pursuit and evasion skills, which are so useful in an urban setting. They brought out a fleet of beat-up cars—Pontiac Grand Ams and maybe a few SUVs—and put us in situations that demanded a lot of finesse at the wheel. We wore helmets, face masks, and protection for sensitive parts, but the instructors took the air bags out of our vehicles, because they just got in the way.

In these drills, we developed the reflexes we'd need to drive effectively under fire in a combat zone. We drove those old clunkers as though we were the Dukes of Hazzard. At one point I was barreling around the track, minding my own business in the driver's seat, doing about eighty, when an instructor suddenly put a piece of cardboard in front of my face. A couple of my teammates heckled me a little, slapping me on the head, while I was speeding along blind. An unknown distance farther ahead, some orange traffic cones stood in my path. When the instructor pulled away the cardboard, I had a split second to see the cones, gauge their distance, and avoid them. It was a test of sight recognition, nerves, and reflexes. If I stopped more than ten feet away from the cones, I failed. If I hit them, I failed.

If we passed a test during the day, the instructors upped the ante, sending us out onto the track at night with no lights, speeding around with night-vision goggles strapped to our faces. Amplifying ambient light from the stars or the moon, NVGs cast the night in a glowing green. No doubt they're a great tool. The only drawback is that they leave you with almost no depth perception at all. Objects in the windshield are *much* closer than they appear. It was almost enough to make me miss the air bags. When the instructors sensed that the novelty was wearing off, they broke out the rifles and we all started shooting at each other as we veered around the track. We'd take an M4 carbine and replace its barrel with one designed to shoot "sim rounds," plastic bullets that contain a load of paint to mark hits. This wasn't paintball—police use weapons like these to suppress riots. But although all this was crazy, it was also fun as hell. It was thrilling to get back into the game.

Our instructors had tactical skills to match those of anybody on the planet. It was no fun to be in their sights, getting hit with paint rounds as we barreled around the track. The rounds left contusions, even through heavy clothing, and they could do worse if you were unlucky or not careful. It was a full-contact sport, as close to real-time life and death as we could get without actually killing each other.

After we finished with the full-size sedans, we graduated to armored Suburbans and Tahoes. The heavier SUVs were much tougher to take through the high-speed turns in motorcade and getaway drills, but the exercise got us ready for a type of work that SEALs often do in a combat zone: escorting dignitaries to extremely dangerous places and running tactical convoys. Our instructors chased us, shooting and ramming into our vehicles, trying to knock us off the shoulder or flip us over. Without warning, they'd pull out in front of us in their clunkers, forcing sudden evasive action. Our job was to get our valuable cargo out of harm's way. You have to think fast. Do you have enough space to swerve around the road-block? Should you plow straight through or drive right over it? Sometimes they trapped us so well that there was nothing left to do but dismount and shoot it out, the instructors closing in, guns blazing. This was no mindless romp. It was a thinking man's game, a test to see if we had what it takes to get our principal out of harm's way regardless of our own safety. And it really opened our eyes to what works.

In these drills, we pushed our aggression levels to the limit. We didn't miss a chance to drive up onto another driver's hood, or to rip out the sun visors and throw them at each other. At the end of the day, our tires were flat, our fenders were caved in, and we were stained with paint from head to toe. When we ran out of working cars, a new fleet was at our disposal in the morning. The welts stayed with you for a while. So did the lessons.

One afternoon at the track, Morgan had a rough go of it. I was busy doing a shooting drill when it happened. I heard him before I saw him: the screech of tires, then the sound of metal grinding on dirt, then a series of heavy, crunching thumps. My brother rolled that brand-new Tahoe three times before it finally came to rest. Fortunately, like race-car drivers, he and the other guys with him were securely restrained, and were wearing helmets and other protection. When he opened the door and rolled out, he walked away to laughter, loud *hooyahs,* and applause. The disclaimers in those auto advertisements on TV always say: PROFESSIONAL DRIVER ON CLOSED COURSE.

I don't know who Mercedes hires to drive the cars in their commercials, but I'd take a job like that in a second.

By the time that training block was done, we were flying around the course, catching all the straight-line angles and working the accelerator and brakes with no wasted motion in our feet or heels. Most people have no need to avoid armed pursuit, put a bad guy's vehicle into a ditch, make a J-turn, or bust through a roadblock. But team guys live in a different world. What we learned there was applicable everywhere, from an urban war zone to downtown Houston. Whether SEALs are driving convoys, moving out in a Humvee jocked up for a raid, or escorting dignitaries in a BMW 7 series while dressed in a suit, driving skills are paramount. If you can finish a training block like this in one piece, you've gotten some valuable combat training under your belt and lived an overgrown adolescent's dream all in the same program. Sometimes it was hard to turn the training off. Leaving the track, we would have to restrain ourselves from racing home in our badass minivans. The cops knew our psychology and were usually waiting for us along the highway. But sometimes the juice is worth the squeeze.

Hollywood does a great job of making what we do look sexy. Jumping out of airplanes and locking out of submarines is pretty cool, but let me be the first to tell you: 90 percent of the time, all we're doing is working from sunup to sundown, wearing our asses out practicing, practicing, practicing. Because it's true: the more you sweat in peace, the less you bleed in war. Still, few training trips were as fun as driving school. It was like the best bumper-car track in the world (with no lawyers or insurance agents hanging around to keep the vehicles limited to walking speed).

A SEAL team has three troops, or task units, each of which has two platoons. I got lucky when they assigned me to Troop 1, whose two platoons, Alfa and Bravo, were under our troop commander, Lieutenant Commander Ryan Thomas. He was a terrific combat leader, and his troop chief, Senior Chief Petty Officer Warren Steffen, was in my view one of the hardest, most experienced, and capable operators in the community, the consummate quiet professional. Because of his build and the slight gray streaks above his temples, I always thought he looked like Mr. Fantastic from the Marvel Comics superhero team the Fantastic Four. Standing a lean and strong six foot three, about 220 pounds, Steffen had served two years in the fleet before entering BUD/S in 1993. He'd served in the finest units in the special operations community, but, like the good ones, never talked about it. SEALs are hard to impress, but we all respected him. His presence was low-key, high-impact. He was always looking out for his teammates. The more quietly he spoke, the closer we listened.

When Steffen mentioned to me that he considered Lieutenant Commander Thomas one of the most tactically sound officers he had ever worked with, I knew we were good to go. I was assigned to Alfa Platoon. Morgan was sent to Bravo Platoon, under Lieutenant Clint. We were both fired up to have been assigned to an outfit that was stacked from the top down with solid operators. We had a great mix of new blood with fresh perspectives and old hands with valuable experience. As we found our stride during workup, we developed an easy chemistry that made the natural competitiveness among us very productive.

Boss was one of the training instructors during workup. Our friendship didn't move him to cut us any slack, however. Let's just say that when you spend a few months getting tormented by a guy with Boss's abilities, you come out the other side with your senses heightened.

In the second phase of workup, we put our individual skills into a team context. This phase is all about the tactical basics. Making a fighting team out of skilled operators, bringing everyone up to the same level with the ability to understand what each man's responsibilities are and how we need to fight, survive, and win. We were in the middle of a mobility training exercise when Senior Chief Steffen told me I had been promoted to LPO, or leading petty officer, in Alfa Platoon.

The leading petty officer works directly under the platoon chief and basically makes sure his will is carried out. I sensed they were sending a message that they wanted me to raise my game as a leader and invest myself in the team. As a petty officer first class, I had served as a leader of a small fire team before. Now that I was an LPO for an entire platoon, things were getting serious.

The SEALs who run a platoon—the officer in charge (OIC), the assistant officer in charge (AOIC), the platoon chief, and the LPO—are objects of constant scrutiny. If anyone shows himself to be arrogant, or if it becomes evident that he cares more about himself than about his men, his reputation is history and soon he'll be finished. As a leader, you either earn your place and keep your team aware of the connection between your capabilities and your privileges or things slide until you find yourself in a sorry place where you can neither lead nor trust your men.

I wondered sometimes if I was up to it. Friends are friends but business is business. Good operators make the distinction and don't let it interfere with work.

As an LPO, I now stood in range of my teammates' judgment of their leader. I sensed the change in my status the first time I walked into the platoon hut and noticed how the boys quickly hushed up. Lips tight, eyes on the walls, they no longer allowed me to be privy to what made their world go round. My promotion took me out of their community and turned me into management. I didn't mind the job itself, but I hated the fact that I was separated from the boys.

The men in Alfa were some of the best I have ever known. I never had to get onto them or tell them what to do. When I got orders of instructions from our chief, I passed them along, and by the end of the day they made me look good. That in turn made the chief look good, which made the officers look good, too.

The synergy of Alfa Platoon was amazing. No matter how bad things got, we all stuck together. Everybody was a packhorse. Even our new guys were squared away, keeping their ears open and their mouths shut. They kept their problems to themselves and their minds on their jobs.

Instructors often drew on past operations during training. If you can learn from past mistakes, your future will be a little less painful. This is part of a frogman's ethos. A willingness to learn from the past is part of who we are—and part of the reason we can pull off some of the impossible missions that every now and again make it into the spotlight. Whenever an instructor went over something, I'd review my performance in Afghanistan and ask myself, "Did I do it that way?" I wanted to reassure myself that I hadn't let my boys down. I wanted to be sure that if I ever got in that position again, everything would end differently.

I learned at one point that some higher-ups wanted to leave me behind in a "beach detachment" when the team finally went overseas. But Master Chief enforced Skipper's wish to keep me on the line. Their confidence in me was energizing. As we prepared to begin the final stage of training, I wanted nothing more than to reward them for their faith.

2

SEAL Team 5, Alfa Platoon

When word came down that we were headed for Anbar Province, the boys were fired up. We had been following the work of the teams that had preceded us over there. Upstairs at the team house, after-action reports had been coming in daily. Ramadi was hot. It was a shooter's field day for the team that had been there since April 2006. Team 3 was stacking up the shit bags as though they were cordwood.

Since late 2005, Anbar had been the bloodiest part of Iraq. Its capital, Ramadi, was a hornet's nest of terrorist activity. Located about sixty-eight miles west of Baghdad, the city of about five hundred thousand people, almost all of them Sunnis, had been a stronghold of support for Saddam Hussein. He cut deals with the tribal sheikhs to secure his control.

After U.S. forces seized Fallujah in November 2004, killing most of the insurgents who had chosen to make that city their Alamo, the leadership of Al Qaeda in Iraq, including its supposed chief, Abu Musab al-Zarqawi, fled to Ramadi. Even after al-Zarqawi's death—a blind date with a JDAM—Al Qaeda had the run of the place and insurgents attacked coalition patrols and outposts almost at will.

Ramadi sits on an ancient smugglers' road, a dusty highway that leads from Baghdad west to Iraq's border with Syria. In 2003, it was a terrorist pipeline. When coalition forces invaded Iraq that year, Syria and Iran, fearing they were next on America's hit list after Saddam paid the piper, allowed throngs of foreign terrorists to enter Iraq through their sovereign territory. They came in the name of Arab brotherhood to fight the American infidels. Unfortunately for the Iraqi people, the terrorists didn't mind slitting Muslim throats to influence their various agendas.

The fighting in Ramadi was intense as far back as 2004. Street by street, block by block, our Army and Marines fought until their trigger fingers bled. After Al Qaeda declared Ramadi the capital of the worldwide Islamist caliphate in 2005, our forces twisted down the vise, relentlessly increasing the pressure on the enemy. But in spite of those heroic efforts, the enemy kept coming. The explosions, heavy gunfire, and terrible human casualties never seemed to let up. The murderers claimed the city as their own, an ongoing insult and a mounting threat to the stability of the region. Anbar Province was hell on earth.

Which meant we would be right at home there.

Alongside their Marine Corps and Army brothers, SEAL Team 3 took a greedy harvest from the ranks of the Al Qaeda and Iraqi insurgents in Ramadi through the summer of 2006. Led by an aggressive, battle-hardened troop commander, Lieutenant Commander Willis, they were doing great work both in and above the streets. Working from rooftop overwatch positions, their snipers were scoring heavily. One of their best, Chris Kyle, was racking up a confirmed-kill record that surpassed that of every sniper the United States had ever sent to war. By the time he was done, it would reach an official count of 160, and I know it was far higher.

I know Chris well, because we started our careers in the teams together. He's down-to-earth and laid-back, a country boy with a huge love of family, God, and country. He has saved a hell of a lot of American lives in combat, too, hanging himself way out there under fire, taking the fight to a savage enemy. Chris Kyle is a hell of a warfighter. Team 3's performance motivated us, and gave us a bench-mark to shoot for, though our leadership kept reminding us that numbers meant nothing in the long run; what counted was the strategic impact of our work once our time in Iraq was over.

The last phase of workup brought together all our supporting elements as a fully manned squadron, readying our entire unit to deploy into Iraq. Our medical teams, explosive ordnance disposal (EOD) technicians, intelligence crews—everyone—learned to function together as we would in Iraq. For months, our officers and senior enlisted had been getting briefed on unconventional modes of warfare such as counterinsurgency (COIN) and foreign internal defense (FID), in which U.S. forces help train another country's military or police to fight an insurgency. This was the strategy our head shed was driving for our deployment, working to tie in our efforts with all the forces working our area of operations and across the region. This mode of war, dusted off and reengineered after years of disuse since Vietnam, was all about understanding the culture, developing a viable government and security force, taking care of the local people, and giving them the confidence to fight for themselves. It isn't as sexy as kicking in doors and laying on a sniper rifle, and it wasn't what most SEALs bargained for when they joined the teams. We weren't wearing Tridents to go out into a cold, hateful world to train others to fight and build churches and schools. But it's how real progress would be made, we were told. You can kill bad guys all day long, but they will always find someone else to step up, even their kids. When you really break it down, the locals are the key to everything. It's their job to take their country back.

Soon enough, word came down that Team 5's two Iraq-bound troops would set up shop in two of the biggest hell-holes in Anbar Province: Habbaniyah and Ramadi. Troop 1 drew Ramadi. Skipper and the head-shed boys would locate in Fallujah, close to their higher headquarters, the I Marine Expeditionary Force (or I MEF). Commanded by General Richard Zilmer, I MEF oversaw all thirty thousand U.S. personnel serving in Anbar Province. Locally, in Ramadi, our operations would be conducted under a U.S. Army brigade that reported to General Zilmer's headquarters.

The rough company of Team 5 was my family and fraternity, and Skipper, Master Chief, Lieutenant Commander Thomas, and Senior Chief Steffen were our patriarchs. Overseas, we would fight in the name of God and country. We would do it in support of the Army and Marine Corps infantry, tankers and engineers who were each doing their part to clear out an Al Qaeda hornet's nest in the middle of Mesopotamia. And never far from my mind was something else: I would do it in the names of Mikey, Danny, Axe, and everyone on the rescue op who lost their lives on June 28, 2005.

Sometimes, as our training wound down, thoughts of that mountain would back up on me. Exhausted from the bone-crushing pain, I'd suddenly feel the slash of shrapnel and the burn in my lungs, the labors of a body under assault in thin air. Sometimes the memory of that pain gave way to numbness. I'd find myself feeling as though Operation Redwing hadn't actually happened, that it was a story I had read somewhere.

I was still learning to keep those memories in a box. When things slowed down, the rage and feelings of futility would sometimes well up in the face of the reality that there was nothing I could have done. Sometimes I'd take a walk through the utility area behind the team house, chewing things over. For instance, I'd learned that when rescuers found Mikey and Axe, they saw that each of them had been wearing some kind of bandage. I was proud that in their last minutes they still did all they could to stay in the fight. But what could anyone say about me? I was the doc and it was my job to see to their wounds. They had each needed help, and I just couldn't make it work. I knew there was nothing I could do while bullets were flying, just send bullets back the other way. But my thoughts would circle this track as I wandered among the big steel MILVAN containers that held our gear ready for quick loading and shipment overseas. Sitting down among them, I'd let some of the emotional overpressure of the past year flow out of me.

When I realized how little I was sleeping, I told Morgan I didn't know what was wrong with me. "Nothing is. Suck it up," he said. And I tried. Morgan was the one person in the world who could always reach me. In his many deployments in the teams, he's done almost everything there is to do, several times nearly losing his life. But even Morgan hadn't been through something like Redwing.

One day it came to a head. Morgan went to Lieutenant Commander Thomas and told him that he and I had talked and agreed that something needed to be done. He and Senior Chief Steffen pulled me in to see Skipper and Master Chief. We talked about the workup, about Iraq, about what Team 3 was doing, and reviewed our plan for taking their place. Soon enough someone broached my own state of readiness. Long story short, it was agreed that I needed a break. Physically and emotionally, I was basically spent. They took me off-line and sent me home for a while. They told me I could reengage when I got back, and the timetable would be up to me.

As Team 5 finished running through its paces, I returned to Texas. Back in the Lone Star State, at our family's horse ranch outside Huntsville, near Sam Houston National Forest, I found a quiet world, a place where people didn't run around the country from training block to training block, practicing house runs, crawling through brush with instructors in pursuit, driving cars like madmen on racetracks at night. I don't sleep much now and I didn't then. But there, in the wind-rustled silence, away from Coronado's constant press, I found time for prayer and rest. I looked to the Lord and my family for strength.

As I took sanctuary in the East Texas piney woods, the story of what I went through in Afghanistan was beginning to get out. I never thought that news of such a sensitive and classified operation would leak out. But the families of my lost teammates were understandably pushing for it to be told. The Navy seemed unmoved until the media started doing its thing. When stories, many of them inaccurate, began to surface, my command decided the NSW community needed to get out in front of it. They decided I should write a book about the mission. I'm glad they allowed it, because I felt a powerful calling within me to honor the memory of some great warriors I once knew.

Over several weeks during my downtime, I went to Massachusetts and sat down with a writer and pulled together my part of the story. When I was done, I sent the manuscript to the Navy so they could make sure no classified information was published. The process was cathartic—painful, but necessary. And also strange: as SEALs, we'd been taught to hold our stories close, to say nothing to outsiders, especially the press. But we also knew how to get something done when the chain of command spoke. So I put my heart into it, mostly because, more than anything else, I wanted to let people know what, and who, America had lost.

Back in Coronado, the head shed did a good job of keeping my absence inconspicuous. Workup was often a circus anyway, with everybody moving around all the time, missing various training blocks when opportunities for more important work came along. When my medical appointments had pulled me away from the team, or when I was in Massachusetts, people were too busy to notice.

Back in Texas, I found time to see old friends. I walked in pastures and woodlands, and horsed around with my most loyal friend in the world, a yellow Labrador retriever who had been given to me as a puppy after I came home. She was a service dog, selected for her calmness and gentleness, traits that settled and grounded me. I named her DASY, an acronym for my lost team—Danny, Axe, Southern boy (me), and Yankee (Mikey).

As we sometimes say in the teams, if you have a bad day in the pool, get back in the pool. After calming my nerves, all I wanted was to be around team guys. I returned to the Silver Strand centered and refreshed. Alfa and Bravo Platoons were in the final stages of workup.

The last evolution the higher headquarters had in store for us before we went overseas took place at a base outside San Diego. It was a certification exercise that would officially validate our squadron's readiness to deploy. We basically put ourselves into deployment mode, and then jumped into a no-joke combat simulation that lasted for a while. This exercise hit us with everything we'd find downrange except for real bullets and roadside bombs. In this dry run for taking on Iraq, we worked through our concept of operations, the whole counterinsurgency scenario. It was two tough weeks, but a great training exercise, with all the bells and whistles. More than anything else, it was good to have everyone together, working on the same objective. Our new guys showed some initiative right off the bat. They bought one of those plastic backyard kiddie swimming pools, set it up on the training range, and invited some women from a supporting Army unit over for a makeshift pool party right there in the California desert. (I'm still getting over the fact that, as someone with a leadership position, I wasn't entitled to an invite.) Thinking outside the box—Bravo Zulu, guys.

As the LPO in Alfa Platoon (E-6 pay grade), I did more than I ever did as a regular shooter, running and gunning with the rest of the E-5s (second-class petty officers) in the train. I briefed my teammates, filtered plans and reports back and forth between the leadership and members of the platoon, and helped draw up tomorrow's plan. On one of our last training ops, one of those doors turned out to hold a surprise I'll never forget.

We were ordered to hit a series of houses, clearing them of bad guys, rounding up detainees, and identifying people to interrogate. One of the buildings we entered was a wooden barn. When we stacked up on the door, breached it, and crashed inside, we discovered a scene of carnage, the smell of blood as thick as a mist.

Someone shouted, "Mass casualties! Medic! Medic!" Though I had been elevated to LPO, I am still a medic. As we entered the barn, my brain did a skip-step, then kicked into gear. Elliott Miller, a Bravo Platoon medic, was spot-on as he went around with me, triaging the wounded. "That guy's gone, forget him! What do we have over there?" It was fast-paced and urgent. Elliott and I were all over it. I heard our platoon OIC call in the quick reaction force and request an extract.

The blood was real, so it was easy to miss the fact that its source wasn't a room full of wounded men: the barn was full of pigs. In consultation with a veterinarian, they had anesthetized the animals, then inflicted wounds for us to treat. It was the most realistic mass-casualty simulation we had ever seen. We practiced a variety of procedures to deal with trauma, arterial bleeding, abdominal wounds, bone fractures, and penetrating or blunt-force internal injuries.

And before you judge it, know that exercises like this, though controversial, have saved thousands of American lives by giving our medics realistic live-tissue training. They are an absolute must for any combat unit heading off to war.

I had just come out of a surgery myself when we went through this evolution. My right hand was still in a cast. After it was over, I noticed that I'd have to get it changed as soon as we got back to the Strand. The plaster was soaked through with blood and mud. Back at the team house, I went to Medical to see about getting some new plaster. The facility was a busy place when a team was doing a workup. Someone's always getting jacked up. Looking around for the officer on watch, I leaned into an exam room and saw some Navy physicians huddled around a guy. He was a blond-haired kid, muscular and stocky. They were tending to one of his knees. If his manner and the look in his eyes were any indication, he'd just returned from a combat deployment. Poor dude was really white-knuckling as the docs worked on his left knee, which had been ripped up pretty good.

Our eyes met.

"Where you been, bro?" I asked him.

"Ramadi."

"Team Three?"

"Yeah."

I considered this as the docs probed his wound. When one of them moved out of the way, I wedged myself farther into the room.

"How y'all rollin' over there?"

He didn't answer.

"I'm with Five," I offered. "We're hearing wild stuff coming off the wire."

He winced as the docs worked on him. He didn't speak, and he really didn't have to. The expression on his face was worth a thousand words. I remember that pain. Hell, just looking at him made my knees hurt.

We already had the big picture of how U.S. forces were taking on that city. A big base, Camp Ramadi, was set up on the west side of town. Our main compound over there, known as Shark Base, was like a little appendage to Camp Ramadi, nestled between the base and the Euphrates River, which traces the northern edge of the city. A smaller base, Camp Corregidor, sat on the eastern outskirts. That place wasn't much more than an outhouse surrounded by walls. I felt bad for the crew that had to live there.

Though I knew this guy had other concerns at the moment, my curiosity got the better of me. I wanted to hear it straight from the mouth of an operator who had just come back from this circle of hell.

"We're fixing to go wheels-up," I said. "Got any advice before we head downrange?"

With the docs continuing to treat his wound, he seemed to welcome the distraction I provided. He did have some advice for me, but it was just a single word. His pale face turned my way and he looked at me with weary eyes.

"Pray."

3

Never Quit

As I go through my days, I've tried to make it a habit to lift my troubles to God. Some guys put their faith in their rifles. Me, I put it all in the grace of the Lord. I know who's in charge and understand whom I serve. When all hell breaks loose and people start falling, God becomes priority number one. Still, the more I learned about the fight for Ramadi in 2006, the more clearly I saw that it might be helpful to take my prayer life to another level.

Soon enough, another Team 3 veteran turned up at the Strand, full of stories and good advice. It was my friend Chris Kyle. Thanks to his insane confirmed-kill total, the insurgents in Iraq knew him as al-Shaitan Ramadi, the devil of Ramadi. When he found out there was a bounty on his head, the sniper was flattered.

Chris has a fighter's heart, and a little luck, too. Some team guys chase wars their whole careers and never experience the heavy stuff. He's thrown out more lead than a pencil factory. When Chris ended his deployment a little early—guess he ran out of rounds—we took advantage of it to have lunch and he talked to me about the daily bump and grind in Ramadi.

We talked about how he kept his fighting edge, both mentally and physically, in the middle of a full-on urban war zone, where plenty of people want us dead and are willing to take themselves along for the ride. He told me dozens of little things to look for when walking down the street, what neighborhoods and villages to be wary of, how to work with the *jundis* (the Iraqi troops and police whom we'd be charged to train). He and his teammates had perfected the craft of building urban sniper hides— shooting positions in the upper floors or roofs of city buildings. Only someone with a death wish made trouble for our patrols on their watch. Yet there was always someone willing to grab a weapon and go toe-to-toe with us.

One time Chris spotted two guys on a moped speeding along the road down below him. He saw them drive past a big hole in the road, drop a big backpack into it, and keep puttering along. The next thing to drop was both of those IED emplacers, straight to the ground, taken down by a single shot that skewered them both through the neck.

When Chris Kyle was serving in Fallujah in 2004, he started out as a sniper during the beginning of the coalition offensive against that insurgent-held city. Setting up in buildings outside the fortified city as our forces went in on November 7, choosing the clearest and longest lanes of fire down the major streets, he had a couple days of very good shooting. At one point, the prime minister of Iraq himself, Ayad Allawi, visited the area and walked by Chris's position. Looking down at his field of view, Prime Minister Allawi saw insurgents running around. He asked Chris, "Why aren't you killing them?" Chris muttered something about the cosmic injustice and hopeless futility of the universe, also known to SEAL snipers as the rules of engagement. The Iraqi leader replied, "They have had four months of warnings to surrender or leave. Therefore, everybody in that city is to die." Chris and the other snipers started carrying out the wishes of the prime minister of Iraq, all the way out to sixteen hundred yards.

In Fallujah, Chris never met his equal, but one enemy sniper came close. His name was Mustafa. Word was he had been a shooter for the Iraqi team in the Olympic Games. This SOB was a pretty bad guy. With his high-dollar Accuracy International sniper rifle, he had built a track record picking off the turret gunners in our Humvees. His skill was testified to by the fact that he sometimes landed head shots on Americans in moving vehicles. When we finally got intel on where he was operating from, one of our snipers sent him up with a .50-caliber round.

Whether they're Marines, Army, or SEALs, snipers are said to be guardian angels of the troops. Elite shooters who endure rigorous specialized training, they strike from on high, unseen. When the enemy wised up and started keeping their heads down, Chris's mission changed. First he took his sniping into the city. Then he joined them in the city's mean streets.

Killing didn't bother Chris. What did bother him was seeing kids die whom he had the skills to save. Thirty years old then, he had been around long enough that it really got into his heart to see eighteen-year-old kids get killed doing room-entry work, a craft that's a SEAL specialty. Having trained for years to master high-speed house runs, and probably knowing more than a sniper needs to know about ballistic breaching (blowing a door open with explosives), he went to a Marine Corps platoon's leadership and asked that he serve as their point man, leading the way as they kicked in doors, house by house. "I can help you out here," he said. The Marines are great warriors and dedicated patriots who, I can tell you, have saved our butts more times than I can count. But adding a highly trained SEAL's speed and proficiency to their arsenal made them even more lethal. The platoon he worked with didn't have an officer at the time, and its enlisted leadership was glad to have him. Sometimes a frogman finds room for a little improvisation after the shooting starts.

At that point, Chris took the guardian angel business to a new level. He waded right down into the fight with these young Marines. In quiet moments, he'd pull them aside and show them how special ops guys enter houses and clear rooms. He wasn't showing off—Chris never does that. Interservice rivalry has its place, but there was no ego in this instance; it was simply about saving lives. Cooperation and flexibility make our combat forces way more effective. As the offensive rolled into Fallujah— four battalions of Marines and two from the Army— Chris shed his frog skin, put on a set of Marine Corps tricolor camos, and went to war with the Corps. *Semper fi.*

After two weeks of this, Chris's uniform was covered in blood. More times than he liked, he held mortally wounded Marines in his arms, shot in the gut and bleeding out. Chris would always tell them that they were going to be fine, even when he knew otherwise. And he channeled his anger into action, alongside that crew of pipe-hitting Marines.

By Christmas, the battle for the city was over. The seven-week campaign claimed the lives of more than a hundred U.S., British, and Iraqi soldiers, as well as thousands of insurgents. It all felt like ancient history as I sat with Chris, trading stories like this day and night in Coronado. When I asked him, "What was worse, Fallujah or Ramadi?" he didn't have to think before answering. "Ramadi," he said. "Ramadi was ten times worse."

What happened to Team 3 in Ramadi in the late summer and early fall of 2006 was an indicator of what awaited us. No one was beyond death's reach.

The first U.S. military operations there, in 2004 and 2005, consisted of raids by our special operations forces, who were working with newly trained Iraqi army units. Conventionals later set up in bases outside the city. They pushed in to attack enemy strongholds, kicked around for a few hours, and then returned to base. But by the summer of 2006, the Army and Marine Corps began moving into the city proper with the intent to stay, ordering their engineers to build combat outposts, known as COPs, right in the heart of the place. Setting up in the enemy's midst was part of the new counterinsurgency strategy. We no longer commuted to the fight. SEAL Team 3 helped install the first of these outposts in the city that summer. They started the fight that we would try to finish.

During workup, Skipper and Master Chief brought in some impressive guys from other branches of the SOF community and academia to talk about their experiences in Anbar. I think we understood there would be plenty of heavy fighting in the months ahead. But these briefings on counterinsurgency warfare gave us notice that the upcoming deployment was likely to be the most challenging thing many of us had ever been part of.

The plan to win Ramadi back from the terrorists was a mixture of traditional offensive operations—with our forces going block by block, doing "cordon and search" missions—and raids. It was a lot of police work, too: traffic control, ID checks, biometric screening, searches, and curfews. The goal in the end was to make the city livable again, leaving the place in the hands of its citizens for good and making sure the enemy never again found sanctuary there.

In Afghanistan, the fight was mostly about muzzle velocity, windage, defilade, and time to target—that's what it was about for our SEAL teams, at least. In Anbar Province, however, we would deal with a full range of targets, hard and soft. We targeted the enemy's fighting forces, but we also never forgot that the security and confidence of the people were paramount. "You can't kill your way out of an insurgency," was an often-repeated bit of wisdom. (Though some of us sometimes felt the urge to try.) We needed to bring security to the people so that they could fend for themselves. Brigade headquarters put a lot of effort into shaping perceptions, too, including setting up a news service that broadcast to the locals.

There always seemed to be enough bad guys to go around. Casualties were high from 2004 through mid-2006. President Bush remembered the summer of '06 as "the worst period in my presidency." In his memoirs he wrote, "I was deeply concerned that the violence was overtaking all else.... If Iraq split along sectarian lines, our mission would be doomed. We could be looking at a repeat of Vietnam—a humiliating loss for the country, a shattering blow to the military, and a dramatic setback for our interests." I take my commander in chief at his word, no matter who he is.

Yet confronted with a grim outlook and an impossible problem, what does our military do? We wade right into the middle of it and tell the enemy to bring it on. What other option was there? Quit? Politicians may go that route (see "Vietnam, war in") but our military forces don't.

None of us thought it would be easy to square the circle of building a nation in a place as irredeemably violent as Ramadi. The SEAL who gave me that ominous advice at the team house—"Pray"—had been wounded in a hotly contested fight in the worst part of the city. On August 2, 2006, he and Chris Kyle were part of a squad supporting a U.S. Army tank unit, augmented by Iraqi forces, doing a block-clearance operation in the rough and untamed southeast part of the city, the Ma'laab district. Team 3 had helped install an outpost there known as COP Falcon. An Al Qaeda cell was discovered nearby, so that morning our tanks and Bradley Fighting Vehicles rolled out to tackle it before first light. Wisely, the insurgents in the neighborhood let the armor pass them by, hiding until they could turn their weapons on our infantry.

Much as we're eager to fight, most of our leadership would say it isn't our job to do a block-clearance operation like this—that's the work of the larger conventional units. But the Army was strapped for personnel and Team 3's troop commander, Lieutenant Commander Willis, simply couldn't tolerate Americans being put at risk without our support. Chris and two other SEALs decided to establish a sniper position in a building near the COP. They dismounted from their Bradleys, humped their gear up to the rooftop, set up a fighting position, and started scanning for targets.

It's hard to confront skilled enemy snipers who enjoy a home-field advantage—they tend to know all the angles. And sure enough, good as those boys from Team 3 were, they soon ran into trouble. As they scoped the streets, they began taking fire from the surrounding rooftops, windows, and streets. Chris was watching the area north of their position, another sniper had a sector to the west, and a third SEAL, Ryan Job, manned a machine gun and looked out to the east. When shots rang out from the east, nicking their parapets and raising clouds of dust, the SEALs took cover. Chris hollered to Ryan, "Did you see where that came from?" Hunkered down behind a parapet, the machine gunner didn't answer. He had been hit. Actually, it was his rifle that took the hit. The metal shattered, throwing a spackle of lead fragments into his face.

Chris put out the call, "Man down, man down," and right away reinforcements came up to the roof. When a SEAL corpsman finally got to Ryan, he noticed that the machine gunner's right eye had been pierced straight through. Ryan told everyone he'd be okay, but few thought he'd make it with his eye socket and face shattered. He sat upright to avoid choking on his own blood. Marc Lee, a damn good SEAL, ran up and took his place on the roof. As Lee laid down suppressing fire to cover the extract, Chris threw Ryan over his shoulder and hauled him to the stairwell. About halfway down, Ryan began spitting up blood. He told Chris he couldn't breathe and said he wanted to stand. Chris realized that Ryan's chest was being compressed by its own weight pressing down on

Chris's shoulder, causing blood to pool up somewhere inside his chest. So Chris set Ryan down, resituated, and helped him hobble down the stairs. An armored personnel carrier was waiting on the street outside to evacuate him.

As Chris eased him into the vehicle, Ryan asked for a shot of morphine, then went unconscious from blood loss. The docs eventually stabilized Ryan and arranged to medevac him out of the combat area. With their brother taken care of, Chris and his team returned to the COP to plan their next move.

The Army stayed in heavy contact with insurgent forces throughout the day. Our guys had their hands full. Aerial reconnaissance revealed large bands of insurgent fighters moving toward our positions, bounding through streets and alleyways on either side, looking to envelop the Americans. As the battle was escalating, intel pointed to a certain house as a suspected location for the enemy sniper who had shot Ryan Job. There was no chance to get him if they didn't move fast. So Chris and his guys decided to push out again, jumping into a couple of Bradleys and returning to the fight. They were powerfully supported by several tanks from an Army outfit that all the SEALs respected, Bulldog Company, First Battalion, Thirty-Seventh Armor Regiment, under command of a fast-moving captain named Mike Bajema. He stood out front; his own tank led the way.

A block or two from where Ryan had gotten hit, the Bradleys stopped and the SEALs dismounted, taking fire almost as soon as the ramp dropped. As Captain Bajema turned his tank's gun on the wall of the target building, blowing a hole in it, the SEALs moved quickly up, formed a stack, and poured inside. Hostile fighters were lighting them up from every angle. Nearby, unseen insurgent machine guns were making it rain with bullets.

As Chris writes in his book, *American Sniper,* he believes they had been drawn into a trap. As the SEALs secured the first floor, Marc Lee led the way to the second deck, running up the staircase. Then, through a window on the stairs, he spotted an enemy shooter in the building next door. The insurgent saw him, too. Marc turned and laid down a burst of suppressing fire. He was opening his mouth to alert his teammates when the insurgent popped back up, drew on Marc, and pulled the trigger. The bullet went straight into Marc's mouth and cut his spine, making him the first SEAL to be killed in action since Operation Redwing more than a year earlier, and the first team guy to die in Iraq. He went out with his boots on, fighting hard for his country. He's remembered as one of the great ones. He died for his teammates. There's no greater gift than that.

The death of Marc Lee and the serious injury to Ryan Job, both in the same day, was a heavy blow to Team 3. No matter how many men we lose, it never gets any easier. They reported the casualties and called the Army for extract. The men of Team 3 had served the Army well. Now the soldiers returned the favor. A pair of M1A1 Abrams tanks, sixty-seven tons apiece, and four Bradley Fighting Vehicles moved into the neighborhood. They are built for one reason: to inflict total destruction on the enemy. At that point, they started doing what they do best. Captain Bajema's tanks sealed the neighborhood so the enemy couldn't escape or be reinforced. Trapped, the insurgents came out in force and presented themselves just as Big Army wanted them to: openly, wielding rocket-propelled grenades, heavy machine guns, and AK-47s. With help from an aircraft on station overhead, which carried excellent cameras, Bajema's tankers saw them coming and turned loose on them. When a vehicle loaded with insurgents came barreling out of an alley and bore down on Bajema's tank, he turned his fifty-caliber machine gun on it and cut them down like weeds in a garden.

After wreaking this destruction, Bajema announced over the radio, "Winchester." That meant his vehicles were out of ammunition. By the time they returned to their bases elsewhere in the city, the insurgent stronghold was coughing up a column of black smoke that was three blocks wide. One man was lost, another was badly wounded, and the angry city burned.

Back home, as Team 3's deployment came to an end, the situation in Anbar Province made for bad headlines. On September 11, a major newspaper ran an article with a headline that declared Anbar Province "lost." This conclusion came from people who had read a classified Marine Corps intel report about the situation in Ramadi and thought they could use it to score political points by leaking it to reporters. The situation, readers were told, was "beyond repair." Someone neglected to inform the U.S. military of this fact, because our guys in Ramadi saw things differently. And so did we, back on the Silver Strand, working hard to get ready for our turn downrange.

For starters, even if there really is no way you can win, you never say it out loud. You assess why, change strategy, adjust tactics, and keep fighting and pushing till either you've gotten a better outcome or you've died. Either way, you *never quit* when your country needs you to succeed.

As Team 5 was shutting down the workup and loading up its gear, our task unit's leadership flew to Ramadi to do what we call a predeployment site survey. Lieutenant Commander Thomas went, and so did both of our platoon officers in charge. It was quite an adventure. They were shot at every day. They were hit by IEDs. When they came home, Lieutenant Commander Thomas got us together in the briefing room and laid out the details. The general reaction from the team was, "Get ready, kids. This is gonna be one hell of a ride."

I remember sitting around the team room talking about it. Morgan had a big smile on his face. Elliott Miller, too, all 240 pounds of him, looked happy. Even Mr. Fantastic seemed at peace and relaxed, in that sober, senior chief way. We turned over in our minds the hard realities of the city. Only a couple weeks from now we would be calling Ramadi home. For six or seven months we'd be living in a hornet's nest, picking up where Team 3 had left off. It was time for us to roll.

In late September, Al Qaeda's barbaric way of dealing with the local population was stirring some of Iraq's Sunni tribal leaders to come over to our side. (Stuff like punishing cigarette smokers by cutting off their fingers— can you blame locals for wanting those crazies gone?) Standing up for their own people posed a serious risk, but it was easier to justify when you had five thousand American military personnel backing you up. That'll boost your courage, for sure. We were putting that vise grip on that city, infiltrating it, and setting up shop, block by block, house by house, inch by inch.

On September 29, a Team 3 platoon set out on foot

from a combat outpost named Eagle's Nest on the final operation of their six-month deployment. Located in the dangerous Ma'laab district, it wasn't much more than a perimeter of concrete walls and concertina wire bundling up a block of residential homes. COP Eagle's Nest was named in honor of the Army unit that was making its mark in Ramadi: the First Battalion of the 506th Infantry Regiment, 101st Airborne Division. Nicknamed the Currahees, but better known today as the Band of Brothers, these paratroopers had built a great legacy in World War II that included seizing Hitler's last holdout, the fabled Eagle's Nest on the German-Austrian border. That legacy meant something to all American servicemen. I think I've seen the HBO miniseries *Band of Brothers* at least fifty times. Watching it always fires me up.

That night, Team 3's snipers were ordered to set up in the urban high ground, in sniper overwatch positions supporting Marines who were stringing razor wire as a barrier to insurgent movement near the southern boundary of the city. It was around three in the morning when the SEALs got into position. Not long after daybreak, one of their hides began taking fire.

Drive-by shooters fired small arms into the roofs and parapets around the Team 3 position. Then an RPG streaked in and exploded against the roof, casting a cloud of dust over the snipers. Faced with harassing fire for most of the next hour, they hunkered down, not worried much by the haphazard shooting. But not long after that, an insurgent managed to sneak in close. Using the urban maze of buildings for cover, he lobbed a single fragmentation grenade at the team.

The grenade arced down and hit a young SEAL named

Mike Monsoor in the chest, bouncing to the floor. In the seemingly endless few seconds that it rolled around at his feet, Monsoor—positioned next to a stairway that offered the only exit from the roof—knew he could have made a quick and easy escape. As the frag lay there cooking, Monsoor didn't hesitate: he jumped on the grenade, smothering it with his body. When it exploded, it threw all of its immense force into him. Mikey took the entire blast and allowed everyone else around him to live.

The SEALs at the other sniper positions were moving to support their brothers at the first report of contact. The gunfire that greeted them was so insistent that the Iraqi troops who were working with them refused to go along. (This was all too typical.) As the SEALs sent a troops-in-contact alert to the tactical operations center (TOC) at Camp Marc Lee (prior to August 2, the SEAL compound had been known as Shark Base, but the boys from Team 3 had honorably renamed it in memory of our fallen brother), and a man-down call as well, they requested vehicles to evacuate their casualty. Meanwhile, the guys from the other sniper element raced toward them through the gunfire. They arrived within minutes.

Securing the perimeter, they provided overwatch and covering fire for two Bradleys dispatched from COP Eagle's Nest. As the vehicles took Mikey away, no one failed to understand what he had just done—and that the price he paid was the ultimate one. By the time the case-vac vehicle reached the base hospital at Camp Ramadi, that twenty-five-year-old frogman, that hero, was already gone.

Never forget.

Mikey was a great kid and a solid operator, a guy

everybody liked. He was a hard worker, young, just starting his career. His example reveals why certain guys make it into the SEAL teams and others don't. I think the guys who make it are the ones who are willing to give their lives for their teammates. It's not all about muscle, stamina, or brains. It's about heart. You can't train a person to react as he did to danger. It comes from your heart, because it all boils down to love of your teammates and the commitment you've made to protect the freedoms of your country. There are no questions to ask—you act because you could not do otherwise, because you know your teammate would do the same for you, because this is all about more than one man. What is service? Mike Monsoor is the answer.

4

Into the Hornet's Nest

On Saturday, October 14, 2006, I went to Naval Air Station North Island in San Diego to jump onto a bird headed for the Sandbox. An Air Force Boeing C-17 Globemaster III airlifter was waiting for us. Sixteen months ago, they'd flown me home in a plane like this one. Now at long last it was time to return to the war. The commander of Naval Special Warfare Command, Rear Admiral Joseph Maguire, was there to see us off.

Everyone has his reasons for serving. Sometimes the reasons we often give to people are kind of flip—"I can't do anything else"—maybe because the real reason is beyond words. It's not just the thrill of shooting automatic weapons and blowing things up; my reasons are deep in my heart. I can't tell you how much the sight of the flag means to me, or the heritage of the military men who came before me. It's about this country, and its people. Mostly now it's about the company of my teammates, those men whose values track mine and whom I would die to save.

The memories of my service alongside these great men runs deep. When I tasted the cold air in the aircraft's cavernous fuselage and felt the power of its engines hauling us aloft, and I caught my first sight of the distant peaks of the Rockies, I had a little moment of déjà vu. I remembered an op we had done in 2005, right before Redwing.

Up there in the Hindu Kush, three of us—Dan Healy, Shane Patton, and I—had loaded into a Chinook helicopter with two other recon teams and risen through the clouds toward a snowcapped mountain. After a short flight, we landed and found ourselves on the nose of a promontory maybe two miles from the border with Pakistan. Once the helo inserted us, we quickly began building our hides.

I remember the commanding views we had, six thousand feet above sea level—an unbroken curve of horizon in three directions. Taliban insurgents were set up in these mountains, working over an Army forward operating base (FOB) near the border with rockets and artillery. Our mission was L&E—locate and eliminate. We were supposed to take them down. Our radio call sign was Irish 3.

From my vantage point on the end of a long, narrow ridgeline in the clouds, I could see the Army FOB to my west. To the east, I could see a cluster of primitive buildings, well camouflaged as natural features of the land, stone built into stone. We kept an eye on things, watching every side for signs of enemy movement. Every now and then we stretched our legs a little and went to check on each other.

It was on the third day that we finally found them. A barrage of rockets came raining down toward the American base. The enemy was beyond our reach, so we did the next best thing: Shane radioed the grid coordinates to the Army's artillery guys and waited. We saw the impact of the Army artillery hitting the mountainside, then its muffled thud. From down in the valley came the delayed *thrump* of the muzzle blast. Shane passed down corrections until the big guns weren't missing their marks anymore. At a distance we saw insurgents running on mountain trails and a train of camels slugging along behind. Let them all die.

Tired of the same damn rock sticking up my backside, I stood up, removed my helmet and body armor, and went looking for Senior Chief Healy. Walking through a cut in the rocky ridge that resembled a bowling alley, then passing through a wooded area, then through another bowling alley, I found him holed up in brush and trees on the side of a cliff. I told him about the houses and the men I'd seen. Normally when we were set up on a recon mission there was no small talk and little or no movement. Any comms were done over the radio. It was good to make some conversation in the vast, lonely silence.

Senior chiefs, however, will only carry it on for so long before it's time to get back to work. "Okay, Luttrell," Healy told me. "Back to your rock."

"Check," I said.

Walking back to my position, where I planned to wedge my butt back onto that rock (I can still feel it after all these years), I was passing through the second bowling alley when the ground began ticking up violently at me. A spray of rocks scattered in all directions—*pfft pfft pfft*. I crouched down. Scanning the mountainscape, I saw three guys on the other side of a pile of small boulders, looking directly at me. They were barely fifty meters away. One of them had his AK-47 leveled right at me. As I ran toward them, seeking cover along the way, the other two opened fire, stitching the ground right across my path. I took another shower of shattered shale. But thanks to their lousy marksmanship, my shorts were still clean. I went prone and pulled my rifle to my eye. I saw an insurgent swing over on me with an RPG. The fight was on.

I pulled the trigger a few times, then got up and moved. I sprinted as fast as I could, covering maybe thirty yards, then stopped to make myself small, hiding behind a wall of rocks. I rose to a knee and fired again. I don't know how I wasn't hit, given how exposed I was. Somehow the guy with the RPG circled around below me and unloaded on Senior Chief Healy's hooch. The detonation turned that big tough bastard loose in a hurry, and he came out of the brush, angry and focused, looking for targets. Meanwhile, on the back side of the hill, Shane Patton had his radio out, calling, "Troops in contact."

"Where the hell you at, Luttrell?" Healy shouted.

"I'm trying to find the sons of bitches who're shooting at us," I said.

Unholy ghosts, those bare-handed butt wipers. After that first dustup, they were swallowed up by the rocks. We never saw them again. The contact lasted no more than five or seven minutes.

Shane Patton's radio call brought reinforcements, fast. At first an AH-64 came on station—an Apache attack helicopter. Then a Chinook arrived with a dozen more SEALs. Weary from four days of cloud-top air, constant vigilance, and little to eat, we were glad to let them take up the hunt. We climbed on board the helo and choppered

back to base. Our relief would spend two more days looking for those insurgents, long enough for a huge thunderstorm to roll in and make their lives miserable for a while.
No matter what you see on TV, frogs don't like to be cold
or wet, and our reinforcements got a double dose of it
because of the storm.

As I sat in the huge C-17 on my way to Iraq, a lot of things
were on my mind, memories both priceless and painful,
pushing each other around in my head. As I looked
around the plane and watched my teammates, my greatest
hope was that every one of them would come home from
Iraq, just the way they were now, nothing missing, nothing scarred. But in a place like Ramadi, what were the
odds of that happening? The chances of losing someone
were high, in spite of everything we did to minimize the
risks. The workup. The constant advice and input from
experienced senior operators. The pass-downs and intel
from the team that preceded us. You put it all together and
you tilt the odds in your favor. But bad things are likely to
happen. It's simply a fact; that is war.

After landing in Germany, we laid over for five hours,
went wheels-up again, and touched down in Iraq's desert
city of Habbaniyah around 2:30 a.m. local time. We spent
the night offloading and staging our gear for the drive
west to Ramadi. In Habby, I got to see some old friends
from SEAL Team 4, but as usual the time together was
short. We hit the rack at about 5:30 a.m. The following
afternoon, we loaded up, piled into our Humvees, and
began the drive to Ramadi.

A hot and desolate place, hard terrain settled by even
harder men. A land of myth and legend, with a long tradi-

tion of war, pillage, and slaughter. A people tested by war and famine, baked hard by the sun. It was a land where the warrior's code binds all men into a ferocious brotherhood, where ancient traditions of honor attempt to govern the indifferent forces of life and death.

I'm talking, of course, about Montgomery County, Texas. But even the place I come from met its match in Iraq. It was a territory with complex tribal politics, ancient legends and even more ancient grudges, and a fickle corruptness that always seemed to push back and challenge unwanted outsiders. Here we were, driving into this wild terrain.

The road west from Baghdad traces the Euphrates River to Habbaniyah and then Ramadi, leading all the way to the border with Syria to the west. This dry, winding path was the cradle of Western civilization. At least four ancient civilizations had their roots in this earth: Babylon, Assyria, Akkad, and Sumer. It was the birthplace of the great biblical figures Abraham, Elisha, David, Jonah, and Noah. In our time, that road carried on its legacy of striving, struggle, and slaughter. Used for illegal trade since time immemorial, in 2006 it was still a principal smuggling route for the insurgency. The road was dotted with safe houses for criminals to hide in, under protection of tribal sheikhs who were always ready for a bribe and even more ready to murder, yet who were motivated all along by the old Arab tradition of giving hospitality to travelers. Since 2003, the road had been heavily traveled by U.S. military convoys. You never knew what fate held for you here.

Basically, it sucked.

It should have taken us thirty minutes to cover those

fifteen miles in our two-and-a-half-ton cargo truck. But knowing about all the IEDs that had been detonated along the main road, we decided to take detours. Using back roads, the trip took hours. I enjoyed the drive, though. A buddy of mine from BUD/S, the officer in charge of Alfa Platoon, Lieutenant Clint, rode shotgun with me, and we used the downtime to talk shop and reminisce. By the time we reached our destination five hours later, we hardly noticed how all the pothole dancing left us numb in the ass.

Ramadi loomed over us like a shadow. The city gave off weird energy. Maybe it was our imagination. Or maybe not. We knew the violent state of things there. Al Qaeda had promised to restore Ramadi to its medieval state. As home to their caliphate, it would be run by strict Islamic law. They enforced their vision with a brutal willingness to slaughter innocents by the houseful. Hundreds of American troops had been killed in its streets in the past two years. About five thousand troops were now at work trying to return the city to a rudimentary level of livability. SEAL Team 3 was on the sharp edge of the sword with the Army and Marine Corps in the fight to retake it. They had helped start the fight, plunging into a bold new strategy to root out the enemy. Our job would be to help finish it and move the strategy toward a counterinsurgency.

Those of us who had seen Ramadi before—and Master Chief had spent much of 2005 there—were surprised by the shocking destruction that had been visited on the city. The place was a ruin. Buildings were reduced to crumbled facades. Weeds grew up through streets. Infrastructure was destroyed. Dust and rubble were everywhere. Already ravaged by Saddam's excesses and UN sanctions, Ramadi now groaned under the weight of an insurgency and a U.S. military presence that was often, of necessity, quite heavy-handed. The runoff from broken sewer pipes turned street dust into a foul sludge. On a good day, the air came at us as though through an unventilated restroom. Businesses were closed because they lacked electricity, water, or basic security. The schools were all closed. There was no effective police force. Though a lot of people lived there, Ramadi had the feel of a ghost town. I know that makes no sense, but in Iraq, few things do.

And yet, while everything was coming apart, the city hollow and desolate, thousands of citizens had stayed, braving all this, because that's what Iraqis always did, making a tradition out of surviving whatever cruelties the world threw at them. It was heartbreaking to watch, and motivating at the same time. The people were working up the courage to fight for their homeland.

As the U.S. counterinsurgency strategy was implemented, our forces moved into the city to stay. The neighborhoods had to be patrolled regularly and made safe, no matter how much fire our forces took. To make life tolerably secure at our combat outposts, sometimes buildings had to be razed to give our guys clear lines of fire. Once in a while, our snipers and assaulters had to roll out and give the enemy a hard kick in the sack.

The headquarters of SEAL Task Unit Ramadi, the home of Alfa Platoon, adjoined the main U.S. military base in the city, Camp Ramadi, situated on the western edge of town. Camp Ramadi was home to an Army brigade headquarters that included elements of the First Armored Division as well as other Army and Marine

Corps units. Shortly after we picked out our tents, Lieutenant Commander Thomas called me into his office and gave me some news. He told me that I was going to take over as acting chief of Alfa Platoon. Our current chief was needed elsewhere. So he recommended to Skipper and Master Chief that I take over the job. Though I was scared shitless of the promotion, all I could say was "Roger that, sir." It was in my blood to respect the chain of command.

The reason why I was scared was pretty simple. When I was a shooter, a member of the "E-5 mafia," all I had to do was show up, find my place in the stack, hit the target, and be ready to shoot again. The promotion to chief (E-7 pay grade), confronted me with so much more: planning missions, dealing with people, mediating disagreements, and determining accountability. Leadership responsibility was going to force me not only to stand on my own two feet but to climb to a higher level, where my every move would reset my reputation, the personal currency of the SEAL teams.

Though any commissioned officer is superior to him in rank, the chief petty officer is the one who makes Navy life go round. That's the way it is on a ship, on a submarine, or in a SEAL platoon. A dozen times during my career I had benefited from the sure, steady hand of a senior petty officer who steered me in a useful direction. One of the most important influences on any new SEAL is his "sea daddy," the chief of his first platoon, who serves as a mentor and shows him how to be a SEAL. Mine was a chief petty officer named Chris Gothro. When I was a twenty-three-year-old E-3, full of piss and vinegar, he took care of me—showed me the ropes and knots, so to speak. He kept me on the glide path, sent me to the right schools to get advanced qualifications as a medic, a sniper, and a comms guy. He taught me to volunteer for everything. There were rewards for discipline and loyalty—and, always, penalties for failure. Once, in Australia, when my redneck ways took me on an all-night bender and got my ass in a sling so tight I thought for sure my career was over, Chief Gothro was there to help me pay the piper. I begged him just to beat the crap out of me and be done with it. But he handled it as you would expect a good chief to. He knew how to keep my little character flaw from coming back in an even bigger way and really hurting my career. Long story short, punishments were administered and my life really sucked for about three months. (You can use your imagination, but you still won't be close.) My sea daddy knew what I needed, and you can't ask more of a leader than that.

Now I was standing in the chief's shoes. I wasn't sure I was ready for it, but, as with everything, I decided to give it my best shot.

The leadership position was nerve-racking in the beginning, but like everything else in life, it sorted itself out. Life quickly returned to feeling like business as usual. The high caliber of my platoon was one big reason the transition went smoothly. I knew I couldn't be a shooter forever, and in the end I benefited from having had men far better than me show me how to handle the added responsibility.

I was lucky when I got in country to link up with the chief from Team 3. Chief Tony handled the pass-down to the Team 5 guys. He had a great reputation in the teams. He sat us down and gave us the play-by-play on how to fight and survive in Ramadi. He told us what was going on there, what parts of the city were hot, which tactics were working for them, and which weren't. We talked about the operations they'd been running, the Iraqis they were working with, and what the state of play was with their training. Sitting there listening to him talk about patrols, routes, enemy tactics, and several dozen other things that could mean living or dying in this hellhole was an incredible experience. It was crazy, all the things he had seen.

When he handed out the maps his team had developed of the city, it was like looking at an inkblot test, a cluttered mess of markings, shadings, and comments. He told us, "It may look confusing now, but don't worry, you'll get it after a while." He was right: you would be surprised how quickly you pick things up when your life is on the line. And we'd have a lot to learn about Ramadi that wasn't on any map.

5

Shakeout Patrol

We unpacked our gear during most of the night of October 16. Our team house at Camp Marc Lee had been a dictator's palace in older days. Fronted by impressive stone pillars, and situated right on the Euphrates River, the three-story stone building once served as quarters for the Iraqi dictator's personal security detail. It wasn't the most secure building we could have chosen. The riverfront side of our compound looked pretty exposed. Our best protection against the dangers of the street came from the high guard towers of Camp Ramadi. Situated to our west, the main U.S. base served as Camp Marc Lee's rear wall. Because we were within easy range of rifle fire from the street, we filled the windows with sandbags and kept alert for incoming rounds no matter what side of the wall we were on.

The accommodations were basic and functional— spartan, just as we liked them. We spent our first days getting organized with our equipment and our accommodations. We sighted our weapons, worked out in the gym, and studied our maps. With summer at an end, the temperatures in western Iraq were slowly falling. It was eighty degrees on a typical October day. Soon, the winter rains would set in. But no matter the season, we would never have much hot water. Though SEALs aren't high-maintenance guys, this does give us something of a problem. After all the time we spent freezing our asses in the cold surf during BUD/S, and all the diving exercises we SDV types did in icy water, we have little tolerance for cold showers. It's a frogman thing—we'll stink like sewers and bathe with baby wipes before we let ourselves freeze without an operation order. Freaking BUD/S; it ruins many of us forever.

Getting our minds around our new battle space was a high priority. On the night of our first day, rolling past midnight, I joined Lieutenant Commander Thomas, Senior Chief Steffen, our LPO, Marty Robbins, and half a dozen other team leaders on what we call a shakeout patrol or turnover op.

In a new combat environment, it usually takes several weeks to get our battle rhythm—a basic level of ease and comfort with the area we're in and the kinds of things that can be expected to happen there. In time, you develop a nose for what's normal and what's not. You know how the people tend to move around. You learn when businesses are open or mosques are crowded. The goal of the shakeout patrol was to get our feet wet, to get acquainted with the area's angles and corridors, and with its human dynamics as well. We had to get into rhythm with our own platoon, and also with the space around us and the local population. Some guys from Team 3 went with us to show us the ropes. Our first patrol was their last. Most of their teammates had left by the time we rolled out, but the guys who stayed behind earned our gratitude. They accepted risks that had to weigh heavily on them during that last night in country. What they taught us would later save lives, and we will forever be in their debt.

Finding our battle rhythm is the first step in a gradual process of plugging ourselves into our own network. SEALs have a culture of independence, sure, but we also develop a sort of hive mind. We interlink, learn to anticipate, think with each other, through each other, and for each other. Then we do the same with our environment. When we do it right, our senses align with our surroundings and danger can reveal itself in something as instinctual as the hairs standing up on the back of your neck. But it takes time to get there.

Experience has shown us that our casualties tend to occur at the beginning and end of our deployments. At the beginning, we're unfamiliar with the area of operations. At the end, with a flight home close on the calendar—and a steak dinner, a warm bed, and the first sight of a woman in maybe six or seven months (but, most important, the steak dinner)—we can get complacent. It's simply human nature. The casualties that Team 3 took, losing Mike Monsoor less than three weeks earlier, told us we had to get up to speed fast, because the day would come when we'd be going after the same guys who had killed him— and more besides.

I liked the fact that an officer of Lieutenant Commander Thomas's high caliber and long experience was running our show. He and my brother are very close, having practically grown up together in the teams. His friendship with Morgan automatically made him close to me.

Like the center of an hourglass, I was Thomas's conduit to the men. I made sure he knew the pulse of the guys who made it happen. I handled small problems and kept him up to speed on their morale. And when necessary, I took it the other way, letting the guys know what was going on at the top. I tried my best to stay in the middle to protect my guys from all the politics and make sure the head shed never had a reason to get upset with the boys. Luckily, our two platoons were squared away, so I never had to worry about trouble from above.

It's common to think of people in the military as conformists. But that's far from the truth in our community. Some pretty capable and colorful types join the SEAL teams, looking for bigger challenges than their high-flying careers or other interesting backgrounds can offer. Whether doctor, lawyer, longshoreman, college dropout, engineer, or NCAA Division I superathlete, they were more than just good special operators. They were a cohesive team whose strength came from their widely diverse talents, educational backgrounds, upbringings, perspectives, and capabilities. They're all-American and patriotic, with a combination of practical intelligence and willpower that you don't want to get crossways with. Streetwise, innovative, adaptable, and often highly intellectual—these are all words that apply to the community. And the majority are so nice that it can be hard to envision their capacity for violent mayhem. BUD/S filters out four of every five aspirants, leaving behind only the hardest and most determined—the best. I was so proud and humbled to be a part of the brotherhood.

Adam Downs was a good old southern boy who reveled in his reputation as the platoon hillbilly. Though he told everyone he was from Kentucky, he actually hailed from Illinois. I respected this guy big-time. He carried his ferocious southern way on the battlefield—we called him the redneck mujahideen. But make no mistake: he was a solid operator, reliable and trustworthy, and one of our best snipers. Adam liked to chew cigars, and was superstitious, too. He kept a soggy old stogie with him that dated to his previous deployment. He thought it was good luck, and said his platoon never took a casualty when he was chewing it. And when you go overseas, trust me, you don't leave something like that behind. By the time he got to Ramadi, that cigar needed so much duct tape to hold it together that at the end of an op, when we returned to base, he could stick it underneath the visor of the Humvee, ready to use again the next time we rolled out.

As we unloaded at Camp Marc Lee, we found that a few of us had brought our compound bows along with us. Blowing arrows through targets on our range was always a way to kill time between ops. Then someone dared Adam to take the bow with him on a mission. We thought it went without saying: the first SEAL to take down an insurgent with an arrow would be an instant legend. With no muzzle flash, a bow might just be the ultimate sniper weapon. Wielding it to lethal effect would be an amazing feat of old-school military art. Of course, it was just crazy talk. The idea would never have gotten past our leadership. We left the Rambo act to the screenwriters. But man, it sure would have been cool.

Adaptability is at the very heart of the way a SEAL team does business. Our tactics are classified, of course, but I can tell you that they change from deployment to deployment based on what we see the enemy doing. I had been out of the war for more than a year and I had to be flexible: no matter how good workup was, you could never start getting comfortable until your boots hit the ground. Throughout a deployment, we'd be one step up on them or one step behind, depending on the day.

When we walked out the front gate of Camp Marc Lee, down the road a little ways to the left was a huge building, a glass factory. Located right on the Euphrates River, it had been used as a recruitment depot for Iraqi police. Earlier in the year, the insurgency rolled a huge truck full of explosives into it when there were several hundred recruits gathered outside. Scores of people died in that blast, a tragedy our forces were powerless to stop. Since then, the building was occupied from time to time by insurgent snipers looking to enfilade our camp. We took a lot of fire from that glass factory before we finally took back control of it and, with it, our own neighborhood.

We relied heavily on the Army and the Corps for intel that helped us maintain our one-up position. All of us appreciated what those Marine Corps and Army companies, and of course the boys from Team 3, had done prior to our arrival. Taking fire every day and returning it many times over, the conventionals and Lieutenant Commander Willis and his guys had cleared out a lot of brush for us, so to speak. He was a straight-up warrior, a gunfighter. He didn't sit around and wait for things to happen—he led his men out into the streets and *made* it happen. If you wanted a fight in Ramadi, it was never hard to find one. All you had to do was hop into a Humvee and drive into the middle of town, and, soon enough, the insurgents started maneuvering on you. We usually had just enough time to adjust ourselves before something interesting went down.

The enemy we faced had been winnowed down substantially by Team 3. But that meant they were a little bit sharper than they were over the summer. The worst of them worked (and probably lived) in the dangerous south-central and southeast parts of Ramadi, the Ma'laab district, areas we called the Papa sectors. Generally we could count on a certain level of incompetence on the part of the jihadists; plenty of them were just opportunists looking for a chance to make some money by killing Americans. Others seemed to have gotten their tactical skills from PlayStation 2—they were more aggressive than the idiots were, but never knew what to do without a memory chip and a reset button.

But in the Papa sectors, they were flat-out crafty bastards. Because Ramadi was one of Saddam's strongholds, it made sense that many of his former Army officers were still living there. That may have been why the enemy in the Ma'laab district was so adept: they were professional or at least trained by professionals, a cut above the fighters elsewhere in the city. When they weren't going out at night, digging holes in the road to plant IEDs, these insurgents were hiding in crowds, using women and children for cover, maneuvering on us, then slipping away to avoid our return fire. Skulking through narrow alleyways and across congested urban rooftops, they looked for that uncovered angle from which to hit us with gunfire, grenades, or RPGs. The crackle of gunfire and pop of explosions was as common as car horns in Manhattan.

Our enemy was a diverse group. Their ranks included fighters from the Mujahideen Shura Council, a shadowy outfit that tried to unify various Sunni Islamist groups fighting us "infidels." Basically they were Al Qaeda types, many loyal to the AQ leader in Iraq, Abu Musab al-Zar-qawi, killed in an air strike that June. Right before we landed, that group released a video declaring Iraq an Islamic state and changing its name to the Islamic State of Iraq. Incurable optimists, these people. They'd have to go through the U.S. military to make that happen, and try they did. Needless to say, their bravado attracted a lot of bad guys to Ramadi and encouraged a lot of reckless violence. The insurgents in Ramadi came from all over the world—from Syria, Egypt, Pakistan, Jordan; there were even some American-born extremists. You name a flag, there was an asshole there who was flying it.

One group, Ansar al-Sunnah, was a cadre of Sunni extremists that rivaled Al Qaeda for its hatred of Americans. Some of them were foreigners who had come to Iraq at the invitation of Saddam Hussein as our military gathered strength on his borders. Another faction was made up of criminals who exploited the opportunities of the moment. Smuggling was a big one. They snuck weapons into the city, sold them to the enemy, then came to us and revealed where they were hidden in order to collect rewards provided by the coalition's buyback program. They made a good living on dumb money. Then there were tribal fighters whose sheikhs didn't want any outsiders in their neighborhood, and especially us Westerners. We had to deal with Al Qaeda and other "insurgent" supporters drawn from the ranks of the poor. It was easy for AQ to find an old man or an orphaned kid who would take payment in exchange for crossing two wires together when a cell phone rang, thereby clacking off an IED against the next U.S. convoy to roll by. Blackmail and threats worked just as well. God help any Iraqi who let one of his bad personal secrets slip into the hands of some Islamic nut—he'd be working for him right quick. Then we had young Muslim kids coming in from all over the world, insurgents who were looking for a fight and eager to prove themselves in action against us. In that one respect, I guess, they weren't all that different from us.

So we faced no one kind of enemy. But there sure were a lot of them, hidden in the city's secret places. Master Chief opened my eyes when he told me of estimates that showed, all across Anbar, probably only a few hundred foreign fighters opposing us in a coordinated way. But there were thousands and thousands of dangerous men who were at their beck and call by way of force, persuasion, or bribery. Given the complete breakdown of law and order there, it was easy for extremists to blame everything on the Americans. The most murderous of the terrorist leaders often claimed the title "emir," a term of tremendous respect in the Sunni culture. Al Qaeda gave that title, typically reserved for men of great power and wealth, to any insurgent who had a sufficient number of American KIAs to his credit. These men reserved for themselves the authority to kill, steal, rape, and pillage as they saw fit. Without some pushback, it would have spun completely beyond anyone's control.

A city is a hell of a battlefield. Every window is a fighting position, every rooftop a fortress. There was always a doorway, an alley, a wall, or another place where the enemy could get the drop on us. They had home-field advantage and knew it. And they could hide in plain sight. A guy in sweatpants and a T-shirt is an innocent civilian; a guy in sweatpants and a T-shirt holding an RPG is a dangerous threat. Four of them together are even worse.

They could sneak through a narrow alley, invisible to our planes, pop up, fire their weapons, then toss them through a window and rejoin society. If we shot the wrong guy in response, we could have a whole neighborhood turning against us.

I had to hand it to them: they had it figured out and were very smart about the way they engaged U.S. forces. If we were to make it out of there, we had to be as unpredictable and fast-moving as the bad guys were.

Having served in Baghdad in 2003, I had experienced urban combat before. But Ramadi was nothing like that. Back then, the enemy hid and we went in and rooted him out. The high-value targets we looked for—bomb makers, terror financiers, former officials of Saddam's criminal regime—were basically craven cowards. They weren't nearly as well organized or militarized. Pursuing them was a thrill, but it didn't seem as dangerous as what we would be asked to do in Ramadi. Here the aggressive ill will was percolating in the air. Everyone felt it. There were so many ways things could go wrong. In a counterinsurgency fight, we had to battle the criminals, persuade the military-age men to work with us (or at least not against us), and spend time and money training them—all while standing ready to jock up on a moment's notice to blow in the door of a fortified insurgent safe house and deal out "medication" in 5.56mm doses while taking care not to disturb the neighbor's goat, for fear he might get annoyed and end up on the enemy's payroll.

Moving through the city, we learned to be hyperalert, "ballooning" our rifles the whole time—keeping them pointed to the sky as if they were attached to balloons floating through the air. This was an exhausting way to work. By the end of a patrol, we felt like we'd been doing curls and shoulder presses for hours. But it saved us a critical fraction of a second if we had to draw on an enemy who had the high ground on us. We were always ready, and always respectful of Murphy's Law—the minute you decide to skip a window, that's where the next insurgent will be, rifle at his shoulder, with you in his sights. The minute you got complacent, you were dead.

The insurgency's bomb makers were relentless. Most of the American servicemen who died in Anbar Province were killed by IEDs. The enemy would take artillery shells and bury them in the street, using concealed wires to detonate them. By breaking sewer lines to flood the dusty streets, they would use the muddy, sewage-laced mess to conceal their trigger wires. They'd plant their charges under the water, making them hard to detect, especially at night. They'd lay monofilament trip wires in the streets, with fishhooks tied to them, to catch a guy by the boot, trigger a bomb, and blow him to kingdom come. The electrical command wires they used were those thin copper wires used to wind small electrical motors— really hard to detect. A street that we patrolled and swept at noon could be thick with hidden explosives before the lunch hour was over. All of Iraq seemed stuffed with stolen ordnance, stockpiled anywhere you can imagine. You make the wrong move, boom—you're in a bag. If you really screw up, they'll be picking you up with a sponge.

The insurgency's bomb emplacers were in constant battle of wits with our EOD guys. Andy Fayal and our other bomb techs were expert in detecting the telltale traces of a bomb that was ready to ruin your day. About 80 percent of the IEDs in Ramadi were what our techs called victim-operated. These devices work with pressure plates or other mechanical components that close a circuit when someone steps on or drives over them. About 15 percent were command-wire detonated—remote-controlled, set off by triggermen in hiding. The rest were remote-controlled by a radio or infrared signal. And the insurgents weren't content merely to blow us up: they added kerosene and other incendiary accelerants to the charges, aiming to set us on fire. When they really wanted to spice things up, they added payloads of chlorine, mercury, or other nasty elements to the bomb packages. (We found their chemistry labs on any number of the raids we did.) When our route-reconnaissance guys got good at using their magnetic detection gear to find buried artillery rounds, the enemy put their homemade explosives in rice sacks. Surviving in those streets took guts, nuts, and smarts.

On that first patrol out of Camp Marc Lee, we drove out to one of the combat outposts in the southern part of the city and shook hands with the conventional commanders who controlled the area—who "owned" the battle space, as we say. The Army would lead the way during our time in Ramadi. Colonel Sean MacFarland, commander of the First Brigade Combat Team of the First Armored Division, would be a major player in this fight, and our leadership was right there at his side. We were the long blade he held behind his back.

In my new position, I frequently dealt with Army and Marine Corps officers face-to-face, because we had to ask them for permission to go into their areas. We certainly stood apart from them in many ways—in everything from experience and training to matters of grooming, appearance, and attitude. We're often allowed to go unshaven and can be a bit more cavalier in outlook. We don't blouse our pant legs over our boots or wear insignia, as they do. But make no mistake: the Army and Marine Corps outfits we worked with were balls-to-the-wall warfighters. They understood urban combat. They had raised their game for Ramadi's challenge, training for weeks, day in and day out, at rifle ranges and "shoot houses," guided by contractors who had served in special operations. They did ballistic breaching, close-quarters battle, and so on. Over and over again they rehearsed what the Army calls Battle Drill 6a: entering a building and clearing a room. They did it in single-room, multiple-room, hallway, and staircase settings, standardizing their tactics so that platoons from different companies could play from the same sheet of music. Some of their leadership had done the special operations training course at Fort Campbell, Kentucky. Their snipers refreshed their skills at Fort Benning, Georgia. We were more than impressed.

It was dark by the time we ditched our vehicles at the COP and set out on foot on our shakeout patrol. It turned out to be a real nut dragger. In urban environments, we travel heavier than we do in the mountains. In the city, where distances are shorter and the air is easier to breathe, we wear our body armor, all the plates. My M4 rifle had an M203 grenade launcher attached to the barrel. I had eight magazines of 5.56mm bullets and ChemLights. As team lead, I carried flares, an extra radio, and an extra antenna stuffed in a cargo pocket. I had a computer and a medical pack containing QuikClot, bandages, needles, and tourniquets. I had water and food, too. I weighed about 250 pounds without my gear, and more than 325 with it. With every step I took, I could feel my spine compressing like a shock absorber.

And the noise—good Lord. We would never have been allowed to move in the wilderness the way we did that night in the city. Half of us sounded as though we had cowbells hanging around our necks. At night it was easy to stumble into things. Running around in the darkness, using night-vision goggles, which remove most of your depth perception, I tripped and found myself lying legs up in an open sewer pit. It's easy to plant your face in the ground when you're slogging around an unfamiliar area wearing NVGs, hyperventilating from excitement, and feeling your heart rate pegged to the right. I'm always glad to entertain my SEAL brothers, and here, lying in that sewage, I didn't disappoint. I radioed up and reported that I had found the shitter if anyone needed to go.

After the first hour of humping through the city's filth, the exhaustion wore on my lungs, muscles, and bones. Our patrol took us through an open area in the southern part of the city. We halted there, and I found myself kneeling in a depression in the earth. I thought at first that it was a foxhole of some kind. It was nasty. It smelled of death. And for good reason: the field we were in turned out to be a cemetery, and the hole I was standing in was an open grave. Mine was the only body in it, fortunately. I remember how the wind carried the aroma of decay. I remember the burning in my lungs—and in every muscle of my body. And now the grave beckoned to me.

I felt like I'd need to get shot at a few times to know that I was still alive as a gunfighter. I wanted to know I still had my edge, and could trust myself to perform in the line of fire. In the teams we reach a place where that edge percolates in the air between men who have arrived at the pinnacle of fitness and training. I prayed we'd make contact with the enemy and take a little incoming fire. If nothing else, it would be an opportunity to hit the dirt, take the weight off, and catch my breath. After all my years in the teams, I felt like a new guy out there that night.

When we finished our patrol and returned to the outpost, Senior Chief Steffen brought us all together and got right to the point. "Now you know what this lousy place is like," he said. "You've smelled it and you've felt it. Start shucking your gear." Serving during the peak of summer, the Team 3 boys had carried a lot of water. The big dromedary bags they stuffed into their rucks added fifty or sixty pounds to their load, forcing them to economize in other areas. They packed just three or four magazines, maybe a couple of grenades, and left a lot of their body armor at the base. It took one patrol for us to learn to go light, too. We got rid of the extra magazines we carried in our vests. I removed the grenade launcher from my rifle and switched out its long barrel in favor of a short, ten-inch upper receiver, better for close-quarters fighting. When we did sniper overwatch missions, which were largely stationary, we could afford to go heavy. But an assault element had to travel light.

Back at camp, I called our guys together and told them we had work to do before I would consider us competent to patrol in a nighttime environment. So we practiced over and over, moving with all our gear on, marching up and down along the wall of the camp, back and forth, deep into the night. We finally got streamlined, tucking in our loose straps and securing all our gear, making sure we were quieter and more agile. I hit the gym hard. Working out on the treadmill, I wore all my body armor to get used to the rattle and the weight. My abused joints and bones howled in protest—especially my spine. I was in decent shape, but I wasn't in *Ramadi* shape. I'd have to get there fast. Spiritual fitness was important, too. I never allowed myself to forget who was in command as I went through these paces. In the journal I kept, the final words in each entry were the same every day:

"Thank you, God, for one more day."

No matter how bad things would get, I'd never forget to tell Him that.

Two days after our shakeout patrol, the rest of the task unit arrived at Camp Marc Lee. I never even got a glimpse of Morgan—my brother's outfit, Bravo Platoon, was bound for a camp across the city, Camp Corregidor, a smaller base built on land once used as a date farm and as a training camp for Saddam's army. It was a lousy dump. The camp had barely enough fresh water to provide just one shower a day—for a single man, not for everybody—so Morgan got used to showering in water pumped from filthy canals. It was said that the fleas and bedbugs that assaulted them daily rode to the attack on the backs of the rats. Still, as home to Bravo Platoon and several companies of conventional infantry, Camp Corregidor would be the center of gravity in our effort to get control of Ramadi's violent east side.

The crosstown road that led from Camp Marc Lee to Camp Corregidor was known as Route Michigan. It was an IED-choked nightmare. Fortunately, the bomb techs with the EOD mobile unit attached to our squadron spent lots of time with the intel shop getting the latest dope on enemy bomb-making tactics. They ran with our fire teams wherever we went, their simple tool kits always handy—a multitool, some heavy-duty shears, and small explosives (det cord and C-4) to countercharge any bombs they found. And these guys smoldered with their own desire for revenge. In February, a bomb tech named Nick Wilson was killed in Ramadi while tracing a thread of copper command wire over a berm near a road. Andy Fayal accompanied Nick's body home to his family, while the others vowed to track down the bomb makers responsible for their friend's death. At Nick's funeral, Andy was impressed to see a number of SEALs in attendance. I think he finally understood then how much we respected the EOD community's skills and dedication to their craft. Our camaraderie ran deeper than blood. God bless all the EOD guys.

The Army engineers who did route reconnaissance in Ramadi did a damn good job, too. Their work was similar to what our EOD detachment did, but on a larger scale. They rolled out in formations of vehicles designed to detect and take out the big subsurface explosive devices. Each vehicle performed a different function—detecting IEDs, marking them, sweeping the street of debris, and finally digging them up and disposing of them. The Army used a type of heavily armored truck known as a Buffalo, which has a big arm that can be fitted with various attachments and extended out front to sweep the roads and uncover planted bombs. They also used these lunar-lander-looking monsters known as Joint EOD Rapid Response Vehicles, or JERRVs. Those bad boys could absorb huge blasts and keep going. It was a talent they used often. The guys inside would be fine as long as they wore their five-point harnesses and helmets. The Army also deployed tracked robots known as TALONs, which are tricked up with sensors and a mechanical arm to deal with the deadly toys they dig up. Sometimes it was just as easy to roll over suspected bomb positions and take the blast. They could work faster that way and cover more ground.

These convoys rolled through the city streets at two miles an hour, creeping along the most dangerous thoroughfares all night long, bright lights blazing, and continuing through the next day and into the next night as well. If a JERRV got hit—and acting as a blast magnet was definitely part of their job description—the recovery team would move in, hoist the wreck onto a five-ton flatbed, and take it back to Camp Ramadi. A replacement would take its place and the formation would continue roaring along at its snail's pace, never losing a beat.

It made a big impression whenever one of their vehicles was dragged back to camp, all the tires blown off— basically a capsule. But every night they went back out, going into the kill zone and staying there because they couldn't stand to see regular infantry get caught there instead. They saved hundreds of lives, and the men who drove them impressed us with their bravery.

Driving Route Michigan, we made good use of our crazy week learning tactical driving. SEALs don't run convoys, as the regular Army does. The conventionals usually travel heavy, motoring slowly across the road, often in broad daylight. This gives the insurgency's IED triggermen plenty of time to see them coming and hit them. By contrast, in Ramadi, we drove like bats out of hell, our vehicles blacked out like shadows. If there was a triggerman along our path who was counting on a few seconds' notice, well, he would be sorely disappointed. The threat of roadside bombs was downright grave already. We didn't need to make it easy for him.

Watching a battered Pathfinder return to Camp Ramadi one morning, I said to Lieutenant Commander Thomas, "Sir, those guys are getting beat to hell. The enemy has to know they're coming. How else would they be sitting on them like this?"

If our troop commander heard any fear in my voice, his easy response didn't acknowledge it. He said to me, "Marcus, if we thought about that too much, we wouldn't be able to do our job. We'd never get out there into the fight."

"Roger that, sir," I said. "Let's go get some."

The boys at Camp Corregidor didn't waste any time getting their rifles into the fight. One day, at his spartan digs across town, Morgan had a quick in-brief from EOD, then turned in for the night. He awoke early the next morning to the sound of enemy mortar fire coming into camp.

Smaller than Camp Marc Lee and more exposed to its surrounding neighborhoods, Camp Corregidor took fire regularly. The boys there just had to live with it. They wore body armor even for a quick run to take a dump. Men were still sometimes killed by mortar fire while in the chow line. The camp was bounded to the north by Route Michigan. An irrigation canal separated it from a nasty part of the city that was home to COP Eagle's Nest, the neighborhood where Ryan Job and Marc Lee got shot back in August. Several lookout towers were located on the camp's western perimeter wall. One of Bravo Platoon's snipers, Cowboy, ran to one of those towers and climbed up to take a look. He had his sniper rifle with him.

From the tower, Cowboy had a good view of the major road that skirted the residential district of the east-central part of the city, intersecting with Route Michigan. Eventually it would be known as Sniper Alley because of the high volume of sniper fire hitting Camp Corregidor from the street. On this day, though, Cowboy was sending it the other way. Through the scope of his rifle, more than six football fields away, he spied a red Opel sedan parked on the road across the canal with its flashers on. A man was standing in front of the car. He looked up and down the road, then lifted the hood, walked around the side of the car, and looked around some more, up and down the street. The guy was expecting something, but Cowboy sensed it wasn't a tow truck.

Apparently believing he was unobserved, the man gave a little hand signal and two other guys came running out of a nearby house carrying rice sacks that seemed to hold a heavy load. They heaved the payload into the car's trunk.

Cowboy didn't need another set of eyes to know what he was looking at. He fixed his crosshairs on one of the bag handlers and squeezed the trigger. A round of .300 Win Mag flew 680 yards downrange. Hit, center mass. The other bag handler began dragging his buddy back toward the building. The driver slammed down the hood, jumped into the car, and began to drive away. Cowboy got on the radio to the tactical ops center. "This is Cowboy in Echo Tower. We've got one EKIA [enemy killed in action] and a VBIED [vehicle-borne improvised explosive device] moving down the street in a red Opel. They're right out in front of you now." In short order some *jundis* hustled out and took that driver and his car into custody. They found explosives in the trunk. It was indeed a VBIED, quite literally hell on wheels. Thanks to Cowboy, they took it off the street before it could find a target. He went back to his quarters and said to his platoon, "Y'all ain't gonna *believe* this...." From then, Cowboy followed the same ritual every morning, climbing to the top of Echo Tower and having a look at his exciting new neighborhood.

6

Firecracker

For a SEAL team looking for work, the action never comes soon enough. Team 5 had taken the nickname Task Unit Red Bull. We wore a patch showing a head-down, horns-low longhorn with the Team 5 logo branded on his rear. Our slogan, "If you mess with the bull, you get the horns," had a sort of Texas twang and was also fitting because of all the Red Bull energy drinks we went through every day just to stay awake. To this day the SEAL teams do their part to keep that brand in business.

The teams can be pretty strongly personality driven, and some of us took the liberty of personalizing our uniforms. My brother and I wore a small three-by-five-inch Lone Star flag front and center on our chests. On his shoulder, Adam Downs had a patch honoring the New York City fire department's Engine 53, Ladder 43, in memory of the 9/11 attacks. Once in a while Morgan brandished a patch with the colonial-era "Don't Tread on Me" flag on it, modified SEAL-style: the snake was replaced by the skeleton of a frog, and the famous command was replaced with something a little more provocative: DON'T F——K WITH ME. Team 3 stenciled the bare-skull image of the Punisher, a Marvel Comics character, on their vehicles, gear, and weapons. In Team 5, we took a more modest approach. We named our Humvees after characters from the *Transformers* movies—Optimus Prime, Ironhide, Bumblebee, Soundwave, and so on. Our comms truck and troop hauler was known as Omega Supreme. Folks don't typically run this way in the conventional military.

Our first job in Ramadi was an important one. We were assigned to push out into a neighborhood about three miles east of Camp Marc Lee to set up sniper overwatch positions protecting U.S. forces who were building a new combat outpost. Both squads from Alfa Platoon—Blue and Gold—went in, all told about thirty guys. On the morning of the twenty-sixth, we rolled out in our vehicles. We drove to an Iraqi checkpoint, where we picked up the *jundis* and two excellent men who served as our interpreters, or "terps"—Moose and Riddick, military contractors who lived with us full-time. Staging our vehicles there, we spent the day briefing with them, then, joining up with a patrol of Marines, we set out for our target on foot after dark.

As we proceeded down Route Michigan by night into the center of the city, all was quiet, a strict curfew in place. Maneuvering through the night, we kept about twenty feet between each man. As I kept pace with our fast-moving point man, Special Operator First Class Studdard, my radio crackled and burped with reports of American patrols in contact with the enemy, out there somewhere. The glow of small fires cast the low cloud ceiling in a spooky, shifting palette of reds. Skeletons of buildings loomed darkly all around us.

Finally, we reached our destination—an abandoned four-story building situated on a circular chain of streets that everybody called the Racetrack. Formerly an Iraqi military post, then a school, it was about to become a stiff thumb in the eye of the insurgency, a forward base for a company from the First Battalion, Sixth Marines (or 1/6). We all knew the enemy would come after it hard. We were sent in to keep things cool enough for construction to proceed. It would be known as Combat Outpost Firecracker.

The building was full of reminders of the evil confronting us. As we entered and cleared it, room by room, evidence of its recent darker uses was all around us. It had been an insurgent base of operations, and also a prison or interrogation center. Its filthy walls echoed with the cries of the tortured. Blood stained the tables. Ominous steel implements well suited to a barbecue pit were left behind (there wasn't any brisket in Ramadi). No telling how many innocent Iraqis had been abused there, but as we took control of the building, its vicious aura gave clarity to our mission.

We decided to set up our command and control element on the fourth floor. One of our officers, another SEAL, and the Navy pilot who served as our JTAC and arranged our air support made their home on the north side. Studdard, Wink, and I led the rest of the group, including all our snipers, around the rest of the floor, looking for positions with the best lines of sight and avenues of fire.

Ten of our thirty SEALs were qualified snipers (the

rest were expert marksmen), so we had five pairs to deploy. Putting a two-man sniper team in each room, we arranged an assortment of desks, chairs, pillows, and blankets for functional comfort. Where windowless walls covered up potentially good lines of sight, we sledged or blasted spider holes through them and otherwise redecorated the place. Senior Chief Steffen was with us and I was glad to have him there—and glad to serve in a position that reflected his trust. Once we were dug in, we lay low and waited for trouble, scanning the wasted city cast in shades of black and green through our night-vision goggles.

Before sunrise we had some small excitement when it was discovered that a mule had gotten inside the huge enclosed open playground behind the school. In Ramadi, nothing was as it appeared. When we noticed a hole in the brick wall nearby, we thought it possible that an insurgent had forced the animal in there with a bomb hidden inside him. They were known to plant explosives in animal carcasses, so nothing was impossible. That jackass certainly could have made a hell of an IED. We called our EOD bomb techs and they checked out the mule, which turned out to be packing nothing more than its usual kick.

Shortly after our arrival, an Army captain showed up, looking to coordinate with us, and I greeted him. Since SEALs don't wear rank, he seemed interested in figuring out where I stood in the chain of command relative to him. *Whatever, dude,* I thought to myself. I asked him what he needed from us.

"I want protection for my guys," he said.

"Roger that," I said. "Just keep your guys away from

mine while we're working. We'll take the fourth floor. No insurgents will touch you."

I have to hand it to the men who built the COPs. The whole U.S. military runs on the backs of its smart and resourceful engineers. It's been that way since the old days: engineers, sappers, Seabees—whatever you call them, good dudes all. The guys we covered worked incredibly fast, usually getting the COPs built overnight. They operated like well-oiled machines, efficiently standing up those outposts and connecting their electrical grids so that our forces could get to the task of taking something essential from the enemy: the trust and goodwill of the citizens of Ramadi. Working in full combat gear in the unbelievable heat, they set up concrete barriers, laid concertina wire on top of walls, layered sandbags into big piles, hooked up generators, and built guard towers, all the while taking harassing fire—and sometimes worse. You talk about hanging yourself out there. Good Lord.

A few of us tried to grab a little sleep as the eastern sky warmed before dawn. We planned to stick around for as long as it took to make sure ours was a long-term lease. But come morning, all hell broke loose in our little sector of Ramadi's shithole.

In Baghdad, we had rolled through the city in unarmored early-model Humvees, our legs and weapons hanging out the open doors on both sides. We looked pretty slick, but were very vulnerable then. Three years of IEDs and RPG attacks had helped us evolve. Now, on the street below us, a Humvee started taking fire from a position beyond our line of sight. Several RPGs hit the vehicle and the road around it. As that Humvee took several more hits, all of us watching were sure its occupants were goners. But somehow, it emerged from the swirl of dust and smoke and continued on. Those up-armored models could really take a beating.

The attack on the vehicle was followed by a barrage of mortar fire, falling on us in high arcs, lobbed from far away. They were big shells, 120mm rounds, and accurately targeted. Three of these bad boys straddled our building. One blew a huge crater in the street right where that Humvee had been. Another went off in the playground. The closest detonation shook the plaster and knocked paint from our walls.

As the attack continued, the streets rattled with the sound of American small arms fire as well as enemy PKC machine guns, AK-47 rifles, and rocket-propelled grenades. Once in a while, people would appear on the streets. Whenever we saw them milling around, we fired warning shots; when a wall splintered behind them, they usually disappeared quickly. The children were widely believed to be harmless, but we always had our suspicions that they served as lookouts and probes for the insurgency. Whenever we saw an older one acting aggressively, we paid attention and didn't quit paying attention until we figured out what he was up to. Polyester tracksuits and old-school Adidas-style sneakers—the ones with three diagonal stripes running down each side—seemed to be the uniform of choice for many of their fighters.

Adam got our team's first kill in Ramadi, earning him a case of beer the next time we got somewhere that had beer. He was always a source of laughs. One time after that, he was doing an overwatch when he needed to take a dump, so he stood up and dropped his drawers, only to be spotted by an American sentry across the way, who opened up on the sniper with his M60 machine gun. Apparently word of our position hadn't gotten around. The sentry ceased fire pretty quickly, though. (I think what saved my teammate was the New York Giants ball cap he was wearing, which must have been visible from quite a distance.) The experience was sure exciting for Adam—and particularly memorable: as he ducked the gunfire, he fell right back into his own crap. Needless to say, for the next few days he was alone in his sniper hole. (Sorry, bro; that moment was too funny not to immortalize in print.)

Confronting shooters of Adam's caliber, our cowardly enemies used any dirty tactic to gain an advantage. They exploited defenseless civilians and forced them into the crossfire. They understood that we were men of morals, governed by laws, and uncomfortable seeing innocents harmed. I remember three terrified women who showed up near COP Firecracker pushing a large handcart with an oil drum in it. An armed man moved along behind them, using them for cover. One of our snipers fired into the drum and another took aim between the women and fired right between the guy's legs. At this, all four Iraqis turned and ran. The guy moved so fast he bolted right out of his flip-flops. When the Marines checked out the oil drum, it turned out to be full of explosives.

By noon of the first day, our snipers had three kills. The streets became quiet.

The next day was calm until the late afternoon. The Army had three Humvees and an Abrams tank parked about 150 meters north of us, near a traffic circle. Just before dark, the insanity resumed. The street outside COP Firecracker came under heavy attack as dozens of insurgents opened up on the Hummers parked there. It sounded like they were firing everything they had.

As I watched from our top-floor sniper gallery, a Humvee parked near the traffic circle started taking machine-gun fire. The rounds were just ricocheting off the vehicle's up-armored hide, so the enemy brought out the heavier stuff. With a loud *whoosh* came an RPG. They shot it low, I think trying to skip the rocket under the vehicle to strike at its vulnerable underside. Through my binoculars I could see the vehicle begin to burn.

I was on the radio calling for a quick reaction force when the guys in the Humvee surprised us all, popping open the turtle shell and jumping out into the street. Running around to the back, under direct attack the whole time, they opened the hatch and pulled out a fire extinguisher. They sure cared about that Humvee, I'll say that for them.

I was expecting to see every one of those guys get hit, but without a visual on the enemy shooting at them, there wasn't much we could do to help. That was when the other Humvees showed up, bringing additional U.S. forces into the fray. These new arrivals compelled the insurgents to make other plans. The crew of the damaged vehicle was quickly extracted from harm's way, and the enemy force, which was fairly sizable, vanished into the alleyways of Ramadi.

Insurgents took big risks when they took on our forces like this. A big part of the reason why was the Navy pilot who ran with our assault element whenever we did sniper overwatches. His name was Brandon Scott, call sign FSBO, or Fizbo. His squadron buddies in Norfolk hung that name on him—an acronym for "for sale by owner"—after he and his wife bought a house and promptly got reassigned to another part of the country. In the military you never live down something like that, and if anyone senses that a nickname bugs you, you're stuck with it forever. (The best pilots usually have the most unflattering nicknames. The pilots I know say they don't generally have much confidence in anyone with a call sign like Maverick or Viper. If you meet one named Outhouse or Dumpster Diver, however, it's a safe bet he's good to go.)

Fizbo, as a JTAC, was basically a traveling fire-control station. Ours was one of the first platoons to let JTACs run with us on missions. Carrying as much as 150 pounds worth of portable radios into the streets, Fizbo kept in constant contact with pilots and lined up air support and overhead reconnaissance for us. He spoke the incomprehensible language known as Pilot and made life a lot easier for us, calling down hell from aircraft circling high above the clouds. Every request for close air support was like Christmas, though you never knew how Santa would deliver your gift. Sometimes he arrived on an F-16 or F/A-18 jet. Other times he rode a Predator drone or an Apache helicopter armed with rockets. Whatever the case, he and his sleigh were always welcome.

Working with a SEAL team wasn't what most high-flying fighter jocks like Fizbo wanted to do, but he wasn't like most pilots. After Redwing happened, he told his squadron mates at Norfolk all he wanted to do was grab a rifle and a radio and get into the fight down on the ground. That's our kind of flyboy. When he joined us at Camp Marc Lee, he got his wish. We did, too. His AN/PRC-117F multiband tactical radio plugged us into a network of aircraft operating from bases all around the region.

SEALs can earn a JTAC qualification, but I prefer having someone who speaks Pilot doing the job. They understand the problems facing the guy in the sleek Plexiglas cockpit up there—believe me, his problem is our problem. Although the assignment of a pilot to our platoon was out of the ordinary, our leadership saw the value in it and supported the effort to get some pilots into the mix. Doing time out there with us outside the wire, Fizbo took down a lot of bad guys and saved our butts many times.

So this Humvee is burning out there in the streets. The enemy has withdrawn, and probably thinks he's gotten away from us. He hasn't. Not with Fizbo sitting there next to me, talking to a buddy of his sitting in the cockpit of a Super Hornet twenty-five thousand feet above us. Thanks to some great technology, he can see what the pilot sees. Taking control of the aircraft's targeting pod, which mounts a powerful camera, he spots the squad of insurgents who launched the attack withdrawing through a warren of streets. Following them, he observes them entering a courtyard several blocks away. Three other insurgent teams, about twenty-five dudes in all, were gathered there. On the jet's infrared camera, some of their weapons glow brightly, still hot from being fired. What a target. Fizbo checks in with our platoon OIC, Lieutenant Nathan, and tells him we've found our boys.

We have a couple of options now. We can push out and launch a ground assault. But that isn't our mission at the moment. We can direct another patrol to their position, but that has risks, too. The easiest approach is a nice, clean bolt from the blue—a missile or bomb strike from Fizbo's airborne brother. Fiz agrees, so he calls in a strike request to brigade headquarters at Camp Ramadi—their approval was a standing requirement in the sensitive counterinsurgency fight—verifying that he's achieved positive identification on a hostile force. With all of them in that courtyard area, he wants to light it up with a five-hundred-pound bomb.

The reply from headquarters arrives quickly. "Request denied."

Fizbo's next course of action: beat head against wall. The look on his face was priceless (and his words unpublishable). He sourly considered this news, then asked that the request be pushed to the next level of command. He was denied there, too—and each time questioned on the validity of the target. When Fiz pressed the case, emphasizing that he had never lost sight of the enemy unit since its attack, a senior commander at brigade headquarters got on the radio. "Sorry, my friend, I'm not giving you this bomb," he said. Headquarters then passed control of the camera on the Super Hornet to its own Air Force tactical control team. Fizbo was out of business.

The head shed air controllers tried to keep watch on the cell. They saw a car pull up to the house. The bad guys started loading their weapons into the trunk. Then they began driving away. The air controllers did their best to follow the car, I guess, but they soon lost it in the maze. That aircraft never got any ordnance off the rails.

Fizbo and I couldn't believe headquarters had let them get away. We let the senior chief know it, and Lieutenant Commander Thomas, too.

Day five was quiet at COP Firecracker. As we kept the lookout, we also started filling sandbags and installing communication systems. Fizbo blew off some steam by standing watch with a sniper rifle on a key alleyway. (We had prepped that flyboy on the range, so he would be ready if events demanded action.) Looking for a quick nap, I stretched out some thermal camouflage netting and tied it off on two walls as though it were a hammock. I had no sooner reclined and closed my eyes when a ruckus woke me up: a pair of Army privates were fighting outside in the hall. I ran over and separated them, then hauled them by the arm into a classroom. I asked them what the trouble was. When it turned out to be a trivial thing—a fight over rations or something—I whipped up some choice Navy language and spread it all over them. I reminded them who the enemy was. I asked them if they understood their mission.

In the middle of my ass-chewing, I heard the cracks of gunfire, followed by an outburst of raw, terrified screaming from the roof. A U.S. soldier came falling down the stairs to our floor. He had taken a bullet in the back. It blew straight down his leg and came out through his knee. He was stabilized quickly and evacuated to a hospital somewhere.

When the excitement was over, I turned to the two teenagers who had been fighting and told them to listen closely. What had happened to that soldier would happen to them if they lost focus on their mission. "The enemy is out there. He's trying to kill you," I said. "You fool around, stop thinking, or start fighting like idiots over an MRE, and some asshole with an AK is going to put one through the both of you." Sometimes in the daily grind of combat, eighteen-year-old privates will be eighteen-year-old privates.

This was unlike any war I ever imagined. There was

no territory to hold in the normal sense. It was a war of constant patrol, a war of potshots and snipers, a war that was small-scale and personal. When someone got hit, we usually never saw the enemy, and when we did there were often questions about his identity or intention. But suppose everything checked out: his hostile intent was established, and we took the shot, taking down the bad guy. Well, here comes a military lawyer, interrogating us as though we were criminals and asking us to fill out a "shooter statement," explaining exactly why we killed the enemy. I understand now that we had to make sure every person killed in battle had a purpose—a purpose that propped up a government and supported the people of Iraq, while not feeding into the efforts of the insurgency. It is hard operating in the gray areas of a COIN environment, for leadership and ground-pounders alike. In the heat of the moment, though, I couldn't get over how our judgment as operators seemed always to take a back seat to the caution of the lawyers. Sure, political problems can sprout up quickly as a result of what happens on the battlefield, but that's bullshit right there. The rules of engagement change constantly in a combat environment, and our operators are rigorously trained to adjust accordingly, depending on their mission and the situation. Certain things should be left to experienced warriors to decide. Does anybody really think a guy riding a bike toward a firefight wearing a black scarf around his head and carrying a rifle slung on his back is looking for a barbershop quartet rehearsal? The lawyers often seemed to want to give him the benefit of the doubt. As a result, we couldn't always engage the enemy the way we felt we needed to. We couldn't touch mosques or hospitals, no matter how many bastards might have been shooting at us from the minarets and pediatric wards.

I could think of at least one way to get everyone on the same page. Let's put the lawyer on the rooftop—let him experience the sensation of having his own skin in the game—and see how far his note-taking skills get him.

7

Old Men of Anbar

When we returned to Camp Marc Lee from the mission to overwatch COP Firecracker, Alfa Platoon's favorite naval aviator was still plenty hot about being denied the chance to unload a wing rack on that buzzing enemy nest. After dropping off his gear at the camp, Fizbo made a beeline for the brigade combat operations center at Camp Ramadi, looking for some answers. He must have been pulling a few g's when he stormed into the office, because an Army captain noticed him and hurried out of his work space to engage him.

"Hey, what's going on?" he asked Fizbo. "I can tell you're upset. What are you trying to do here?"

"I'd like to see the officer who turned down my air strike."

Fizbo laid out how we watched those shitheads assault U.S. forces, and how we tracked them back to a courtyard where two other armed gangs were gathered.

"Yeah, we were watching that in real time," the captain said. "We really tried to make the right call." He explained how strategic objectives had affected the tactical decision that day. He said they were all concerned that Ramadi could become another Fallujah—total rubble, in other words. Ramadi had been so badly battered by collateral damage in several years of fighting that another rough six months of it might end civilization there altogether. The challenge, the captain said, was to kill the insurgency without killing the city. And that would require a new way of war.

Having defended his commander's decision, the Army officer then remarked, "You know, everything considered, we probably *should* have let you drop the bomb."

As it happened, the officer with the fine diplomatic touch was one of a handful of Americans involved in the sensitive effort to win Ramadi's tribal sheikhs over to our side. His name was Travis Patriquin. A civil affairs officer and a former Green Beret, he was an authority on Middle Eastern cultures and customs and was fluent in seven languages, including the colloquial Arabic dialect that people spoke in the streets. We had seen some of his briefings near the end of workup, and Lieutenant Commander Thomas noticed him as a standout as soon as he got in theater. He recommended that Commander Leonard, our skipper, meet him and hear his thoughts on the tribal dynamics in the city.

When they met, Patriquin explained to Skipper that the Sufiyah district, north of Camp Corregidor, was an opportunity for us. The tribe there, the Albu Soda, was neutral toward us at best, and allowed Al Qaeda to roam. Their sheikh and his people seemed angry at the terrorists, but they needed guns and assurances of support before making a move. Skipper learned that the tribes were establishing their own "emergency response units," which needed training. An outfit like this could be a windfall for us. Properly trained and equipped, locals serving as police could identify and get rid of the foreign terrorists in a hurry.

Captain Patriquin spent a lot of time meeting with the sheikhs in their homes, breaking bread, drinking chai, and smoking cigars. He sensed that some of them were seriously considering the idea of turning on Al Qaeda, which had done so much to ruin their city. The sheikhs considered Patriquin someone they could deal with, and he became a sought-after dinner guest. One of these sheikhs was named Abdul Sattar Abu Risha. The thirty-four-year-old Iraqi proved to be very effective at getting his peers to come on board the anti–Al Qaeda effort. Patriquin had so much influence with the sheikh that Sattar began calling him his son. Sattar was the first sheikh to ally himself with us. It was a brave move, but it might have been the only thing a man of honor could do, because Al Qaeda had murdered his father and two of his brothers. I can't imagine the pain he had gone through, but I could understand what motivated him. He wanted to fight, and he was smart enough to realize that the Americans were the toughest fighters in town.

The tribes of Anbar Province are generally quite secular. They're not unlike the ancient clans of Scotland: membership is based on bloodlines, and loyalty to tribe trumps loyalty to the state. It's hard to ask an Iraqi to do something in the name of his country. Loyalties don't typically run that far, at least they hadn't yet. Since the tribes are full of internal divisions and shifting alliances, their leaders are paranoid about threats to their status and authority. Saddam Hussein had manipulated their insecurities with a Machiavellian finesse, buying the cooperation of the willing and pitting rivals against one another. But with this powerful movement gaining steam, it was clear that Sattar was putting himself on the line in a way that went beyond his own self-interest.

By late 2005, American commanders realized that it might be possible to ally Anbar's tribes against Al Qaeda. The commander of an armored battalion, Lieutenant Colonel Tony Deane, began providing security for the meetings Sheikh Sattar was holding with other tribal leaders at his compound, north of Camp Ramadi. These meetings were the start of what would be called the Anbar Awakening.

Skipper said Sattar reminded him of Sonny Corleone, the hotheaded son from *The Godfather*. He carried a beautiful Walther PPK pistol under his gold-braided white robes, liked whiskey, and enjoyed telling tall tales. He cultivated a reputation of being violent. His brother Ahmed was more like Michael Corleone—cool and political. Yet to me, the comparison wasn't to Francis Ford Coppola but to John Ford: in 2006, Ramadi reminded me of the American West in the 1840s, rife with lawlessness, with Sattar as a maverick dust bowl sheriff and our SEAL team standing in for the mounted Ranger service. There were some in our headquarters who didn't want us dealing with local strongmen at all. They wanted everything to run through the national government instead. Problem was, the governor of Anbar was little more than a figurehead. Sattar's Texas-size confidence didn't bother us. He was someone our commanders thought they could work with.

At a meeting at Sattar's compound on September 9, the

sheikh told Colonel MacFarland and Lieutenant Colonel Deane that he would encourage men from his tribe to join the Iraqi police. "We're with whoever is against Al Qaeda," Sattar told the Americans. He said his tribe would treat an attack against Americans as an attack against themselves. He persuaded twenty sheikhs to form an organization known as the Anbar Salvation Council. Our leaders felt it was an important step down the right path and supported the tribes' change of heart.

Once gathered, the sheikhs asked their people, "When are you going to be able to send your children to school? How are you going to live a normal life, when these thugs are in charge? These people are wearing masks. They cannot build the country." Sheikh Sattar said that members of Al Qaeda were murderers and drug addicts. "They abuse our traditions and generosity," he said. Another sheikh on Sattar's Anbar Salvation Council said, "They are bastards. And the people who follow them are also bastards." The Salvation Council finally declared war on Al Qaeda, basically so they could rebuild their society and get on with their lives.

The political side of all this was outside the reach of an assault platoon's daily mission planning. It was a city full of good guys, bad guys, and a whole lot of innocents who risked getting caught in the crossfire every time they set foot in the streets. Mostly we were concerned with the bad guys—finding them, targeting them, and killing or capturing them. That was our work, night after night.

I'll tell you one story that got into our hearts. After a firefight against American forces, an insurgent who nearly had his arm severed was treated and saved by a medic from Team 3. His time in their care turned him around to cooperating with us. He came to understand that the IEDs he planted had killed many innocent Iraqis, and that he had an obligation to repair his honor in service to his country. He began to work with us against Al Qaeda and the insurgency. His family did, too. He was passionate and proud of his work, so much so that he resisted our efforts to protect him. With such a high profile, he was bound to attract Al Qaeda's attention, and he did. They captured him and brutalized him unmercifully. They tore off his newly healed arm and worked on him with a cordless power drill. They dragged him over to his family's house and shot him dead while they all watched.

Though the Sunni tribes didn't trust the Shiites any more than a Southerner trusted a Yankee in 1864, Al Qaeda proved itself the enemy of both Muslim groups. The terrorists were more brutal than Saddam's goons ever had been. Yet thanks to two years of hard fighting by our soldiers and Marines, these insurgents had turned out to be powerless to expel U.S. forces from Ramadi. The death and destruction they spread were the ultimate in hypocrisy. Muslims murdered Muslims to restore Islam's glory. And after our forces had flexed their muscle and made a down payment in blood on the security of the city, the sheikhs found the courage to rise up.

The Anbar Awakening was a gift that kept on giving, as Iraqis came forward to volunteer as police and offer intel on insurgent leaders. Armed with that useful data, we kept up a high tempo of raids and other operations through the fall. Every time an Iraqi turned away from Al Qaeda and began cooperating with us, it was a double blow to the enemy. Sure, there were still large neighborhoods in the city where it was extremely dangerous to tread. But with the rise of the Anbar Awakening and the goodwill of more and more Iraqis coming our way, we had a chance to finish the job that American forces had been struggling with for years: grabbing hold of Al Qaeda and ripping it out by the roots.

Back home, the American press was writing a different story. Two days after the deal was struck with the sheikhs, western Iraq was said to be "beyond repair." The reporter who wrote this wasn't out there with us, witnessing reality. Instead, he was writing from Washington, D.C., working from rumors about a Marine Corps intelligence report that supposedly deemed Ramadi "lost." He hadn't actually seen the intel report in question, and relied on characterizations of it by "officials familiar with its contents." Once President Bush's political opponents got hold of that newspaper clipping ahead of the midterm congressional elections, reality took a backseat to calculation. And so an untruth became the conventional wisdom: Ramadi was lost.

The five thousand U.S. military men and women serving in Ramadi were working from a different narrative. Change was coming fast, under the radar of journalists working on the other side of the world. Change was in the streets. It was change we could believe in. We, the combined forces from the United States and the Anbar Awakening, were the change the people of the city had been waiting for.

Earlier, I mentioned that a good number of SEALs love the movie *The Boondock Saints,* in which two brothers, Connor and Murphy MacManus, go after the murderous gangsters plaguing their city. In Ramadi, that was us—Army, Navy, Air Force, and Marine Corps—taking on an enemy who was virtually begging for the righteous to step forward and end their barbarism. They had taken the lives of many innocents and many American servicemen who were fighting in their defense. We mourned the loss of our own and were eager to exact the price.

Every time our assaulters and snipers came together at Camp Marc Lee to brief a new mission prior to stepping outside the wire, we recited the MacManus brothers' Irish Catholic prayer.

And shepherds we shall be
For Thee, my Lord, for Thee.
Power hath descended forth from Thy hand
That our feet may swiftly carry out Thy commands.
So we shall flow a river forth to Thee
And teeming with souls shall it ever be.
In nomine Patris et Filii et Spiritus Sancti.
Amen, and let's roll.

8

Under Fire and Blown to Hell

It's a mysterious force, this thing we call battle rhythm. But after our successful overwatch operation at COP Firecracker, I felt like we were establishing one, finding our ability to adjust to the daily grind, and adjust to the environment and the operational tempo. Getting there always takes time. Our snipers, with four confirmed kills, had kept the enemy at bay. We were learning to read the streets. We were finding our groove.

The morning after we got back to Camp Marc Lee, I went to the gym. I was working hard to stay physically worthy of the honor of leading Alfa Platoon. Our missions are high-tempo and the pace never quits. We work like hell, and success becomes an expectation. After a good op, the new guys in the task unit return to camp all jacked up and eager for more. Most of them don't realize how bad it can get. I knew I never wanted to get into something like Redwing again—surrounded, outnumbered, buddies dying and you can't do anything about it. I wasn't sure how I'd perform if I were ever thrown into those circumstances again. I suppose no one ever is.

Shortly after I returned to base, Lieutenant Austin, the OIC of Gold squad, tapped me to join him in another foray into the city. It was no sniper mission this time. It was a DA—a direct action, or raid—an assault on two houses that were thought to be storing weapons for the insurgency. We were also to capture an insurgent leader who had popped up on our radar.

The "concept of operations" came down from Lieutenant Austin to Senior Chief Steffen. As acting platoon chief, I put the teams together and scripted out what everyone would do. Choosing a point man was the first big decision. The point man has huge responsibilities. Leading our train, the first in the stack, he navigates (using maps and GPS), keeps us oriented by the compass, counts paces, and locates the landmarks that serve as set points for our missions. All that, and he's the first guy to take fire if the enemy ever sees us coming. But that decision made itself. Special Operators First Class Studdard and Salazar were our two best. They were smart, aggressive, and experienced. Dark, intense, charismatic, and ferocious, Salazar was built as if he resulted from the coupling of an angry bull and a fire hydrant. A great frogman, he ran point for Blue squad the whole six months we were there. Studdard was with my squad most of the time and he proved to be as reliable as the sunrise.

I asked Studdard and Salazar to find three ways into our target and three ways out. The comms guys, Guzman and Hanks, had a huge job managing their advanced single-channel ground and airborne radio systems (SINCGARS), keeping their clocks synced with those of other commands, and staying ready to let us talk to everybody. Our EOD bomb technicians went over the road like hound dogs, looking for bombs. Breachers, assaulters, intelligence, surveillance, and reconnaissance—I put all the details into PowerPoint along with the force list and passed it up to Lieutenant Austin, who would sign off on it. Senior Chief Steffen was the final authority. He'd either kick it back down to me for revision or he'd sign off, too, and then it was ready for Lieutenant Commander Thomas's final okay.

Marty Robbins, the Blue LPO, and I moved miniature buildings around on the sand table until we had a handle on the neighborhood and how we would maneuver through it. We laughed bitterly at the idea that the brigade commander seemed to consider Iraqi houses more valuable than we were. That might have been unfair, but the idea stayed with us after Fizbo was denied his perfect air strike. Part of me longed for the old days, when I didn't have to worry about the big picture, when I could just line up in the stack and get after the enemy.

When Lieutenant Commander Thomas's approval came down, we went to the tactical operations center and went over several dozen details of the op. Lieutenant Austin explained that the guy we were going after was an emir. We fixed our attention on the profile intel had on him. We reviewed the contingencies, along with the tactics, techniques, and procedures we'd use. Then up came the last slide: a prayer. After the amens, we had fifteen minutes to get jocked up with all our gear and be standing tall beside our vehicles, ready to go.

One of the consequences of my hard-won wisdom was insomnia. I never did sleep much during that deployment.

Every thirty minutes I bounced awake. I eventually realized it was pointless to try going back. It didn't help that the Army had a big artillery battery in Camp Ramadi, just across from our camp. Whenever their guns cut loose—and they were liable to start at any time of day or night—the blast was deafening, and the overpressure shook the whole camp.

With any luck, our op that night would deprive the enemy of the ability to respond in kind. As I mentioned earlier, arms and ordnance are stored everywhere in Iraq. Some of the secret stashes—such as those buried in pits under trash bins—were easy to find. Others turned up in the damnedest places, like inside plaster walls. (We'd go into a house and sledge a wall for a sniper hole and there it was: a whole arsenal of small arms and RPGs.) We often found that the shortest path to these hidden treasures ran through the kid on the corner. Why would he lie to us when we're the ones handing out candy? Worked every time.

Sometimes when we took down a building to clear a line of fire, it was like digging up Fort Bragg and Fort Knox all at once: weapons and piles of cash. That's what we were looking for the night of November 3 as we drove to COP Falcon and pushed out, walking down Baseline Road under a full moon.

The road had high walls on both sides. I was concerned about this lack of visibility on our immediate flanks. Walls were not our friends. When we took fire, we always tried to stay away from them. They may seem to offer cover, and it seems instinctive to stay close to them. But in combat, bullets, thanks to ricochets, always seem to run along the walls. So we kept moving; as ever, the hardest thing to hit is a moving target.

We were heading toward our objective, with Studdard on point, when I noticed that the road, with its high walls, was narrowing. It was, as planned, leading us toward the house we were supposed to hit, but the side streets that we expected to find had all been blocked off. I felt like we were being drawn toward a position with no alternate routes or avenues of escape. If we were walking into a channelized trap, there would be only one way out.

SEAL platoons are small units that often depend on larger ones for support. Sometimes, when the mission requires it, we gladly go out on a limb—us against the world. But we fight smart. We stay alert for the signs that something's about to go down: a guy standing on the street corner with a camera; a car pulling up a few blocks ahead and the driver honking the horn, signaling to his buddies that we're on the way. You always need an exit from the kill zone, and we constantly keep track of escape routes in case we take fire—such as a house to push into. In that case, we would kick in the door, secure the first room, separate the women and the children from the men, put security on them, and head for the roof, where we could set up a perimeter and call in reinforcements. Advancing down that channelized road that night in Ramadi, I was all too aware that my team would have nowhere to go if the worst happened.

That was when the bullets started flying. They were 7.62mm rounds, from AK-47s. Good weapons, but not very accurate from medium to long range. (And there are many times I've thanked God for that.) I heard the bullets first, snapping in the earth and walls around us. Then came the echoes of the rifle reports themselves. On the squad radio, somebody called, "Contact left." The gunfire

That's me, at Camp Marc Lee, Ramadi. *(Courtesy of Brandon Scott)*

Task Unit Ramadi, Task Unit Red Bull. *(Courtesy of Brandon Scott)*

Brandon "Fizbo" Scott, our JTAC, outside the SEAL camp. *(Courtesy of Brandon Scott)*

Inside Camp Marc Lee. *(Courtesy of Brandon Scott)*

Looking south from camp down the Euphrates, toward the glass factory. *(Courtesy of Brandon Scott)*

Chris Kyle and Team 3 preceded us in Ramadi and put a dent in the enemy's numbers. *(Jim Hornfischer)*

DQ. Good man. Good friend. *(Courtesy of DQ)*

Thanksgiving... Just another day out there. *(Courtesy of Brandon Scott)*

The streets of Ramadi held a thousand dangers. *(Courtesy of Brandon Scott)*

Our EOD guys saved our lives every day. L to R: Lieutenant Paul, Brad, Andy, Shane. Bottom: Nick. *(Courtesy of Paul Craig)*

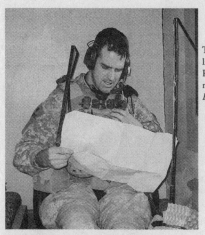

The glamorous life of a JTAC—Fizbo consults his maps. *(Courtesy of Brandon Scott)*

Adam Downs, our
redneck mujahideen.
*(Courtesy of Brandon
Scott)*

Elliott Miller
*(Courtesy of
Brandon Scott)*

Whenever we got in trouble, Army and Marine Corps Abrams tanks like this bailed us out. *(Courtesy of Brandon Scott)*

A long day's done in Ramadi. *(Courtesy of Brandon Scott)*

Iraqis in training, dressed in their Sunday best. *(Courtesy of Brandon Scott)*

When Sheikh Jassim (center) called for help, we moved. *(Courtesy of Brandon Scott)*

(Courtesy of Brandon Scott)

was coming from our left side, from higher ground, from buildings that were shrouded in the dark. The shooters had the drop on us. They were impossible to pinpoint from our position in the street. Taking cover meant we couldn't return fire effectively. Then someone else called, "Contact rear." That's when the picture came into focus for me, and darkened.

There were two or three shooters somewhere to our left. A round ricocheted behind us with a sharp zing. Another zipped right over my head—*thpff*—and punched a hole in the cinder-block wall next to me. A spattering of dirt and dust hit me in the face.

I remember freezing in that moment. Despite knowing better, I leaned against a wall, my mind blank.

These were the first bullets to come my way since Redwing. I had wondered what it would be like. Staring down into the dusty street, I sensed that I was scared. No denying that now. At least there was no belt-fed stuff, thank goodness.

Ernest Hemingway once wrote that "There is no hunting like the hunting of man and those who have hunted armed men long enough and liked it, never really care for anything else thereafter." Let me flip that around: there is, in fact, no fear as deep as the fear of being hunted. Those who experience this fear find, later in life, that they never have reason to be afraid of anything else. Still, you can prepare for combat all day, you can read, think, and study, but you'll never know if you're really ready for it until an enemy gunner sends one flashing past your temple.

My hesitation couldn't have lasted more than three seconds. But all these years later I can still replay the whole time-stopping scene. It seemed to last an eternity.

Scared though I was, I had an even greater fear: that Lieutenant Nathan, Senior Chief Steffen, Wink, or the E-5s in our train had noticed my mental stutter step. I was glad Studdard was in front of me. I valued his opinion, too, and I didn't need to be standing in his line of sight when I went blank.

I took two short, hard, deep breaths. And there—a switch was thrown. *The edge.* It was back again. I felt a clarity and a will to act. A rush of adrenaline and an after-taste of bile. I thought to myself, *I got this.*

The road ahead curved around out of sight and there was no telling what awaited us there. We had to find another way. I knew what the right call was and I made it: the best route of egress from our channelized area was to double right back the way we had come.

I keyed the radio. "Blue and Gold: center peel! *Let's-go-let's-go-let's-go!*" The center peel is a standard maneuver for breaking contact with an enemy force. We do it fast, like a machine, and practice it often. If you can't do it that way, someone's likely to get shot.

Our mission that night wasn't to get into a street fight. It was to come down like a hammer on our target house and seize some weapons. We weren't going to get it done with half the turds in Ramadi throwing lead at us. Life in the SEAL teams isn't always a warfighter's nirvana. We run plenty of missions that go nowhere. Sometimes we have to recognize when the "cank bird" has flown and an op has gone south. That described our little job the night of November 3. We fell back, knowing that, in those cir-cumstances at least, discretion was the better part of valor.

So it didn't bother me to be returning to base. What

bothered me was my standing in the eyes of my teammates. I figured they must have noticed the three critical seconds I spent with my brain in a sling. We lost some good men on Redwing. I had been unable to save them. Eager though I was to fight, I didn't need to see my name tattooed on another episode like that. I had a vision of me surviving another terrible ambush, with several SEALs lost, and going back to base. Some time later, someone on the chow line would invariably make light of it—"Damn, Luttrell, what the hell kind of dark star were you born under?" Laughs all around. And my story would be written.

We were happy to discover what a great working relationship Team 3 had with the conventional units in the city. One of the Army units working out of Camp Corregidor was from the 101st Airborne, the First Battalion of the 506th Infantry—those legendary Currahees. We were uncharacteristically awestruck in the presence of the fabled 1/506. An officer from Team 3 asked the battalion's commander, Lieutenant Colonel Ron Clark, if his frogmen could wear the paratroopers' famous ace of spades insignia. Colonel Clark granted the request, prompting the SEAL to say later, "We earned the right to call ourselves soldiers." In turn, some of the Army boys had given the frogmen a nickname after six months of serving together: they called them Army SEALs. Talk about the universe being turned on its head—say that to a frogman in Coronado or Virginia Beach with the wrong tone in your voice and pretty damn quick you might find yourself crapping out your teeth. But in Ramadi, the rules were different. The brotherhood of battle had grown and spread. And we liked it. We liked it a lot. Still, as some of us saw it, the erasure of boundaries was threatening to erode the unique nature of our special operations mission. Master Chief was visiting Camp Corregidor one day when an Army sergeant major walked up to him and said, "Man, I love you guys. You're the best. It took us a while to learn how to task you, but you have become one of our *best assets.* Whatever we need, *you'll do it.*"

That old warrior meant this as a compliment, of course, and Master Chief was gracious and cool with him—he respected and cared for our brothers in arms—but the exchange bothered him. He and Skipper saw SEAL teams as strategic-level assets, not regular infantry. "If we're stuck running around the streets doing the infantry's bidding," he said, "we're not focused on the larger strategic mission, which is winning the war for the long term." Using elite special operations forces to do patrols and block clearance didn't get us there. Hooking and jabbing with enemy gunmen in the street was only the beginning of what we needed to be doing. "We're here to do the right missions for the right reasons," Master Chief said. "The work of a SEAL team goes far beyond racking up numbers against low-level fighters." The ultimate aim was to make a more lasting impact. Figuring out exactly how to do that was part of our challenge.

As Master Chief put it, the difference between counterinsurgency warfare and assault operations is like the difference between shooting paper targets and shooting steel targets. "Shooting a steel target is damn fun," he said. "It's dynamic. The target clinks and falls down. You see paint and lead splash off it. There's an instant effect.

"A sniper mission is like a steel target. If you kill a

bomb emplacer, congratulations, you just did something for America—you see and feel the satisfaction of saving an American life. But counterinsurgency, that's more like shooting paper targets. You shoot from a distance and you don't see an immediate effect; the bullet passes right through without disturbing the paper. You have to run up close to the target to gauge your success. In the same way, training an Iraqi cop and putting him on the street doesn't make a dramatic difference right away. But somewhere soon, maybe weeks or months from now, the effect will be dramatic. That Iraqi will influence others, maybe train ten more men, and together they'll bring security to a whole neighborhood. If we keep at it consistently over several deployments, we can change the landscape and save a lot of lives—including Americans." Often he would lay it out as a matter of simple math: "Shoot an IED emplacer and save an American life, maybe three. But put Iraqis on the street and take our American brothers and sisters off for good—you will save hundreds."

Commander Leonard and Master Chief struck this match everywhere they went, hoping to start a wildfire among us. Leaving the head shed's extremely capable operations officer, DQ, and executive officer, Mark Starr, to run the Fallujah headquarters, Team 5's two top dogs traveled the province like Old West circuit riders, settling local disagreements between commanders and urging everyone to take up the challenge of setting up the Iraqis to defend themselves. I guess you could also call what they did preaching. They knew taking a backseat to Iraqis, as part of the training mission, was hard for some of us to swallow. But Master Chief had lived it a year earlier in Anbar. We knew how to fight and win. It seemed crazy to many of us to emphasize putting less-capable forces in our place when our conventional brothers needed us. But they wanted to balance slogging it out in the streets with performing missions that would drive the larger COIN strategy. It was the modern-warfare version of the "Give a man a fish…Teach a man to fish" proverb.

None of this was brand new. Counterinsurgency strategy came from an almost-forgotten playbook. General Petraeus and others had revived it in the years before he became commander of all U.S. forces in Iraq, and we believed that if we did it right, we could root out the city's violent elements once and for all. If everyone pulled together as a team—all the U.S. forces in Anbar—we could bring peace not just to Ramadi but to all of Anbar Province.

At Camp Marc Lee, the tension between doing kinetic ops and counterinsurgency was always present. The "thinking soldier's war" gave all of us a few headaches. Lieutenant Commander Thomas, Senior Chief Steffen, and others thought we shouldn't separate ourselves from the immediate, urgent needs of the soldiers and Marines around us. We were intensively trained gunfighters. We couldn't very well deprive those guys of our help when they were right there, running life-and-death missions alongside us. Three Marines, lance corporals from the 1/6, were killed right in our area on October 20–21, reminding us that it could happen any time to anybody.

It could happen to one of us. It was important to keep that knowledge in its box.

As always, the only easy day was yesterday.

With the Anbar Awakening under way, the citizens of Ramadi were buying into the idea of retaking their city and owning their own security. They became ever more helpful, offering tips that kept us hot on the trail of the murderers and opportunists who were happy to destroy the city on their perverted journey to power and glory. Skipper and Master Chief were out front with the brigade leadership, encouraging the Iraqis to support us, and U.S. forces to commit to the training piece of the COIN strategy. The number of police recruits we pulled into the system was growing by the week. As we trained them up to a basic level of proficiency, they served as leadership for the new guys in the pipeline.

Still, we were well aware that large parts of Ramadi were firmly in the insurgency's control. The areas south of Route Michigan and east of the stadium were hotbeds of violence. The fights that took place down there had a different feeling. In that part of the city, the insurgents were skilled, well armed, and fully supplied. They fought like pros, making coordinated tactical movements, assaulting us from multiple positions, then slipping away, "going slick"—tossing their weapons into a house—and blending in with the populace. It was the enemy's home turf, and he was hell-bent on keeping it that way.

As team lead of an assault element, I didn't have much to do with training Iraqis. We always worked with a few *jundis* when we went outside the wire, but they didn't operate at our speed—and that's an understatement. The SEALs who were training them told us the stories with a mix of disgust and hilarity. At the shooting range, some of the Iraqis set their rifles on the wrong shoulder, had the wrong hand on the trigger, and looked through the sight with the wrong eye. But our instructors kept at it, teaching them to patrol, clear houses, investigate crime, and handle themselves like cops. We were multitasking—juggling raids, sniper overwatches, and training. A separate team of guys would get up in the morning, take Iraqis to their training camp, and lead them through simple tactical exercises, such as room clearances. As comical as their antics on the training ground might have been, and as suspicious and squirrelly as some of them seemed to us, what they gave us—intel—was a boon to our efforts to hit the enemy's leadership.

November 7 of that year was a day of rain and mud, memorable mainly because it was the first time that Morgan and I had seen each other in a couple of weeks. He had arrived at Camp Marc Lee in a fast convoy the previous night. The occasion was a major combined operation that the Camp Marc Lee and Camp Corregidor contingents were going to do together.

Blue squad was just back from a sniper overwatch mission near COP Falcon, located on the western edge of downtown. When they'd returned, Lieutenant Commander Thomas told everybody that a big follow-on operation was scheduled that very same night. This was pretty unusual, so we all geared up and gathered in the chow hall to hear the plan. It sounded big, but there was a surprise waiting for Morgan and me.

When we got there, a cake was sitting on the table, and it turned out the op was simply cover for a quick, impromptu thirty-first birthday party for me and my brother. I'll always be grateful to Lieutenant Commander Thomas for allowing it—he knew how to keep our spirits high. I remember someone producing a big combat knife and handing it to Morgan to use on the cake. "Which one of you is older?" someone asked. Morgan is, by seven minutes, and he said so, adding with a grin, "I'm king." And then it was cake for everyone.

But it was quickly back to work. I had an operation to help plan with Senior Chief Steffen for the next night. A Marine had been killed at COP Firecracker that day, the victim of an IED. We were going to roll out the next night on a sniper overwatch and reconnaissance mission that we called Operation Steel Shield.

I struggled through a night of fitful sleep and spent most of the next day in the gym, studying the ops plan, and emptying a few mags at the range. Come nightfall, I got Gold squad together in the TOC and helped Lieutenant Nathan go over the final details. At about 2300 hours, we rolled out.

Shortly after midnight, we arrived at Combat Outpost Steel, located in the Ta'meem district, southwest of the Habbaniyah Canal. I had a short face-to-face with the commander. Discovering he was a Texan was almost enough to make me forget the full moon that hung ominously over Ramadi that night. We set up our sniper teams to provide a 360-degree perimeter around the outpost. Our interpreter, Riddick, and I took the bottom floor with two other guys. Sleeping on the floor, we found out how cold Iraq can be. We froze our butts off.

The next day was entirely too quiet. We spent it watching the streets. Nothing moved. I remember a cloud of shitty-smelling smoke flowing in from the window. Turns out some idiot was burning a shit barrel right outside our house.

Around 7:30 p.m., we were all set to roll, but the driver of the Bradley that functioned as the entry gate to COP Steel was asleep on watch. We raised a little hell trying to awaken him, but our rifle butts pinging on the hull must have sounded like gunfire—hardly enough to disturb him in his much-needed sleep. It took a call to Camp Ramadi to rouse him, and soon he rolled the vehicle out of our way and we were pushing out. Leading the column was the Humvee we called Optimus Prime.

Our EOD tech, Andy Fayal, felt a cold chill come over him when he realized the implication of that Bradley driver being asleep for so long. More than just serving as the gate to the FOB, that vehicle was there to monitor the street outside as well, and keep it clear of bomb emplacers. If the crew was snoozing, well, who had been watching the road? Plus, we were pushing out early—another no-no. The guys from Team 3 had warned us not to go out before 11:00 p.m. or after 4:00 a.m. The insurgency's IED crews were too active during those times. But with things on the street pretty quiet, I thought we could get the job done and get the guys home for some badly needed rest.

As we left COP Steel, Andy, nervous about the unmonitored road, advised the driver of our lead Humvee to swing his vehicle into the wheel tracks of another convoy that had just come down the road. He scanned the road through his NVGs as though he were a jeweler examining a diamond.

We weren't two hundred yards outside of the gate when I realized what a mistake we had made. I was in the Humvee behind Andy's, looking out at the city through my NVGs, when everything went white. I felt a powerful shock, but I don't remember any sound. It was a hell of an explosion. Andy heard a metallic *brrannggg* and was thrown upward, smashing his head on the top of the vehicle. His vehicle had hit an IED.

Our EOD guys were among the most important people in the squadron. They're different from SEALs. They're the techies of our world, intuitive, interested in how things work, and more than a little paranoid about what type of infernal mechanism might be waiting for us around the next corner. They were gearheads, and warriors, too. Lieutenant Paul Craig, the OIC of the EOD mobile unit at Fallujah, was a twelve-year veteran of Marine Force Recon. And Andy Fayal stood five foot eight but was built like a brick shithouse. He owned the record in all of I MEF for bench press: 475 pounds. They spent most of their time studying the enemy's treacherous ways, scanning the ground ahead of us in the streets, hunting for explosives in the roads, shoulders, embankments, and walls.

Andy had developed his approach from his time assisting the Secret Service. His job one day was to go into a hotel the president might be staying in and look for bombs. He'd sit on chairs, jump on mattresses, and open drawers and closets, doing what they call a find or function operation. If there was a bomb in there, he was supposed to locate it, either with his eyes or by detonating it. "Our job is to preserve life and critical infrastructure. My life means nothing," Andy told me. When he was with us, he was ready to do more than just defuse the bombs. He would willingly turn himself into a pink mist to save us if he had to.

Nothing is impossible when you have people like that working with you. I considered our EOD bubbas some of the best in the world at their craft. One reason I felt that way: it was clear that thoughts like that—*I'm the best*—never once entered their selfless minds. We were blessed to be working with men like them.

On foot patrols, Andy and the other techs—incredible men like Shane Snow, Nick Ferrier, Brad Shannon, and their lieutenant, Paul Craig—made sure to check out every suspicious hole in the road or pile of rocks, and stood right between it and us when we proceeded by. Whenever Andy found a wire that looked suspicious, he'd take out his tools and cut it. During our ops, he electrocuted himself on more than a few live power lines, but he took it as a point of pride. He was determined that no threat would escape his notice. That night outside COP Steel, he settled for using his helmet as a bell clapper against the metal roof of his Humvee.

Once we felt the blast ahead of us, those of us in the second Humvee knew we were likely next. After a lead vehicle is disabled, the enemy's next move is often to target the next vehicle in line with more explosives or a ground assault. The first responders for the lead vehicle become easy targets. In our parlance, those guys are "sitting on the X." That was my vehicle that night.

Ahead of us, sparks were pouring out in all directions from underneath Optimus Prime. "Get off the X, get off the X," came the order on the radio. I was more concerned with whether anyone in our lead Humvee was even alive.

I called Lieutenant Nathan, Gold's leader, riding in Optimus Prime. "Status." I was ready for the worst.

Sparks were still kicking out from beneath our lead Humvee. Except for that, all was quiet, a storm of yellow-orange glitter amid an absolute eerie silence in the dead of the wartime night.

All of a sudden, the radio crackled with the reply. "We're all good, bro. What's your situation?"

I exhaled heavily. The only reason they survived was

because the warhead was a shaped charge, meant to penetrate armored vehicles, not to blow up personnel who were less well protected. The explosion punched a clean hole straight up through the right side of the engine block, tore a hole through the hood, blew off the right-side tires, axles, and the front bumper, and virtually split the chassis in half. All the glass on the passenger side and turret was gone. But there were no serious casualties, thank God. They were lucky the engine block took the hit.

As Lieutenant Nathan was radioing his status, the driver of my Humvee already had the transmission in reverse, backing up to get off the X and out of the way of any secondary charges the enemy might have planted to finish us off. As we dismounted and found firing positions, the third Humvee in the column circled around and eased a bumper against our totaled leader. Then the driver started pushing it back toward COP Steel. The night was silent and cold. No follow-up attack came. Optimus Prime was dead, but other than that, we had taken no losses.

Thank you, God, for one more day.

On a raid sometime later, we gathered intelligence that showed that the insurgents were listening to our frequencies and tracing our movements by our *Transformers* call signs. It was also possible we had a leak in camp. Either way, it was clear it wasn't smart to get too attached to our vehicle's names.

Of course, we were always doing a little snooping of our own. The bread and butter of special operations is intelligence, and we never launched a raid without having a good handle on the who, what, where, and when of our target. When U.S. forces built COP Eagle's Nest in the summer before our arrival, we had a toehold in the neighborhood. Once we had a presence, good intel began coming from locals. They'd walk up to us and tell us things. And our patrols found a lot of surprises by beating feet in the street. For instance, there was a whole IED factory hidden inside the soccer stadium. Underneath the bleachers was a workshop containing industrial-grade saws, used for making sharp cuts in the asphalt streets—so fine that it was nearly impossible to detect them visually when the excavated chunks were replaced on top of bombs. They used carbide-tipped saws to cut nearly invisible grooves in the road to hide trigger wires. The huge subsurface IEDs they emplaced in this way were big enough to flip a tank or disintegrate a Humvee outright. Inside that stadium they had everything they needed: bomb-making materials, wires, timers, and explosive ordnance.

In time, our intel network started popping the names and locations of the leadership of the insurgent cell that Team 3 had confronted in that September firefight in which Mikey Monsoor was killed. The idea of delivering justice in this hero's name focused our attention.

Delivering it, of course, meant venturing into "Indian country." In south-central Ramadi, the enemy kept a full-time presence. They patrolled. Eyes watched from every window. Commander Leonard, our skipper, once said, "They were everywhere and nowhere, like a cockroach infestation."

Women and children walked around reporting anything they saw to the insurgents. IEDs were planted on every other street corner and triggermen stood by 24-7 to clack them off on us if we took a wrong turn. Though most of the insurgents didn't have radios or night-vision optics, they still found ways to coordinate their attacks. We'd see a moped driver snooping around—a scout, looking for our positions and measuring ranges. (Often, the mortar fire or ground assault against us would begin as soon as the driver disappeared around the corner.) The enemy could tell Army soldiers from Marines and could sniff out the boundaries between their areas of operation. They'd hit the Currahees, then melt back into the Marines' zone. We adjusted, of course, but we never lost sight of the fact that the hand directing the insurgents on the streets was an intelligent, thinking one. When we were bunkered up in a house doing a sniper overwatch, they'd shoot at our position from one direction, and then try to sneak in from another direction and lay booby traps on the gate if our attention got diverted. In that part of town, we felt like we were on a nearly equal footing with the enemy. One thing we never like is a fair fight.

On November 12, I was part of a sniper overwatch operation supporting an Army block clearance in south-central Ramadi. We moved out from COP Iron, on the south side of the city, late that night, with an Abrams tank leading the way. For anyone looking for a fight, there was no better op than one like this. The term "overwatch" was a misnomer, actually. It suggested that we were standing on passive guard, protecting other forces against an enemy who was attacking them. What actually happened was very different: while we were set up in our positions, the enemy quickly figured out where we were and came after *us,* often ignoring the conventionals doing street patrols. And we generally didn't mind that. Every round sent our way was one that some Army kid in the street didn't have to worry about.

When we reached our target that night—a nice house furnished with a chandelier, comfortable furniture, and an actual heater, which made our night much more pleasant—we cleared it quickly and took up positions on the roof and on upper floors. When we tried to blow spider holes in the wall for our snipers, however, we found it was too thick for our explosive charges. We couldn't even scratch it. Our resourceful snipers managed to work around that little problem and had a productive day.

Around 11:00 p.m. that night, a long day's work done, Lieutenant Nathan made the call to pull Gold squad out and return to our COP. We took some fire from down the street, including some heavy stuff. When we called for our return ride, we were hoping for Bradleys. Instead, we got Abrams tanks. Nothing against those big armored beasts—they were your best friend in a heavy fight—but they weren't what we wanted for a lift. There was no room inside to carry us. So we formed up in columns and jogged along behind the tanks, doing what we call the Mogadishu Mile. During the whole exhausting slog, spirits stayed high. I remember guys joking about who was going to step on the first IED.

We speculated who would fly the farthest, propelled by the blast. "If you're going to go," someone said, "you should do it with distance, and style points."

On November 15, Blue squad went out to set up a pair of sniper positions in south-central Ramadi. It was a bait op, our favorite kind of mission. We almost always drew fire, and whenever we did, we gave it back tenfold. This time, though, the insurgents changed the way they came at us. Seems they had learned they couldn't outshoot our snipers, so early on the first morning, the enemy located the sniper hide and probed it with small arms fire. The guys gave far better than they got and held their position, but by midafternoon, both overwatch locations came under heavy attack. The enemy couldn't outshoot us, but he could use his familiarity with the streets to sneak up on our positions.

Marty Robbins was walking up the stairs to the roof with an armload of water bottles for him and his partner on the roof, when the frags started landing. At least three of these old-fashioned German potato mashers came flipping end over end into the snipers' midst. One of them hit Robbins square in the crotch, bounced to the ground at his feet, and started rolling toward his teammate. With seconds to act, thinking he was a dead man, Robbins hollered, "Grenade!" then kicked that one away, keeping it from his buddy, then dropped his load of water and dove toward the stairs just as the grenades went off. Another SEAL, a chief by the name of Mulder, hit the deck of the roof and curled up tight. When the grenades exploded, they sent a storm of shrapnel into both men's feet and the backs of their legs. The blast slammed Robbins into the door frame as he tried to dive through it, and he tumbled down the stairs. Amazingly, both men made it out of there under their own power in spite of their wounds. It was an incredible lifesaving reaction, and a heroic act. After suppressing the attack and doing triage on the wounded members of his fire team (with no thought to himself), Robbins called the QRF—the quick reaction force.

As the other sniper overwatch position came under attack—that team got into a full-on grenade-lobbing contest with the enemy—two Bradleys pulled up. It was the QRF. Unfortunately, it arrived in front of the wrong house. Robbins and Mulder were forced to run for it. Under fire the whole time, the two wounded SEALs made it all the way over there. As they piled in to the rear compartment, the Brads turned their powerful chain guns on the house that Robbins and Mulder had exfilled from and tore it down, concrete block by concrete block.

I was working on the mission plan for the next night when they returned to camp—twelve hours sooner than we were expecting them. They had gotten a rough lesson in what awaited us in south-central. We were lucky we didn't lose anyone that night. The enemy was getting brave. We decided that next time out, things would roll differently.

9

Frogman Down

We had a big operation planned for the night of November 18–19—a push into the hottest part of the southern area of the city, the Ma'laab district. It was high time for us to shake the bushes and see what came crawling out.

We were rolling out heavy. Gold squad's two fire teams would set up sniper positions protecting tankers from the First Battalion, Seventy-Seventh Armor Regiment, based at Camp Ramadi, and the infantry from the First Battalion, Ninth Infantry Regiment, known as the Manchus, based at Camp Corregidor, as they went block by block, yanking the enemy out by the roots. We found out during planning that Bravo Platoon was putting in three sniper positions of their own in the neighborhood, too. They moved out from Camp Corregidor to COP Eagle's Nest, and then infilled on foot into Ma'laab—labeled the "Papa sectors" on our map—where they would set up three more positions to our east.

Running a daylight block-clearance op in the Ma'laab district was an easy way to get into a fight. Located about half a mile southwest of the soccer stadium, the neighborhood was densely residential and widely feared by the locals. Moose and Riddick, our terps, shook their heads at the mere mention of the place. "It's *baaad* news down there, man."

I wanted nothing more than to have my rifle in that fight. With Robbins and Mulder still nursing shredded glutes, we all wanted payback. But I wouldn't be going out with them—I was on "injured reserve," because my back was a mess. Senior Chief Steffen had some good advice. "Just step back a little, Marcus." He was a man of few words, but these were the ones I needed to hear. He let me know that the guys had it covered, that I could take a moment to heal. In the teams, it seems like we all take a heavy load on our shoulders, feeling like we need to be there at all times to help our brothers. It never hurt to have a reminder about the strength of our team and the capabilities of the men in it, and know that they would be good without me. The teams never depend on a single person— ever. If they try to, what can happen is not far from what happens to a sports team that relies too heavily on a single guy: there's no chemistry, and they're set up perfectly for failure. We have no use for glory hounds, either.

We shuffled our team leads. Wink took Gold squad and, with Marty Robbins down, Senior Chief took over the chief spot in Blue. I already thought he was one of the best frogmen I'd ever worked with, but when he returned to the train, taking the place of a wounded comrade, it was business as usual. I knew it was going to be a busy night, and it sucked to see the boys roll out while we had to stay back. Marty and I would make our contributions in different ways. (Just call me the paper bitch.) One way or another, we were determined to collect on debts that night.

Gold squad, under Lieutenant Nathan—with Wink as his platoon chief, six other frogs, and our JTAC, Fizbo— loaded up at Camp Marc Lee and took a fast convoy to COP Iron. Staging there, they pushed out on foot around 2300 local time on November 18. Carrying enough food and water for two days, they patrolled eastward, along the base of a stone embankment supporting the railroad tracks that marked the city's southern boundary. The nearly full moon was throwing out more light than the sun, but it was good that Fizbo was with them. Using his radio, he kept in close touch with aircraft overhead. Their infrared eyes were lifesavers, their air-to-ground weapons game changers in a pinch.

Coming to an intersection, Gold squad crossed the railroad tracks and patrolled north into the southern part of the Ma'laab district. Moving like smoke through the nighttime streets, they advanced through a maze of narrow alleyways threading between houses made of brick and mud. Stepping over trash and avoiding sewer pits, they could hear people stirring in the houses as they passed. If they weren't careful, they'd end up facedown in a sewer. But unwanted noise—the foul-smelling splash— could exact a price far higher than a soiled uniform.

Continuing north, they passed a schoolhouse. Littered with small arms, tools for making bombs, and bloody whips and other instruments of interrogation and torture, it had been recently used as an Al Qaeda playground. When some dogs began to bark and a donkey began to bray, Gold thought they might have been compromised. Hairs rose on the backs of their necks as they pushed the mission ahead. I know what that feels like; the fear that you might have been compromised can be worse than the actual knowledge of it.

When they finally reached their target, a neighborhood spanning five or six city blocks, they split into two groups and moved to their overwatch positions. Nathan's team entered and cleared a house situated just north of the school. Austin and his boys approached a four-story structure located five houses to the east, on a street corner. With eight guys in the upper floors of each house, they were ready to go to work.

Come morning, around eight thirty, Fizbo and a sniper we called Noise were watching the schoolyard to the south when they saw a line of about ten cars driving past the house. Each time a car went by, the driver leaned on the horn. As they felt the hackles rise on the backs of their necks, Noise and Fizbo agreed that if any of the cars stopped, they'd bring their rifles to bear and light it up. Everyone in Ramadi understood the threat of vehicle-borne IEDs. The only way to stop one was to shoot the driver before he got close enough to clack it off. Sure enough, one of the cars stopped in front of the house.

Noise, Fizbo, and another frog flipped their safeties and were about to fire when a guy came running out of a house across the way and jumped into the car. It sped off. Then they saw a woman in the open field near the school digging with a shovel. She reached down and pulled several sacks out of the ground, the contents of which the snipers couldn't see, then began passing them into the passenger-side windows of cars driving by. Noise pulled his scope to his eye, took aim, and put a round into one of the bags. He thought it might explode, but it didn't. The suspects scattered, quickly escaping Noise's field of fire, and their suspicious activity ceased.

From his rooftop hide, Adam Downs was watching the block to his northeast when an enemy sniper drew a bead on him and fired. The round hit the wall about six inches from his head. Adam returned fire immediately, zeroing on the flash, then displaced, running down the stairs. He was pissed off.

There was no time to dwell on near misses, though, because Lieutenant Austin's boys, five houses to the east, reported half a dozen insurgents leaving a nearby house, on the move north. In this neighborhood the homes were packed so closely together that you could run across the roofs from house to house. Each structure was set back from the street a pretty good distance and had a tall, thick stucco wall between it and the street. This made each house a natural fighting position, but it also meant that anyone outside could sneak up on the house unseen, hidden by the wall.

Though his squad lost sight of the enemy force, Fizbo was able to pick them up using the airborne camera of a Marine Corps F/A-18 Hornet on station overhead. The insurgents ran west through an alleyway three blocks north of his position, hauling heavy weapons and ammunition. It looked like a flanking maneuver. Passing seven houses, the insurgents finally stopped at the northeast corner of an open field about three city lots wide.

Fizbo contacted the Army commander and requested permission to have the Marine Corps pilot make a strafing run. The commander told Fizbo that strafing was prohibited in densely populated neighborhoods, so our JTAC doubled down, contacting his new friends in brigade headquarters at Camp Ramadi and asking for even heavier ordnance.

Meanwhile, Dozer, the JTAC from Bravo Platoon, asked Fizbo to have the Hornet scan the neighborhood around their house a hundred yards in all directions. It seems the element from Bravo Platoon had had quite an adventure patrolling into the city the previous night. They rode in Bradleys from Camp Corregidor to the edge of the district, then dismounted and went on foot. Led by Elliott Miller, their point man and medic, they twice had to find alternate routes when Dozer told them that a pilot had detected hot spots on the road. These were likely newly emplaced IEDs. So now the Hornet pilot reported that no one was moving in the streets, but there was a cluster of suspicious vehicles gathering a few blocks to the north.

It was hard for a single aircraft to serve many customers at once. A pilot couldn't, for instance, watch the streets surrounding Bravo while also lining up an air attack somewhere else. In addition, the pilot had to worry about the perpetual thirst of a modern military aircraft. After scanning Dozer's area, he came back on line saying that he needed to leave station momentarily to refuel from an airborne tanker.

Fizbo used the short break to double-check the tactical situation and finalize his request for an air strike. Known as a nine line, the request specified the coordinates the aircraft should hit and the type of weapon to be used, and confirmed compliance with the rules of engagement. To avoid collateral damage, headquarters ended up giving Fiz a Laser Maverick—a laser-guided air-to-ground missile—instead of the more powerful five-hundred-pound bomb that he preferred. When Fizbo's Marine Corps brother returned from refueling, he scanned the area again and reported that the enemy force had doubled in size. There were about a dozen fighters ready to move out and attack. The guys couldn't afford to wait for headquarters to decide what to do with Fizbo's nine line.

Wink used data from the plane's camera to find his target, then, as a pair of his teammates began laying down automatic weapons fire on the insurgents' building, four other operators began lobbing 40mm grenades. Their aim was true. The aircraft reported several direct hits, and a number of wounded fighters crawled away from the field. Fizbo passed corrections to the grenadiers and more frags flew. By the time they were finished, no one was left in the field. The survivors had crawled (or were dragged) into a house just to its east.

The teams were only getting warmed up. Adam Downs pulled out the heaviest weapon in the platoon's arsenal, a recoilless rifle that we call a Carl Gustav, heaved it to his shoulder, and sent an 84mm rocket downrange. It slammed into an empty house that stood between them and their quarry. Equipped with a time-delayed fuse, the projectile punched through the empty house and exploded in the neighboring house a split second later, after it had penetrated the wall between them.

The pilot promptly reported an explosion in the house where the enemy was holed up. Fizbo, standing in a stairwell in Lieutenant Nathan's sniper's nest, updated his nine line to make that new house the Hornet's target. As he awaited approval, Wink turned loose another Carl G. with a fiery roar. The backblast blew out the windows around him and shook the house. The Marine Corps pilot reported another direct hit on the enemy's hidey-hole, and told Fizbo that four insurgents were hauling ass, running south into the next house. Our JTAC relayed this to Wink, who sent another Carl G. to visit the next house.

In spite of the SEALs' deadly handiwork, the Hornet pilot told Fizbo that an even larger group of insurgents than before, as many as twenty of them, was in a house just north of the one Wink had hit. It was then, finally, that Fizbo got approval to unleash the Hornet's heavy weapons. He verified the coordinates and confirmed compliance with the rules of engagement for close air support missions. Then he contacted the pilot, verifying the target and the weapon of choice, and finally spoke the magic words into his microphone:

"Cleared hot."

Hustling in from the south, the aircraft dropped a Laser Maverick from the rails. "Rifle," the pilot announced. Fizbo told his teammates to duck and cover.

When that delta-winged weapon hit, its three-hundred-pound warhead detonated with a thudding roar, cloaking half a city block in a cloud of dust. When it began to clear, the guys could see that much of the target building was gone. The pilot reported seven insurgents escaping to another building across the street. That left, of course, more than a dozen bad guys buried inside the house. When brigade headquarters denied Fizbo's request to use another missile, Wink and his rocket team were on the survivors like sand on a BUD/S student, throwing another Carl G. at them and scattering those who were still somehow ambulatory into the northern part of the neighborhood.

It was a hell of a satisfying hour's work, the kind of

thing that SEAL teams, and regular soldiers and Marines, do every day. You seldom see it in the papers. Once in a while some guys get put up for decorations and a ceremony takes place somewhere. You see them in dress uniforms, standing proud. But that's politics and theater. You should see them as I have, downrange, in action. They're amazing to watch, risking their lives to serve their country. I don't like to talk about valor awards. I don't think it's useful to think about them. We just go to work, and it's the work itself that tells us who we are. Our pride is no less without the fanfare.

Alfa Platoon's little live-fire exercise against the insurgents in the sector designated Papa 12 was just the first act of a long day—one that will live in the memories of those who were there as one of the hardest days of their lives. Soon after we heard that the enemy was fleeing, a radio call came from battalion headquarters asking whether any of our guys had requested a casevac.

What the hell was this? the boys in Gold squad wondered. None of their positions had taken casualties, and if the Corregidor SEALs had gotten hit, surely they would have heard from them directly about it. What was headquarters talking about?

No one in Alfa Platoon had any idea. Then, one and all, they realized it had been a while since they had heard *anything* from the two elements from Camp Corregidor.

Not good.

As it happened, the enemy's attack on Gold was part of a larger, loosely coordinated assault on all the units in the neighborhood. As Gold was wreaking havoc on the insurgents in their neighborhood, all three overwatches manned by Bravo Platoon came under simultaneous concentrated attack.

Several blocks east of Alfa Platoon's two overwatches, Bravo had cleared and secured three different houses about two hundred yards apart as sniper positions. With a couple of Abrams tanks parked at the intersections of important streets, and the blocks cordoned off, the infantry was kicking in doors and entering houses. Bravo was set up to provide the Army a wide blanket of coverage while also staying close enough to each other to regroup and fight together if the worst came to pass. A key factor behind what happened in the hours ahead, however, was the fact that the three overwatch positions weren't within visual sight of each other. When one of the squads decided they didn't like the layout of the first house they took, they shifted to the one two doors over. This took them out of line of sight of their teammates. Watching the streets north of their position, they were in a house that backed up to a huge courtyard bounded by the backs of several other houses. In one of the nearby houses, they heard somebody clapping. It was an Iraqi, signaling to some pigeons—real birds, homing pigeons. We suspected the insurgents used them to tell their buddies where the Americans were. Every time we saw a pigeon flying near us, we seemed to get shot at. Like so much else about this ancient country, this stuff was straight out of the Middle Ages. We always had to assume the worst was possible.

Cowboy was with this fire team. He came up over the wall, looking to draw a bead on the birdman, but the Iraqi saw him and dove down a stairwell to escape. Then, out of the corner of his eye, the SEAL saw something in the air, flying toward him from another direction. It wasn't a pigeon. He ducked back behind the wall of the roof as a grenade flew by and exploded some distance away. Then the squad radio crackled with news from one of the other overwatches that all was not well.

The guys at the other position—Lieutenant Clint (who had been switched over to Bravo Platoon), Dozer, Elliott Miller, Johnny Brands, and some others—had sensed a strange feeling in the air as their day began. As they set up their position, the family who lived in the house they were borrowing was behaving nervously. Then, from the loudspeakers on the mosques, came announcements that the terps thought were unusual, perhaps a coded message of some kind. It was around that time that an insurgent managed to creep up on their roof and toss a grenade through one of the spider holes. They reacted by the playbook, hitting the deck fast, with their arms covering their heads and showing their tails to the frag. It exploded amid them and ripped up their backsides. No one was killed, but Elliott took deep shrapnel wounds to the shoulder and arm. With an arterial bleed, he was quickly treated by his teammates.

Then Lieutenant Clint called Camp Corregidor with a troops-in-contact report and a casevac request. The other sniper positions were directed to close up shop, collapse on his position, and await extract. A quick reaction force—Bradley Fighting Vehicles from the 1/77—was en route to pick them up. They were going home—at least, that was the plan. But as the SEALs moved from the rooftop to the first deck, they began taking heavy fire. Realizing that insurgents had infiltrated the roof, they took a head count and gathered their sensitive gear as the crack of small arms fire and blast of grenades sounded just outside the walls.

To defend ourselves, there are certain measures we take as a last resort. In a worst-case scenario, such as the immediate threat of being overrun, we implement these measures, which include setting off explosions that we hope will kill or incapacitate anybody lurking in the alleys and streets outside. With grenades detonating in the interior courtyard and small arms fire popping everywhere, it was clear Bravo Platoon was at risk of being overrun. The platoon's officer in charge, Lieutenant Chris, decided to blow the window-mounted charges, and his bomb technician, Shane Snow, did the honors.

The explosion was more than the guys had bargained for. The wave of overpressure rebounded off the heavy wall of the house next door and slapped back at them, shaking the entire structure. The door leading outside to the front gate was jammed in its frame—definitely not what they needed as they prepared to bust out of that house.

The guys were wrestling with the door when another explosion came. This one felt heavier than anything they had heard during their time in the city. Several blocks away, the Alfa Platoon squads from Camp Marc Lee, Gold and Blue, felt it as well. Fizbo thought to himself, *I hope that's nobody we know.*

Over the radio, Lieutenant Clint informed the other Bravo Platoon elements: "Mass casualties. Calling for extract. Move to extract position, our location."

There was no time to waste. Hearing the order, someone called out, "Time for a Mogadishu Mile." To reach their teammates, they would have to make a two-hundred-yard dash through hell.

Checking the open courtyard to their rear, they forced

their way through the balky front door and pushed out of the house to the gate in the outer wall, which led out to the street. They formed their stack and the EOD, Shane Snow, used his shears to cut the zip ties securing the gate. When nothing exploded, they thanked God the insurgents hadn't managed to booby-trap it with an IED. That was always a risk when you were camping in the enemy's backyard.

Pushing out into the street, the fire team found the situation beyond all contingencies. The scene was straight out of *Black Hawk Down*. A crowd confronted the small element of soldiers. In their midst, gunmen appeared. With Cowboy on point, the frogs pushed out and began moving toward their teammates.

Cowboy went right. A teammate who followed directly behind him, carrying an M60 machine gun, went left. When his teammate fell, hitting the ground hard, Cowboy thought he had been hit, but then the frogman scrambled back to his feet. Fanning out, guns at the level, they moved purposefully and precisely, just as they had practiced a thousand times. Determined to reach their brothers, who had just suffered some kind of catastrophic event, they gave no quarter to their enemy. They knew the only way to stay alive was to move, and move fast. With every step, they earned their Tridents all over again.

The insurgents owned the rooftops, and they were firing madly. Whipping down at Cowboy and the others, bullets smacked into the street, the popping of small arms fire now and then yielding to the occasional hissing rush of an RPG or the blast of a tossed grenade. The bullets were way too close—as Cowboy said, "They were saying my name."

I learned early in my career that when things go south, you milk your cover for all it's worth, shoot often but sparingly, and keep moving fast. That was how these guys worked. They survived on quick reflexes and cool nerves. As they advanced down the street, leapfrogging to cover each other at road crossings, Cowboy, running point, took the long angle, scanning for targets straight ahead. His teammates behind him each took a different angle to the side. Shane Snow did his best to move fast and provide covering fire, but mostly he did what a good bomb tech is supposed to do: sweep his eyes over the ground close ahead, looking for command wires and pressure plates. Their hard-charging train fought together as one, making the two-hundred-yard dash to their brothers. Not many enemy fighters who raised a weapon against them lived to tell about it.

Turning a corner and running down the street, bound for the extract point, they saw a couple of Bradley Fighting Vehicles in front of a house. One faced north, the other south. One of them was lashing out with its turret-mounted 25mm chain gun at a building across the street. Return fire was spitting and sparking off its armored hull like a medium rain. As they neared Lieutenant Clint's overwatch house, Shane noticed smoldering fragments of some kind in the street. There was a large circular black stain on the wall outside the house, about three feet in diameter: an RPG impact. The chief of Bravo Platoon, Crossman, was outside the front door, firing into buildings across the way. Another operator was working a crew-served M48 machine gun on the same targets. The team moved up to the wall outside the front of the house and used the Bradleys for cover.

When Cowboy stuck his head into the Bradley, it was full of smoke. Then it came rushing at him, the horrible smell and sight of an inert human form lying there in the crew compartment. The dead man was an Iraqi, one of Lieutenant Clint's *jundis*. He was missing both of his legs and had terrible burns on his stumps. Baling wire was wrapped around what was left—apparently someone had tried to stop the bleeding. There was no saving that dude. As bullets continued to strike the vehicle, everyone kept calm and focused, counting on their training to tell them what to do. But not even our down-man drill with the pigs could fully prepare a man for a moment like this.

Someone yelled, "Get in the house!" Turning, Cowboy saw Lieutenant Chris motioning him inside the door. There was a large puddle of blood on the ground between them. From the deep red trail that led from it into the house, it was obvious that something had been dragged out of the puddle. Following the bloody smear inside, through more heavy smoke, Cowboy found another pool of blood several feet across. In the middle of it lay an M4 rifle with a torn sling.

Feeling his way farther inside, he stumbled across something that yielded only slightly against his foot. It was one of our own: Elliott Miller. When Cowboy bumped into him he let loose a primal howl. His legs were an utter ruin. A light wisp of white smoke seemed to be rising from him.

A short distance away from him, another man was down. This was Johnny Brands, screaming as several of his teammates tried to apply battle dressing to his feet. They were doing the best they could, given that the platoon medic, Elliott, was in no condition to help. Every frogman is trained up in basic trauma, but it never helps that it's all too often the medic who gets hit.

What had happened to them was revealed in fragments to Cowboy and his teammates as they jumped into the mix, trying to save those two frogmen's lives.

It was the relatively minor wound Elliott had received earlier on—grenade shrapnel to his arm—that led the team to call for extract. When the QRF arrived outside with a couple of Bradleys, the squad moved quickly downstairs and lined up to break out of the house. They tossed two smoke grenades outside to cover their exfil, then burst through the door. Two Iraqis were in the lead, followed by Elliott, hobbling along with help from Johnny Brands. The *jundis* had just hit the street when the world went dark. The IED might have been dropped down on them from the roof in a backpack. Or it might have been planted in the ground or hung on the gate while they were inside. All we know for sure is that it was a trap set by enemies who were obviously wise to everything we were doing and how we were doing it. They knew that straight-on firefights were losing propositions. So they snuck around and planted their bombs where they thought we'd be. They sure got it right that time. An enormous explosion engulfed our guys as they exited the house.

The explosion killed the two Iraqis leading the way; the first man simply disappeared, evaporated by the blast, his scant remnants drifting away in the air, a pink mist, while the second, partly sheltered by the leader, was nearly sliced in half at the waist. The blast still had enough force to devastate Elliott. It tore into his body wherever it wasn't protected by body armor. His legs were shredded from about midthigh down. He had a hole in his right shoulder and the parts of him that weren't covered by plates were being eaten into by a terrible chemical residue.

As we learned later, the insurgents had probably made this weapon from a 122mm artillery shell and an 82mm mortar round with a white phosphorus payload. So-called Willie Pete rounds are one of the nastiest weapons on God's great earth. When that chemical gets blown all over you, it sticks and burns, eating through metal, clothing, skin, and flesh. White phosphorus can't be put out, and it was all over Elliott. There was nothing they could do but watch as the chemical slowly burned all the way through him. I know the guys in Bravo were losing their minds as this happened. But Elliott is a tough SOB; he just took the pain. It was a while before he finally stopped smoking.

Johnny was better off, but that wasn't saying much. Both his feet were attached to his ankles only by the Achilles tendons. The blast had wounded one of the crew on the Bradley, too. When notified of this, the commander of the QRF evidently decided he needed to get his wounded crewman to a casualty station, and ordered the Bradleys to return to base.

Alone for the moment, without a means of extract, the boys of Bravo Platoon groped through the smoke for their brothers, homing in on their screams. When Dozer found his down teammates—two of his closest friends—he checked a surge of grief, then realized, *You've got to get them the hell off the street or you're gonna get shot in the face.* Whoever set that bomb by their gate might still be watching. He could have secondary charges ready to go.

Looking down at Elliott, Dozer saw that his friend's legs seemed loose and detached in the bloody mess of his pants. The steel rifle magazines stored in his front vest pouches had been dished in by the blast. Elliott's watch was charred and black but, amazingly, still kept time. Only his body armor saved him from being killed instantly. Dozer ran his hands under Elliott's plates, checking his torso for wounds. As he removed Elliott's gear, Dozer realized he didn't have the first idea where to begin treating such a seriously wounded man. That was when he heard another explosion, a smaller one, go off in the courtyard. A grenade. The insurgents were still out there, probing them, probably planning another attack.

Elliott was one of the heaviest guys in the teams, a good 240 pounds, not counting his kit, loadout, backpack, and corpsman's gear. Dozer grabbed Elliott by the shoulders and started struggling to move him toward the foyer of the house. When one of Elliott's legs got snagged in the door frame, wrenching around at an unnatural angle, Dozer tried to go back through the doorway to untangle him, but found himself blocked by his teammate's broad shoulders. Dozer shouted to another guy to help, and together they eased Elliott free of the jam.

With two men down and several more focusing on treating them, it would have been easy for a gunman to come in and kill them all, Dozer thought. They continued to be very vulnerable until the guys from the other overwatch positions arrived. Even then, the handful of frogmen—the rest of Bravo Platoon—was hard-pressed to keep the enemy at bay. There were too many avenues of incoming fire. They couldn't see what was going on outside, or on the roof.

As some of the guys stayed with Elliott, Dozer looked after Johnny. He was alarmed to see blood flowing from his teammate's crotch. Fearing a femoral arterial bleed, he ripped Johnny's pants open and was relieved to find everything still intact. He said to his wounded teammate, "I know you're hurt, and I know this may not mean anything to you, but your dick is still there. At least you have that." Johnny, somehow, managed a laugh. Dozer was finally able to find and stop the source of his bleeding—a cut just underneath his groin. "You're good," Dozer told him. "You're gonna make it."

Then Elliott stirred and was conscious again. A SEAL through and through, the medic told his teammates to take care of Johnny first, then screamed and demanded some morphine. No one knew where the morphine had gone. When they found it, the frog who tried to inject it into Elliott had the device backward and injected it into his own hand. The sheer adrenaline rush of the situation kept him from getting too groggy.

When Dozer and Clint were satisfied that Elliott and Johnny were stable, tourniquets secure, vitals stable, wounds under pressure, and at no risk of bleeding out, they had to figure out how to get them out of there. The time had almost come: Dozer had been on the radio, guiding some Bradleys to the house. But how do you move a man whose legs are a mess, whose feet are hanging off his body, and whose body is slowly burning from phosphorus? There was only one way to do it without a stretcher handy. You carry him.

When the QRF returned, Cowboy leaned over Elliott and told him, "We're going to get you out of here, amigo, but you've gotta cowboy up, because we're going to have to hurt you to get it done." Then he bent down and grabbed him behind both of his ruined legs and heaved him up while another guy lifted his shoulders. With his legs torn apart, and a bilateral tibia/fibula fracture and a shattered right forearm as well, Elliott was screaming the whole time they moved him to the street. *"Stop, you're killing me!"*

A couple of guys ran to the roof, cleared it, and one of them leveled his M48 light machine gun and laid down suppressive fire on the buildings with line of sight to the Bradley. Outside, Crossman scanned the perimeter around the front gate of the house, securing the extract point. Then Lieutenant Clint ordered his men to prep for breakout. As they moved to the front gate, he directed the Bradley to turn its main gun on the roof of their own building. That's when the squad carrying Elliott made their move.

Rounds were smacking into the Bradley as they eased Elliott inside. Running into and out of buildings and alleyways all around them, insurgents now and then peeked down from the rooftops and once in a while got brave, taking a haphazardly aimed shot. Looking up, Cowboy got a quick glimpse, barely eight feet above him, of a scarfed head ducking behind a parapet. Thank God that guy didn't have any courage—or a grenade.

Dozer, Cowboy, and the others ran back inside to get Johnny. The first thing to do was get him calmed down. Dozer grabbed Johnny by his shoulder straps. Cowboy took him by the legs. Dozer said, "If you have to bite down on something, I'd start doing that now." What Dozer didn't tell Johnny was that he feared his teammate's legs would come right off when they moved him. But there was no other way. With a hand from two other guys, Dozer and Cowboy lifted him. The wail of pain that issued from Johnny was a sound like none they had ever heard. But they stayed with the necessary task, taking him to the waiting armored vehicle and putting him inside. They all crammed themselves into the tight confines of the Bradley, then pulled the rear hatch shut behind them. Forward of the crew compartment, a soldier stood, manning the vehicle's gun turret. Dozer could see only his lower half. The soldier's legs were shaking hard with fear.

Twenty or thirty seconds passed—an eternity—and still the Bradley did not move. The driver said something about needing authorization from command first. Cowboy grabbed the mike and told whoever was listening that "authorization," whatever that might mean, was hereby granted. That was good enough for the driver. As grenades lit off on the street outside, and rounds ricocheted off the vehicle, the driver hit the gas.

That was when Cowboy's guts turned over. He had choked back as much of it as he could, but in that dark, confined space, the smell of burned flesh, blood, and shit was just too much. He and a teammate lost their lunches right near Johnny, still screaming as his shredded shins and ankles jostled back and forth in the crowded Bradley.

Call it a miracle that all those guys got out of there alive. Elliott and Johnny were rushed to the casualty station at Camp Corregidor, treated by the docs, then loaded into CH-46 Sea Knight helos for evacuation to Al Asad air base, where the trauma surgeons were. Cowboy wasn't about to leave Elliott Miller's side. Covered in his friend's blood, he piled into the bird with him. After the helos took off, Dozer looked around for a ride back to the Papa sector, where his teammates were still shooting it out. He was covered in blood, too. By the time he finally negotiated for a Bradley to drive him back to the fight, it was over. The Camp Corregidor boys had finished it, and found another platoon of Bradleys to take them back to their base.

That was a really bad day. Play with a snake long enough, and even the best snake charmer will get bit.

10

"We're Not Going to Make It Out of Here Alive"

Back at Camp Marc Lee, I was in the TOC, listening to all this go down on the radio. I could hear everything— the gunfire, the explosions, the radio calls between the teams, and the growing desperation of my teammates in extremis. Sitting there in the TOC, I might as well have been a continent away. I remember the paralyzing feeling of helplessness as I sat there monitoring the radio, unable to take any action and forbidden, of course, to communicate, lest my inquiries muck up the more urgent needs of my teammates across town.

Man down…casevac…another man down…he's dead.

But who? It took hours for the details to reach us. Then it was a long, anxious wait for our boys to return.

I drifted around Camp Marc Lee like an unchained ghost, ashamed I couldn't get my gun into the fight. It was impossible to sleep, so I stopped trying. I went to medical for a little PT, and spent some time with people who lifted me up—guys like Marty Robbins, who was still healing from his frag wounds. That dude was as tough as nails, and a fine example for me. He'd fought to get back on the line as LPO and team leader, and when I finally let him start running again, he'd come back after every op and take his boots off, and I'd have to doctor up his feet because his socks were soaked through with blood. If you're a baseball fan, you may remember Boston Red Sox pitcher Curt Schilling's "bloody sock" World Series game in 2004, when he got a win even though his ankle hadn't yet healed from surgery. Marty's bloody socks impressed me a lot more.

I worked out in the gym for as long as my back would allow, then went to the shooting range and amused myself for most of an hour. I know nothing would have changed had I been out there, but it bugged me all the same.

Johnny Brands was flown out to Germany, on a path to becoming a case study in reconstructive orthopedics. I wouldn't see him again until everyone had come home from Ramadi. As for Elliott—Lord, that frogman nearly died on the hop. When he arrived as an urgent surgical case, the docs put twenty pints of blood back in him and patched him up as well as they could, once the phosphorus burned away. More than once they called us to report Elliott's death, but each time he fought back for life. Dozer, his closest friend in Bravo Platoon, finally asked the docs not to call unless Elliott's vitals went flat for more than two hours.

Elliott regained consciousness after about two weeks, but he would never be the same man who quit the Marine Corps after 9/11 to try to make the cut for the SEAL teams. After four deployments, he was a medic and a frogman all the way, and always will be. But he's in a new world now, facing the huge challenge of recovering as much of his life as possible after suffering wounds that would have killed ninety-nine men in a hundred. Not one of us doubted he'd take it on with determination and the utmost courage.

In the days following the battle, the mood at Camp Marc Lee was sullen. About half the guys who had gone out that night came back carrying shrapnel—Purple Hearts were given out all around. I visited with each of the wounded men at the hospital at Camp Ramadi. I also spent more time than usual on the phone with my family and friends back home.

One morning a few days later, I awoke to the sight of Morgan leaning over me, shining a flashlight in my face. He had just ridden over from Camp Corregidor. From the look on his face I understood how bad it had been for him. All through our lives, very little has ever come between us. We've stood together in every fight. Hell, we were swim buddies long before we ever darkened a door at Coronado. What I went through on Operation Redwing was the first thing that pushed us off course from walking basically the same path through life. Now I could see a trace of my new self in him. There was pain and anger, and a new level of seeing, born of the effects of the wounds suffered by Elliott and Johnny. It was visible in his eyes and in the tight set of his jaw, and there was an echo of it between every syllable of every word he bit off, painting the picture for me about what had happened that day. Where once there had been a separation between us, we were now one again.

Then, as fast as Morgan had appeared, he was rolling out again, on to the next operation. Such is the life of a high-speed operator in wartime. But it was very, very good to see him. I don't believe it could have been an accident that, later that day, a package full of good things arrived in the mail from Mom.

When I first got my Trident, I thought fights like the one we found in the Papa sectors would be the be-all and end-all of life in the teams. Everyone in Task Unit Red Bull relished our standing as the guys who were in the thick of it, getting it on in Al Qaeda's backyard. With that costly mission on November 19, we landed a gut shot on a major insurgent cell that was dedicated to pushing Iraq into the Dark Ages. With the enemy body count north of thirty-five, we seriously weakened Al Qaeda's ability to enforce its murderous will in that dangerous neighborhood. But our days, nights, and weeks in Ramadi ground away on my body and soul. Though my muscles were cashing checks my bones didn't have on deposit, I think that mission helped me settle into my new position. I knew that the goal of bringing long-term change to a broken part of the world had to be foremost in our minds. Skipper and Master Chief never stopped spreading that message. Yet as we shifted our focus to helping the sheikhs take back their city, we would never let up entirely on killing the enemy as he came at us. This was the yin and yang of our service as special operations warriors.

Shortly after Elliott and Johnny were hit, our leadership flew in from Fallujah to visit us. Sitting down with the entire complement of both camps, Commander Leonard, later joined by Master Chief, said we had to speed up our transition into doing business differently. Though it might make our conventional brothers uncomfortable to lose us as a direct asset in their firefights, it was critical to the success of our deployment. Since arriving in country, they had been working with leadership on all sides, up and down, and from every unit in our area of operations, including our own task units, to lay the groundwork for tribal engagement and the COIN efforts. This latest overwatch support mission amplified the need to be more careful in selecting how we met the enemy in the street. When we were entering enemy-controlled neighborhoods to set up overwatches, we sometimes had no way out when the shit started flying. Our effectiveness in the overwatch mission was waning, they told us, and our talents had to be used to truly help change the landscape. We all had to avoid getting too heavily invested in the emotional desire to fight it out, seek revenge, and lose sight of our higher purpose, and this included the Skipper and Master Chief. Skipper informed us that from now on, sniper overwatch missions would be carried out only upon his direct command. He didn't like taking autonomy away from his troop commanders and their men, but we had to make sure these missions were carried out with the right strategic intent.

What happened to Elliott and Johnny broke the hearts of our EOD detachment in particular. They felt they had failed us. Andy took it so hard that he called his OIC, Lieutenant Paul Craig, in Fallujah, and pressed the case he had been making for a while: he thought the bomb techs needed to work differently with our assault elements. Instead of following behind in the train, waiting to be called forward, he wanted to run up front with the point man, studying the street for command wires and pressure plates. Whenever we left a house we had been using for sniper overwatch, he wanted his guys to be the first ones out the door, scanning the ground and walls.

Afterward, Lieutenant Craig visited Camp Marc Lee. He and the Master Chief had discussed these tactics in the past and now that the guys on the ground felt the need, he understood it was time to drive the point home. He and Andy sat down with me and made their case. Their message was, "We're not going to make it out of here alive if we don't change things up."

This wasn't a casual request. SEALs guard the real estate at the front of their trains jealously—we're wary of guys who aren't frogmen wanting to play one on an op. The front is a critical position and we need to be sure we have someone there who can handle the worst when it happens. But the bomb techs articulated their special skill set well, and sold us on its value. Fortunately, this same request had been made by Master Chief to our task unit leadership in the past. So, when we took it up the line, our troop commander, Lieutenant Commander Ryan Thomas, was receptive. From then on, whenever we went on foot patrols, one of our bomb techs ran right behind the point man, be it Salazar or Studdard, studying the ground for pressure plates and command wires. On convoys, they sat behind the driver, advising him to go slow, telling him where to turn, and pointing out obstacles to avoid. They were well-qualified backseat drivers. *Watch that crack in the road.... Stop—let me check out that pile of rocks....* Soon our drivers were so well schooled that in their heads they could hear the bomb tech's instructions before they were actually uttered. It was a change that saved lives. We became such believers that we sent Salazar and Studdard to talk to the Army SOF units in town about the value of putting the EOD guys up front.

When Lieutenant Clint and Dozer both argued that we

needed someone else fluent in Pilot to arrange our air support for the Camp Corregidor boys, we brought in another F/A-18 driver, Lieutenant Commander Jake Ellzey, from the head shed at Fallujah. Jake was also a Texas boy. I'm not sure that had anything to do with the fact that our eastside frogs didn't face another attack after he came to town, but we couldn't rule it out, either.

The fight for Ramadi wasn't going to depend on how many enemy fighters we killed. They were replaceable by the dozen. Our goal now became clear: getting the Iraqis ready to take care of this hellhole on their own. It was easy to treat the locals as though they were furniture. Relations with them were never helped when we took over their homes and, in defending them, turned them into replicas of the Alamo, riddled with bullets, leaving the rest of the neighborhood ripped apart by bombs. Sure, a hostile enemy always needed killing, but how could we be sure that the story of how we did that, when it was finally told later in the street, wouldn't end up completely warped and used by our treacherous enemy as propaganda against us? If we were looking to make an impact at a higher strategic level, we had to take control of the narrative. We had to accept a different level of risk to gain the locals' trust.

Many of the guys didn't want to hear it—the talk was always about going out and getting some. Living the warrior way. We saw ourselves as venturing into a savage land and battling a ruthless enemy. Every warfighter loves the history and culture of ancient Sparta, whose heroism against the odds at Thermopylae was one of history's greatest last stands. We identified with the warrior culture that saved Western civilization. But once Master Chief pointed out that the Spartans often won their battles by putting lesser warriors from other nation-states out front to wear the enemy down—leaving out the fact that they sometimes engaged in personal behavior that many Americans wouldn't consider manly—our mission made a lot more sense. "If you want to be like Spartans," he told us, "then start training Iraqis."

It sometimes seemed impossible to bring freedom to a people who had known nothing but war and murder. Living in dirt-mound poverty while their ruler enjoyed luxurious palaces, the Iraqis were so scared of Saddam Hussein that they rarely bucked the system. Those who did were quickly killed. We had to fight the apathy that overtook the survivors. It often seemed they were ready to run to whichever side came out on top, as long as they could have security for their families. Giving the people of this godforsaken place a chance would be the legacy of our service.

When I was in Afghanistan, local culture came crashing into my life unexpectedly, and immediately became the most important thing in my world. The ancient ethical code of the Pashtun people, *Pashtunwalai,* meant so much to Gulab and his people that they risked their lives to protect mine, holding at bay Taliban fighters who were looking to capture and execute me. Here in Iraq, too, we found a country of good people looking after their kids, starting schools, improving their prospects in spite of terrible obstacles. But there were basic problems of law, order, economics, government, and the lack of everyday conveniences that we wouldn't tolerate for a minute in America. Iraqis were doing their best to live through their nightmare. In the short term, though, life for ordinary people was made much harder by our work destroying the murderous cancer afflicting them.

*　　*　　*

As the weather got cold, some of our guys went to an Iraqi outpost where U.S. Army trainers were getting the Iraqis up to speed. Fumbling around in their blue-collared shirts, the *jundis* had a long way to go. Meanwhile, our two platoons also continued operating at high tempo, going out almost every night, often for multiple nights, pretty much without a break. The chill in the air meant that the boys were loaded down with extra clothing, which made movement harder.

One of my duties in mission planning was to give names to our ops. The next two we did were known as Blind Fury and Armageddon. After our losses in the Papa sectors, those words described everyone's state of mind. Blind Fury was a raid to take down a bomb maker and an assassin. Lieutenant Austin and the boys took care of that one. I was in the train with Gold for Operation Armageddon, an overwatch operation to support conventional forces, as well as the follow-on raids the next two nights. It was good to be back, but the good feeling was short-lived. This op would prove to be my undoing.

Thanksgiving dinner was luxurious by the standards of the battlefield—a dry ham-and-cheese sandwich washed down with some Mountain Dew. But there was no joy in the holiday. The weather was wet and cold. That might have been why sleep was difficult.

Our next mission, a raid to capture a high-value target, was known as Operation Mind Freak. It was followed by a sniper mission in a neighborhood we hadn't operated in before. We had some new guys in the platoon for this one. Our straphangers were all solid operators, and some of them were very experienced. We valued their ideas and their input. Just because we had been there for six weeks didn't give us a monopoly on smarts.

In line with the wishes of the head shed, our missions evolved from static overwatch operations to more active, mobile assignments. We used our intel to target leaders more surgically. We moved out fast, doing snatch-and-grab operations. We didn't do bait ops anymore, or patrol to contact, looking for a fight. As the enemy went to ground, the challenge now was to make sense of ambiguity, and to get smart about people. It was about deciding when to blow down a door and when to hand out candy. When you blew down the wrong door, the principles of counterinsurgency warfare required you to call in the home repairman or grab some tools and become one yourself. They say SEALs can operate anywhere, and we do. But this was a whole new battlefield for us. Sometimes a hammer and a pack of nails (and a handful of M&Ms for the kids) did more damage to the enemy than a laser-guided Maverick.

When I was serving in Afghanistan, I couldn't fire my gun fast enough. In Ramadi, though, a rifle magazine was like a can of worms. The battle for the city sometimes seemed less likely to turn on the shots we took as on the rounds we decided to keep in our chambers. One night one of our snipers spotted two insurgents digging a hole in the road, attempting to plant an IED. He shot both of them, killing one and leaving a wounded survivor, who we quickly took into custody and promptly sent to the hospital. Saving the life of an enemy may seem like the wrong thing to do. But ask yourself: Which of the two bullets fired by the sniper that night did more to pacify the area? The insurgent who got killed will never plant another bomb. But the guy who was shot, taken in, cared for, and saved by American forces is likely to come away with his mind changed about what Americans are all about. We were there, it had been said, to steal their oil and their women, after all. Or were we?

Sometimes Skipper and Master Chief went out with us to see how we were doing business. They took positions in the back of the train, and, wanting us to operate naturally, asked us to pretend they were invisible. One time Master Chief joined us while we were overwatching the flank of an Army unit doing a block clearance in a heavily contested part of the city. They had set up a cordon—a secure perimeter of cleared buildings, which no one could approach without being seen. A call came on the radio from one of the snipers. "We've got a mover. A military-age Iraqi male." There he was, down on the street. He was holding something in his hands. He didn't seem to be moving toward our forces or acting threatening. Still, the sniper thought he was highly suspicious, standing in an area he had no business being in, even though he was a good distance from anyone's position and well outside of our "ring of safety."

The team listened as the radio chatter continued.

"He might have a grenade—ah, never mind, I don't think it's a frag."

"I think it's an apple."

"Wait—it looks like it could be a frag."

"No, I don't think so. I think it's an apple."

"It's a grenade. It has to be...."

As the dialogue went back and forth, Master Chief got up and tried to take a look. To his eye, it was hard to determine the guy's exact intent, and besides that he really didn't look more than fourteen or fifteen years old. And that was when the shot rang out. The sniper across the way decided to engage the kid as he approached a block of buildings. It was a tough shot on a moving target heading toward the defilade of a structure nearby. The sniper's bullet missed the kid's head by a matter of inches. Having cheated death, he wisely disappeared. There was nothing in his hands as he left the cordon area.

When we got back to camp, Master Chief walked our snipers through an analysis of what had taken place.

"So what do you make of this? Do you think that was really a grenade in his hand?"

No one had any reason to doubt the shooter's sincerity, but Master Chief didn't get an answer.

"Well, in the end, I think it's fortunate that he missed him," Master Chief said. "Judging by what I heard, I think we *wanted* to see a grenade.

"Think about it. Even if it was a grenade, what was that one kid going to do? There were no American forces in the area, and he was no threat to our or any other position."

One of our snipers suggested that the shot might have served to deter Iraqis from picking up hand grenades, if that's what it was, or from acting suspiciously in restricted areas. Maybe this was a dangerous insurgent who needed to be shot. Maybe shooting him would give a second thought to anyone planning to gather ordnance for money.

Master Chief said, "Okay, let's say that one of those things was the goal, and we shoot this guy, because it's going to keep Iraqi kids from picking up grenades and, we suppose, save an American life somewhere in the future. So now the kid's dead, and the grenade's still lying there on the ground. We're not going to go out and take the grenade off the street, are we? No, we aren't. So very likely it will just end up in an insurgent's hands again. Meanwhile, how did an average Iraqi see what just happened?

"They're going to see a dead boy," he said. "And they're going to say, 'The Americans shot this child for no reason. There lies an innocent boy, killed just because he was standing in the street, holding an apple.' This is the word that gets around on the street, even if he really was holding a grenade.

"If you make the wrong call, you can lose a whole neighborhood," Master Chief continued. "And that grenade, or that apple, will still be lying there in the street. Either outcome harms our mission. If we take the shot, we have to be ready to get out there and influence the perception. I won't ask you to hesitate, but we need to have tactical patience. We need to know the shot is necessary, and if you feel it is, then you have to make the hard call."

Master Chief was tough to beat in this kind of exchange, brilliant at breaking down complexity and casting aside bullshit. He had seen similar situations in 2005, when the rules of engagement allowed our snipers to shoot anyone seen holding a shovel or a bag of trash that could be hiding an IED. Men with shovels and heavy trash bags were suspected of being an IED threat—until it became clear that innocent shopkeepers now and then used shovels and dustpans when they would sweep their stoops clean, and that sad souls were sometimes coerced by the insurgents to carry sacks of rocks and drop them into a hole in the road to test if our snipers were nearby. He learned well from history, from his peers, from anyone who had seen things he hadn't and he took it in to use with his men.

If you couldn't out-argue Master Chief, you were wise

just to keep your mouth shut. He never raised his voice, and always grounded his lessons in reason. That's what master chiefs get paid to do in the Navy, what sergeant majors do in the Marine Corps and Army, and what chief master sergeants do in the Air Force. They live by an idea that many folks hold dear where I come from: There's no education in the second kick of a mule.

As we saw it, a leader should always be ready to ask anyone under him: Are you preparing yourself to make the team better? Are you acting to make the team's record and reputation stronger? Are you staying in good shape—in both body and mind—for the greater good? You don't get people to follow you by demanding it with your words. You do it by *commanding* it with your example. In the chow hall at Camp Marc Lee, we put a sign above the door that read: IF EVERY SEAL WERE LIKE ME, HOW GOOD WOULD THE TEAMS BE?

Team 5's outstanding enlisted leadership kept me wanting to stay sharp, even as my body threatened to collapse under the weight of my plates. A feeling of competent, effective command was just exuded by our leadership and it trickled down from there. Success built upon success, and even after a bad day we felt motivated to get better. I think we all knew we were serving with some special people. Even our oldest frogs still say that about Task Unit Ramadi, all these many deployments later.

I once heard DQ say, "The day will come when the fight for the city will just seem to tip. One day, victory came from putting an artillery round into a building. The next day, victory will come from *not* doing it. The key to success will be recognizing as quickly as possible when that change has taken place."

Every man in Task Unit Ramadi can point to the day when that change came and our fortunes fell clearly into alignment with the people's. It was the day after Thanksgiving, when we copied a desperate radio call on the tactical net.

"My people are being killed. I need your help!"

11

My Enemy, My Friend

The man who sent the message was an Iraqi sheikh named Jassim Muhammad Saleh al-Suwadawi. The leader of the Albu Soda tribe, he controlled the sparsely populated northeastern part of Ramadi, the Sufiyah district. It was the same tribe that Travis Patriquin had identified to Commander Leonard as a likely key ally against Al Qaeda.

Our recent history with them wasn't good. They had been a thorn in the side of the men at Camp Corregidor ever since Americans had been there. Just about every day, Al Qaeda–linked insurgents roamed freely in that neighborhood, firing mortars at the camp from the backs of pickup trucks, then driving like hell to get away before our radar-directed return fire arrived. On some days early in our deployment we could mark time by the cadence of the mortars they lobbed in. Sometimes they came in volleys of five or six at a time. More than a few soldiers were killed on the chow line. You didn't go anywhere in the camp without a full kit and body armor.

We knew that Al Qaeda terrorists were responsible for a great many of these attacks. We also knew, because there was hardly ever a letup, that the terrorists had made a deal with Sheikh Jassim and his tribe.

Then, it seems, their infernal little bargain fell apart.

Sheikh Jassim resented the way his homes and his people were always caught in the crossfire. Al Qaeda militia often fired at Camp Corregidor from schools and hospitals in his area, probably hoping it would deter us from shooting back. Sometimes it did. But sometimes, too, there was collateral damage. Sheikh Jassim didn't care much for Al Qaeda's brand of cowardice, and the loss of life and property it inflicted upon his people, so he tried to put an end to it by banishing them from his neighborhoods. He set up checkpoints to keep the terrorists from getting in. He only had a force of about fifty men in his tribal police, but it took them no time, using their well-placed checkpoints and ability to distinguish locals from troublemakers, to shut them out.

The terrorists issued grave warnings. "Take the checkpoints down within seventy-two hours or we will kill you and everyone in your tribe." But the sheikh stood his ground. That's when Al Qaeda made its move: a huge attack on the Sufiyah district, aimed at wiping out Jassim's people.

The terrorists began by overwhelming the police checkpoints. With just a few dozen rounds apiece in their weapons, the tribal cops on duty didn't stand a chance. Then the killers turned on the tribe's women and children. It was a shocking and deliberate slaughter of innocents. The tribe's population of military-age males was quickly decimated by the attacks—but that wasn't enough for Al Qaeda's killers.

The Americans had long feared that something like this would happen. Captain Patriquin had the foresight to give the Sunni chief a satellite phone and his own personal phone number. That's how Sheikh Jassim was able to reach American forces directly, through a personal phone call to Patriquin. "My people are being killed. I need your help!"

Aerial surveillance gave us a grim real-time picture of what was going on. The terrorists were killing everyone they could find. They shot them dead in their yards, in their houses, and in the streets. They slaughtered their livestock, poisoned their water, and destroyed their electrical generators.

The brutality and scope of the attack was quickly followed by an explanation, thanks to our intel shop: the top commander of Al Qaeda in Iraq, Abu Ayyub al-Masri, had come to Ramadi to organize it personally. I guess the success of the counterinsurgency mission and the Anbar Awakening was reflected in the desperation of the response.

As the closest commander on the scene, Lieutenant Colonel Charles Ferry of the First Battalion, Ninth Infantry Regiment (the 1/9), ordered his tanks and infantry to move out of Camp Corregidor and enter the neighborhoods that not a month before had been virtually off-limits to them.

As the Americans began arriving, Al Qaeda assassins were heading for the sheikh's house. Jassim and his fighters abandoned their compound, falling back toward the Euphrates River. "We're coming, we're coming, hang on!" Captain Patriquin told him.

Meanwhile, from many mosques rose the familiar shrill voices over the loudspeakers. The Sunni imams were calling their faithful to jihad. This time, though, the message was different. Our terps told us the jihad was aimed not at the "infidels"—usually, that was us—but against Al Qaeda.

So here we were, Americans from several units, working together to essentially join a call to jihad. The world really had been turned on its head.

Colonel Ferry ordered aircraft to make low-level runs over the neighborhood, looking to slow down the bad guys. Army artillery began targeting the terrorists. Other strategic air assets began arriving overhead, too, helping to win the fight. Despite its chaotic battlefields, Anbar Province was seen as a backwater by some higher commanders in Baghdad, and we'd never seen this kind of air support before. Still, not everybody wearing a black head scarf and carrying an AK-47 was a bad guy. There were tribal fighters coming over from other neighborhoods to support Jassim's besieged people. But Al Qaeda fighters often stood out by their cruelty. As the terrorists fled the neighborhood in their pickup trucks, they tried to intimidate the locals by dragging bodies of the dead behind them, chained to their fenders. All this did was help our airborne watchers distinguish friend from foe. A Marine Corps F/A-18 Hornet was vectored to attack. The terrorists were blown into pieces, their last stain upon the earth. It was old-fashioned American shock and awe that finally stopped al-Masri's murder brigade.

Before U.S. forces took him to safety at Camp Corregidor, Sheikh Jassim instructed the elders in his tribe to cooperate with us. After all the blood we had shed in fighting the insurgency—taking, no doubt, a heavy price from Jassim's own ranks—we all had second thoughts.

But we are forged to adapt quickly to the battlefield. In Ramadi in 2006, we could sense that things were turning our way.

The night of the attack, our officers at Camp Corregidor helped plan the mission to repatriate the sheikh back into his neighborhood. Most of the Corregidor boys piled into a helicopter and set out into this until-recently-off-limits part of the city. Making several false landings to conceal their location, they finally hit the ground in a rural area about five klicks from his compound and began patrolling it on foot.

It was like entering a lion's den. Jassim's fighters and other allied tribesmen walked up and down the streets with weapons at the ready, while our guys studied them grimly. They were in typical Iraqi ninja gear: full black clothing and scarves, faces covered—the same dudes who had been shelling Camp Corregidor and staging attacks against us all the way west to Camp Marc Lee. There was bad blood going both ways—a couple of nights, while sitting around the campfire, our guys overheard Iraqis talking about how a week ago they were killing American soldiers. But now came the understanding that circumstances had changed and bygones needed to be bygones. It was the way of life out there in old Mesopotamia, a tried-and-true understanding rooted firmly in the ancient earth: "The enemy of my enemy is my friend." Everyone seemed to know what the deal was. War sure is crazy. Still, our guys kept their fingers close to their triggers.

They all thought it was going to be a quick in and out, a three-day overwatch operation with a raid or two thrown in. As it happened, the undersized platoon of about a dozen guys spent most of a month out there, hanging out on a limb, calming things down and keeping the sheikh's people safe from incursions by Al Qaeda. They set up at a power plant, then moved into the sheikh's compound. The EOD tech, Shane Snow, decorated the outside walls of the compound with antipersonnel mines, concealing them with blankets and prayer rugs. Better safe than sorry.

When they began training volunteers to join the Sunni police, our guys ran background checks on the recruits and created a biometric database—fingerprints, retina scans—keeping lists of who'd been naughty and who'd been nice. Several of them popped for having killed Americans. The most charismatic and aggressive of them, of course, had the leadership traits we needed, so we put them—arguably the most dangerous ones—in charge.

It's spooky to work with people who had been trying to kill you just a few days before. Team guys are raised from birth to deal with threats like that forcefully and permanently. I don't need to tell you that my brother and his teammates slept with one eye open the whole time they were out there. Their days and nights were an endless episode of *CSI: Iraq*. But this was the strategy we and so many other units were working toward. It would change the landscape.

Within days, most of our guys had learned enough Arabic to run a shooting range. "Hold the butt stock firmly against your shoulder!"..."Use your right eye to look through the sight!" Much as they didn't care for this mission, they proved themselves in the training role. Afterward, sitting around a fire with the locals, sipping chai, they'd struggle along, telling stories in broken Arabic, with a lot of intense eye contact and frequent recourse to the phrase book. The Iraqi kids seemed to think it was the coolest thing in the world. The SEALs took special care to show respect for the kids' mothers, who, like mothers everywhere, knew how their corner of the world worked better than anybody.

Those who had a handle on Arabic made a real difference, getting good intel from their new friends. This allowed us to raid insurgent cells that otherwise would have remained well hidden. Sometimes they fooled us, dropping the dime on tribal rivals, saying they were Al Qaeda and hoping we'd ruin their day. We learned to vet their leads fast.

Pretty quickly, the Army moved a whole company into the neighborhood—about 150 men—and kept it there for a while. The SEALs and those soldiers from Lieutenant Colonel Ferry's command understood the score. In spite of official coalition policy, which frowned on it, they had clearance to bring in weapons and ammunition and helped arm the new tribal police to defend themselves. Though they were wary of creating a potentially dangerous militia, the greater need by far was to make sure we had allies who could get the job done. We didn't always mind seeing business done that way, and never minded it when it worked as well as it seemed to here. It didn't take long for something remarkable to happen: in less than two days, the daily barrage of mortars stopped raining down on Camp Corregidor.

One day Shane noticed that one of his hidden claymores protecting the compound had been exposed when a strong wind gust blew the prayer rug hiding it out of position. He was watching when an Iraqi clad in black noticed this. Shane raised the scope of his M4 to his eye, steadied himself, and put his finger on his trigger, ready to take the shot. That was when the guy reached down, picked up the blanket, and put it back in place, covering the charge. Shane stood down. This enemy seemed to have become our friend.

The fighting never completely stopped, and we always had to watch our backs, but after Sheikh Jassim reclaimed his neighborhood from the terrorists, with an assist from U.S. forces, it was clear that Al Qaeda in Iraq was on the ropes. We mourned the deaths of all the Americans who had died to put us in that position. We honored the sacrifices of the Iraqis, too. Anyone who was there at the time can testify to the impact of their steadfast and courageous service. We did it, and we did it together.

12

Going South

As I flip through my diary of those days, I see something I never fully realized in the moment: though we all lived it from day to day, from one mission to the next, the battle for Ramadi was epic. Our mission challenged us mentally and physically. It stretched our capabilities in new directions and sharpened our blade for wars both familiar and new.

It stretched me a little, too—nearly to a breaking point, in fact. In early December, as Pearl Harbor Day approached, I knew my days as a door kicker were numbered.

As the platoon medic, I was keeping busy helping guys with their injuries and ailments. But you know what they say about the cobbler's kids wearing the worst shoes. My back and pelvis were busted up so bad that if I sat for more than twenty minutes, I lost all feeling in my legs, and eventually in my arms, too. The pain from the compression on my spine was getting worse all the time. With sleep seldom coming, I got by on little cocktails of Vicodin, Flexeril, Ambien, whatever combinations the doc thought might help. But I wouldn't surrender to the forces that were trying to take me down from within. Staying on the line with the guys was more important than saving my body—and I was always willing to do whatever it took to stay on the line, always ready to do my duty when midnight came.

The last mission I ran with Gold squad, on December 7, 2006, was named Going South—an appropriate name. And this one was going to be it for me.

After Johnny and Elliott got hit, our bomb techs had been itching to take down the "emirs" who oversaw manufacture of the IEDs. Our assaulters had killed or captured plenty of triggermen and emplacers, but the HVTs—high-value targets—eluded us. The assholes who designed and built the IEDs were like the cookers in a drug ring, simmering the meth. With college degrees and professional training, they were smart enough to feel the heat coming when we were after them. They ran when they sensed trouble, and that was probably why the mechanics of the bombs our EOD guys found seemed to change so often.

Andy and Shannon had a hunch that the area west of town known as the Five Kilo district sheltered some of the people we were after. It was quiet out there, sparsely built and rural. We had never run an op out that way before, but I trusted their hunch and passed it up the line. That's how we ended up targeting that neighborhood for a midnight visit.

Within the city, we almost always drove a safe route to one of our combat outposts before setting out to our objective on foot. This time, we did it old-school. We drove out into the unknown streets to the actual target instead of patrolling from the COP. The motorized assault consisted of two ten-man squads, one under Lieutenant Austin with Salazar on point, and the other under Chief Marty Robbins. Each group had a trio of *jundis* as well. Lieutenant Nathan and I had the mobility force: the vehicles. The two squads piled into our two-and-a-half-ton troop carriers, and we left Camp Marc Lee after midnight and turned west onto Route Michigan.

In the desolate area west of town, this heavily potholed main road was known to be full of big IEDs. Buried in the road, they were like speed bumps packed with homemade explosives. As our convoy moved, we noticed different symbols painted on the wall running along the road. They were said to be warning signs to locals that IEDs might be buried along their path. The houses out there were built of mud and straw, scattered around a flat, sun-baked area. One might have taken it for a farming community, if growing dirt could be considered farming.

About five hundred meters from the houses we were going to hit, we stopped the trucks and our two squads dismounted. They formed their trains and begin sprinting forward parallel to the road, offset by a healthy distance to avoid unwanted fireworks. It was a full-on rush to hit the targets: three houses, each suspected of having some involvement in the bomb-making trade. Battle-wise as our guys were, they ran almost silently though they carried a full loadout.

The assaulters split into their two elements. Their point men led them to the doors and the breachers came forward and sledged the bolts. Marty Robbins, the chief, pushed everybody forward, running up their backs, keeping the train moving fast. Piling in, they hoped for resistance and expected a jackpot. Instead, there was nothing. No resistance, no fight. And no bomb materials, explosives, wires, or emplacing tools, either. Instead, the lieutenant and I, who were in charge of the trucks, got a call from the pissed-off operators asking for extract. When we kicked it into gear and drove to the set point, where they had dismounted not twenty minutes ago, the frustration of the anticlimax was vented in the obscenities they unleashed upon the world for hitting a dry hole.

You can't make movies out of raids like Operation Going South. Not every target is what you think it's going to be. There was no drama in this anywhere, except in the full day preceding its kickoff. The preparation of the force list; the infil and exfil routes that we drew up, debated, and redrew; the coordination with the Iraqis; the staging of vehicles; the time-on-target calculations; the shootout procedures and contingencies identified and game-boarded; the comms plan; the QRF plan—all of it prepared with a rushed special operations tempo, the checking and rechecking of gear: rifle cleaned, mags and frags packed, batteries, flares, radios, and so on. The adrenaline surge is even stronger when you're going into a new area. The sense of anticipation and tight nerves—that's war, too.

Truth is, every mission is big, and the fight isn't always where you expect, which is why a warrior's first challenge is to be ready for it, especially when there's no reason to think it will appear. You prepare so you *don't* have to fight, not so you have to fight. You don't always get what you wish for. If you love the fight too much, sometimes she won't love you back.

As inconsequential as it was, this mission was a turning point for me, and I knew it. Or, actually, I should say I knew it as soon as Senior Chief Steffen pointed out to me what a turning point it was. There was no hiding my physical decline from a leader as well attuned to his men as he was. He sensed my pain and my exhaustion. None of it was useful to the squadron.

As I've said many times and will probably never say enough, in my opinion Senior Chief Steffen is one of the most effective individuals in the special operations community. Part of it is his ability to tell you things you don't want to hear, and make you like it all the same. He has this rare talent for climbing into your ass, knocking around a little, and leaving you feeling grateful for the favor. He hammers you like a loving father. He'll tell you that you screwed up, or that you're not on your A game, or that there may be serious questions about your suitability to serve, but at the end of it, all you want to do is say, "Roger that, sir." And go find a way to improve yourself. Our respect for him was commanded, not demanded.

Still, when he came to me one day in early December and told me he thought it was time for me to quit going outside the wire, I wasn't ready to hear it. I remember our conversation well. I pushed back on him. I told him I was still good to go, and that the boys would pick up my slack. We were a machine out there and it had a lot more miles on it. There was no way I entirely believed this myself, but I did my best to make the case. I didn't want a bullshit op like Going South to be my swan song.

I won't describe the language that flew between us that day. When I flared up on him, it was the last gasp of a tired frog's pride. I think he knew it, and I think he knew I knew it. But my pride had to have its say before I went along with what was right. As a member of an assault element, I was more a liability than an asset now. I'd been burning the furniture to avoid freezing to death in my house. It was the senior chief's job to tell me I couldn't go anymore.

How do you get right with the idea, at the age of thirty-one, that the career you've pursued with every fiber of your being has come suddenly to an end? I can tell you it helped that DQ, our squadron operations officer, widely respected in the E-5 mafia, was on hand, visiting from Fallujah. He helped me own the decision. To have a gun-fighter like him look me in the eye and tell me that the war can't go on forever, that a young gun must always become an old hand, made this evolution feel natural to me. He forced me to be honest with myself. He asked me, "Marcus, if something happens out there and you have to vault somebody over a wall, or haul a badly wounded teammate to safety, are you the best man to carry the load for your team?" My back, my knees, and my exhausted mind answered the question for me.

It was the path we all must take. All senior SEALs, including Master Chief, DQ, and Skipper, reached the point where they had to slow down as shooters before they could raise their game as leaders. DQ said there was a new job for me within the platoon, in the operations section. I would be, in effect, his counterpart at Camp Marc Lee. Talking with him made me feel like the ballplayer in John Fogerty's song "Centerfield." "Put me in, Coach." I'd have to get right with the fact that I was no longer operational, but there was a game to play. When my BUD/S class had finished Hell Week, an instructor said, "We've all been there and done that. It's time to get ready for the next step on the ladder."

It was time to be reborn again.

Climbing that ladder involved standing face-to-face with my teammates and seeing how they took the change in my role. I was afraid of what I'd see on their faces. After word got around that I was coming off the line, I walked into the chow hall and a couple of guys came up to me and said they were sorry to hear it. They told me to use the time to heal up, and not to worry, everything would be fine in the train. In about ten minutes, it was business as usual and we were all still tightly bound members of the team. There was always someone ready to fill your post.

As I found a new home in the TOC, in the role as chief of the operations section, I wrapped my arms around the challenge of vetting our op plans, coordinating communications, getting aircraft and drones into the mix, designing routes into and back from our targets, making sure the operators never got their toes stepped on by other friendlies when they went outside the wire, and supporting the training mission. It's easy to think you're there to do whatever you want, and pursue a personal agenda of some kind. But of course we weren't. Our duty is to serve the mission, and if we're not doing that, then we have no right to call what we do service.

Though I knew I was unlikely to carry a rifle into a war zone ever again, I didn't want to be seen as a paper pusher. I wanted to stay close to the fight. So I kept up with what our operators were doing. I checked and rechecked everything. In briefings, I always wanted to be able to tell them, "It's all there, everything you need. I know the route, because I've walked it." I'd always remind them that only one thing was important: "From the minute you jock up, the mission's not over until you're back here, boots on the ground, mission accomplished, and back in your tent asleep. Bring everybody back. If you get into it, fight like you've never fought before. *But bring everybody back.*"

I was thirty-one, but well aware that I was becoming an old man. And I'd earn the right to talk like one, if only those willful young bucks would let me. It helped that I was surrounded by great frogmen who had already made this evolution. As upset as I was by early December's turn of events, I look back today and see that I was never prouder to stand in their company. My teammates from that deployment were, as a group, top to bottom, some of the finest I've ever served with. I loved seeing guys like Marty Robbins and Wink going to work, and doing it with a level of confidence and authority that they had earned as SEALs. Seeing them rise to the occasion, I was left with no doubt at all that our world doesn't revolve around one man. No single person makes our world go round.

Pearl Harbor Day was a terrible day in Ramadi. At least ten U.S. servicemen were killed in insurgent attacks. One of those attacks was particularly nasty and costly.

Some American journalists were visiting town that day. They were interested in the story of the Sunni tribal awakening, and they wanted to see it up close, in the street, so a little embed operation was set up to accommodate them. Given the bad press the war had been getting, most of us saw how helpful it could be to have some truth in the papers. Among those members of the press were a twenty-five-year-old woman from a newsmagazine and a photographer who came to see how our work was transforming one of Iraq's worst places. They were riding

Route Sunset in a convoy, bound for COP Falcon. The road was secure, locked down with 24-7 patrols and surveillance. The only vulnerable spot was a road crossing near a newly reopened school. It was there that Al Qaeda managed to insert a bomb team.

An officer riding in the convoy's second Humvee saw the steel plate buried in the street. He tried to call a warning to the lead vehicle, but it was too late. A heavy rubber tire rolled over it, a fuse triggered, and after a short delay, the third Humvee in line was engulfed in a blast of flames. That vehicle contained four people: a driver, a turret gunner, a Marine Corps public affairs officer, and Captain Travis Patriquin, the Army civil affairs officer whose work with the Sunni tribes had done so much to pacify Ramadi.

The explosion threw Patriquin out of the vehicle. He died on impact. Two others—the gunner, Army specialist Vincent Pomante, and the Marine Corps PAO, Major Megan McClung, were KIA as well. Major McClung became the first female graduate of the United States Naval Academy ever to be killed in action.

Among those who mourned this loss hardest was Sheikh Sattar. Burning with anger and grief, he wept at the news of Captain Patriquin's death. "For some reason when I make good friends with Americans," Sattar would say, "they become my brothers, and they die." The sheikh decided he couldn't bear making any more American friends. "I don't want them to die," he said. At the memorial service for Patriquin, McClung, and Pomante, held several days after Patriquin's body was flown home—and that was one of the largest "hero flights" anyone in Iraq could remember, attended by more than a thousand people—Sattar offered a traditional Muslim burial prayer to his slain friend. "O Allah, admit him to Paradise and protect him from the torment of the grave and the torment of hellfire. Make his grave spacious and fill it with light." He also pledged himself to bringing righteous justice to the killers.

Within forty-eight hours, tipped off by a relative, Sattar and his police got the intel that led us to the prize. In a series of raids conducted on December 19, our forces searched for the three assassins who planted that bomb. Gold team finally grabbed them. As we all suspected, they were your run-of-the-mill Al Qaeda hirelings, teenagers, greedy opportunists looking for a payday. They were turned over to Iraqi police. Sheikh Sattar boasted later on that he had "fed them to his dogs." Was it true? I don't know. It was his city, so I suppose that was his business.

Patriquin's death was not in vain. You talk about one man making a difference—his role in the Anbar Awakening, from his work with Sheikh Sattar to his encouraging of Sheikh Jassim's rebellion against Al Qaeda, was of enormous importance. Those sheikhs knew how to take care of business in their city: Sattar's recruitment work was invaluable, and in his fight up in Sufiyah district, Jassim put Al Qaeda on the run, at a cost of just seventeen of his men. Jassim called his KIA martyrs. Call them what you want; they were heroes to the people of Ramadi. Our estimates put Al Qaeda losses in that fight at around sixty, though in the chaos of mobs, troop movements, and air attacks it was hard to nail down a final number. Afterward, many tribes that had been devotedly unhelpful to us and the cause of a new Iraq came on board and helped us with our police recruitment and training effort. It appeared that a turning point was near. Travis Patriquin's hands were all over this success and his fine touch would be forever missed.

President Bush had been conferring with Iraq's prime minister, Nouri al-Maliki, about our progress. In late November, at a meeting in Jordan, the president first broached the idea of a "surge," pushing another twenty or thirty thousand U.S. troops into Iraq to improve security for the people. Around the same time, another American newspaper article was published claiming that things in Anbar were so bad that "U.S. and Iraqi troops are no longer capable of militarily defeating the insurgency in al-Anbar."

Actually, maybe that was partly correct, because the wave that was sweeping Ramadi clean of terrorists was only partly military in nature. When Iraqis saw that members of Al Qaeda were the real infidels, young Iraqi men everywhere rallied to the idea of defending a just cause. Captain Patriquin put his finger on it when he wrote in early December, "The promise of a life of adventure, steady pay, and being on the side of righteousness has proved to be the right mix." It allowed peace-loving Iraqi men on the right side of the law to serve family, tribe, and nation. All of a sudden a lot of farmers and shopkeepers were up to their hips in marksmanship, assault tactics, checkpoint operations, rules of evidence, and techniques for handling detainees. Those who showed promise were sent to a detective school across town. The change was bubbling up from within. We played a role in helping it along, but we were far from being the conquerors of Anbar Province.

On December 13, President Bush met with the Joint Chiefs of Staff to discuss how to capitalize on our momentum. Five days later, the new secretary of defense, Robert Gates, was sworn in and went to visit Prime Minister al-Maliki. When he came home, Secretary Gates recommended the appointment of a new commander for all coalition forces in Iraq. The man selected was the Army's premier counterinsurgency strategist, General David Petraeus. It's clear from this that our success in Ramadi, building on previous successes in Tal Afar and elsewhere, was a blueprint for what could be done throughout the country.

Confronted with a citizens' uprising, the terrorists seemed to know the days of their reign of terror were numbered. And at Camp Marc Lee and Camp Corregidor, Task Unit Ramadi was fully in its battle rhythm—another big problem for the bad guys. The surge in police recruitment was bringing us better intel all the time, and night after night, our assault elements went out and bagged a growing number of high-value targets. Some of the missions we ran were quite audacious.

Consider, for example, a stay-behind operation. You move into a neighborhood in strength, with forces that have a "large signature"—tanks, vehicles, and a lot of men. You patrol around, entering and clearing houses, making a lot of noise. You plant your footprint on that neighborhood, let everyone know you're there. Then you leave—or appear to leave. The tanks withdraw, the patrols load up into Bradleys and drive away. But not everybody goes home. A lot of guys stay behind. You can only do an operation like this when you're comfortable working in your battle space, when the people and their reactions are familiar to you, when there's a baseline level of goodwill in the streets, and you know basically how the enemy is going to come knocking.

You leave a few platoons of riflemen dispersed throughout the neighborhood. They'll sit quietly with their hosts, talking, being friendly, and explaining that they are there to stop the people who are killing their children and ruining their neighborhoods. The innocent residents of Ramadi are like good people everywhere. They don't want fights going on around their homes. And they don't want their families to be put needlessly into harm's way. They bring out pita bread and their syrupy sweet chai. All the while, our guys are keeping an eye on the streets. Because the enemy, when they see our vehicles leave, is going to come back, looking to set up their IEDs and so on. It may happen at first light of dawn, or after the mosques let out. There will be movement, a gathering. The gunmen and bomb makers will awaken and assert themselves.

When they show up again, that's when we spring the trap. Sometimes it's a tank platoon supported by heavy weapons pushing suddenly out of a hidden position. Sometimes we'd catch them in a crossfire between mutually supporting rooftop sniper positions. There was almost always close air support overhead, with missiles ready on the rails. Those pilots—we loved them. They were always dying to hear the magic words from a JTAC in the city down below: "Cleared hot." And we were always happy to follow what happened next: our guys would see cars and small trucks driving along, full of armed men—and then all of a sudden the vehicle would burst into flames, struck by a missile. We put a serious dent into the enemy's ranks this way. It's a tactic we picked up from the Army. Since the beginning of the teams, we've never hesitated to upgrade our playbook with tactics borrowed or stolen from the conventional side. Whatever it takes to keep our enemies squealing from the feeling.

We used psychological operations, too. A "call to fight" operation would consist of a psy-ops team setting up loudspeakers and broadcasting insulting messages to the enemy. Targeting the insurgents' fragile egos, the psy-ops team would broadcast aggressive messages in Arabic. "Stop hiding behind your women and crawling around like dogs. Come and fight! We are waiting for you!" At this, the enemy would usually go nuts, and when the mosques let out around noon, we'd hear a cryptic call to arms from the Al Qaeda–friendly muezzins. "It's time to harvest in the garden...." "Bring forth the blood donations...." We'd see the troublemakers stir, go to their vehicles, grab weapons out of hidden storage areas, then start moving toward us. We let them come.

Sometimes it was over quickly. Other times it was more profitable just to observe and track their movements. We might find an IED-emplacing team. Those usually consisted of three guys. We'd have a sniper take out the driver and the shoveler, but let the bomb carrier get away. We would watch the survivor all the way home, then snap on the nest and round up all his buddies.

We changed up our approach almost every time so the enemy never figured out our pattern. But there was one constant they almost never seemed to recognize: if you fight us, you're going to lose.

There's no excitement to match heavy-breaching an enemy-held house. If you're serving as point man, you'll be hitting the door before the dust has even settled. Sometimes you get lucky and a bad guy answers the door as the charge goes off—a head start on the room clearance. You step over him and enter the house, your number two and number three men right on your belt, moving fast. You move and fight as one, each man counting on the others to cover his corner. As you flood the room, part of you prays that an armed enemy will appear before you. Whether he has a weapon at the ready or is reeling, stunned, bleeding, and concussed from the charge, you welcome him, and finish him, running down the wall as the stack floods in behind you. "Clear!" "Clear!" "Clear!" come the calls on your headset. Having secured one room—elapsed time, five and a half seconds—we roll into the next. We gather and exploit sensitive materials. Depending on what we find, there may be several days of follow-on raids to do.

This sort of thing is a drug for an SOF warrior, but I had to "detox." The breachers, assaulters, and snipers I helped put into play almost every night became an extension of my own gun sight. We served death to the enemy in innumerable combinations and captured many, many more, usually with an overhead view as the whole thing unfolded. As we looked at these missions roll from the top down, we knew we could get our teammates whatever they needed and took pride in supporting the fight in this way. Supporting our operations became my stock-in-trade in the TOC. When I turned in my rifle for a laptop and a sand table, I stepped back from the fight itself and dedicated myself to running our plays over and over again till we had them perfect, then starting over and running them again.

Shortly before Christmas, our guys were part of an effort to set up a new combat outpost in a tough neighborhood we hadn't visited before, the Qatana district. A company of Marines from the 1/6 had been pushing east from COP Firecracker, which we helped install back in October. But the attacks on them were so intense that they never got very far. They asked us to come in and relieve some of the pressure. Our job was to go in and set up overwatch positions to disrupt and kill insurgents who might resist the push. Senior Chief Steffen went outside the wire, running Gold squad with Lieutenant Nathan. Lieutenant Austin and Marty Robbins took Blue.

Before midnight, they convoyed out to COP Firecracker, which had since been renamed the 17th Street Security Station. (I guess the term "security station" was thought to be less frightening to the public than "combat outpost.") They met with the Marine Corps leadership, then patrolled out. Snaking by night through a landscape of rubble, they found the target building, a three-story structure, southwest of the new COP, just south of the Racetrack.

The family who lived in the house looked scared to death when the Americans arrived; the insurgents had told them we'd kill them all. It was apparent they hadn't seen our like before. When our terp, Moose, heard their fears, he just started laughing. With a few easy words, he calmed the family down and they began breathing again. Out came the tea, syrupy sweet and hot, and bread, served on what seemed to be their finest china.

Fizbo, running with Blue, set up his comms system in a third-floor room. The door that led to the roof had been riddled with gunfire, and it appeared that a large blast had gone off in the room, judging by the shrapnel holes in the ceiling and walls. The snipers sledged a hole in the wall, giving them a field of fire to the east, along the primary axis of threat. A cold, rainy wind rushed through the holey door and walls. It was a miserable winter's day.

Morning was quiet, but activity in the neighborhood picked up around noon. From a five-story building about a hundred yards away, insurgents opened up with small arms and RPGs at a Marine Corps position north of our guys, apparently unaware that we were set up on them at six o'clock. From that one spider hole, the boys of Blue opened up with everything they had. They were practically shoving and pushing to taking their turn on that spider hole. After they had unloaded all that ordnance on the building, it was no longer possible to see it. It was completely obscured by smoke. With the overcast too dense to allow air support, Fizbo worked on getting a ground-launched rocket battery into the mix. But by the time approval came, there was no longer any need; patrols found that all the insurgents had either been killed or had hightailed it out of the line of fire.

That night Blue hit a house farther east. Though a great point man, Salazar, was leading the way, this movement had an unfortunate end. The boys took a wrong turn and moved through an intersection flooded about knee-deep with water. Of course, it turned out to be sewage. Marty Robbins, Adam Downs, and the guys sure loved that.

As the snipers got set up and Fizbo lined up the air cover, Brad Shannon, one of our EOD techs, found three bombs dug into the ground and wired to blow right outside the house. Once again, our SEALs wouldn't have gotten far without the incredible know-how and solid brass balls of our EOD guys. Of course, as Brad was disarming them, some Army cats located a few houses away chose that moment to blow a charge to open a sniper hole. As the explosion echoed through the streets, Brad enjoyed the feeling of thinking he'd just been blown to bits. When he came back inside the house, he was ghostly white. But I'm sure that doesn't begin to describe the terror felt by a band of insurgents a few blocks away, who stumbled into Gold squad.

That unlucky band of enemy shooters apparently had no idea where the U.S. positions were. Groping around through the streets, they learned the hard way. The insurgents were trying to sneak up on a Marine Corps outpost north of us when Lieutenant Nathan's snipers in Gold laid into them. Two insurgents died right off the bat. Shortly thereafter, a mosque put out a request for "blood donations," and the snipers found themselves in a target-rich environment. Those lucky frogs—I wish I'd been with them to face that doomed onslaught.

For Blue it was mostly quiet until, later that day, Fizbo noticed through the aerial camera of the F-16 on station overhead a group of ten insurgents pouring out of a house just a hundred yards away from his position, headed straight for him and his guys. Fizbo figured this was a suicide attack inspired by the morning call. Given how close they were, he realized there was no time to get approval for an air attack. He also realized that his snipers couldn't see them yet because of several houses that blocked the line of sight. So Fizbo used his airborne eyes to tell the snipers on the roof exactly where the enemy was.

That was when one of Blue's snipers, Chuck Norton, turned to Danny Hanks and calmly asked, "Hey, can I borrow a frag?" Hanks didn't think anything of it and handed Chuck a grenade. He immediately pulled the pin and tossed it, leaving Danny to wonder why Norton didn't just ask him to toss it in the first place.

Based on what he saw on his ISR (intelligence, surveillance, and reconnaissance) feed—the approaching insurgents were still about a hundred meters away—Fizbo thought Norton had thrown the grenade way too early, with no chance of reaching the incoming insurgents. But the enemy was moving fast, and, as it turned out, Norton's throw was a one-in-a-million toss, a perfect strike, high and tight. The pilot overhead was in midsentence, saying, "They are headed right for you . . ." when he stopped. "Uh, well, not anymore!" The grenade exploded right in their midst. Instantly, two insurgents lay dead and three more were seriously wounded. Fizbo told the team, "Good effects, good effects. Direct hit!"

From nearby alleys, other insurgents emerged to try to evacuate the wounded. When Lieutenant Austin said, "Hit 'em again. Throw one more," every SEAL on the roof thought the LT was addressing him—so everybody threw a grenade. A deluge of frags decimated the insurgents. After that, no one else tried to attack Blue's position.

Over at Gold, there was a close call. A van rolled up about a hundred yards down the street. A guy got out, stood around, looking suspicious. Senior Chief Steffen was watching him through his sniper hole. He saw one of the rear windows roll down. At that point the senior chief's fighter's instinct told him to hit the dirt, and as he did so, two rounds struck right around his sniper hole. He hopped back up, and as his spotter took the measure of the enemy through a periscope, Steffen got the picture, jumped up, and fired, putting a round dead center into the enemy's forehead.

Our snipers were on their game that day. Around sun-down, Fizbo spotted something suspicious. A dude with a shovel, digging a hole in the street. Four others were hunched around him, assembling something out of parts they had carried there in large sacks. As he tracked them with his aerial camera, Fiz patched his video feed through to brigade headquarters and was preparing a nine line for a Maverick strike when Chuck Norton decided there was no need to impose such an expense on the American tax-payer. He asked Fizbo for the range and bearing of the enemy and Fiz gave it to him: about 150 meters due east. Norton strode outside, carrying an M79 grenade launcher. Fizbo heard a thump followed by a muffled explosion. The pilot of the F-16 reported that only two enemies survived, both of them badly wounded.

Fizbo took note of the houses the two remaining insur-gents fled to. He and Norton stayed by their post that night, working the aircraft, while the rest of the guys, led by Lieutenant Austin, Marty Robbins, and Salazar, went out on raids. They rounded up the insurgents and took them into custody. Later, with Fizbo serving as spotter, Norton found a couple more insurgents stalking his posi-tion. Done and done—just another night in Ramadi.

Fizbo and the rest of them exfilled later that night to begin Christmas on a cheerful note. Back at Camp Marc Lee for the holiday dinner, they spit-roasted a lamb on a bonfire. It was good to see the guys return. We hung out, counted our blessings. I found time later to call home and had a good conversation with Mom and Dad.

13

Sniper One

A lone figure moves swiftly and quietly through the darkness, down a street, into a building. Another figure follows, traversing the city street and moving like a spirit into the building. And another. The building they've entered is an apartment complex, four stories high, large and vacant. It is situated on the southwest corner of a soccer field.

The night is still and their watchword is stealth. No movement is visible unless you're watching the rooftop closely. A small steel rod, a periscope, rises from behind a rooftop wall. The periscope turns, and the eye using it scans an open field just down the way.

The eye in the periscope belongs to a SEAL sniper. Tipped by a source, he and two more shooters are working in a neighborhood west of Ramadi General Hospital, north of the Racetrack. It's a neighborhood where our operators haven't ventured before. They're part of a mission to lay a trap for a large element of the Al Qaeda brain trust in Ramadi on their home field, as it were. They've been assigned to overwatch a soccer field where, a reliable intel source has told us, something big is about to go down. The source says that at 9:00 a.m., certain elements of the Al Qaeda leadership will gather here to brief insurgents on upcoming operations. They will distribute weapons and cash. The snipers lie patiently in wait, scanning the night and standing by.

The eastern sky brightens, then the sun peeks up, banishing the shadows. By the first light of day, the streets begin to show signs of movement. Just like clockwork, the cars begin arriving—sedans and station wagons, small trucks. Several dozen of them turn off the street and into the soccer field.

Cowboy keys his radio mike. "This is Sniper One. I have movement."

The insurgents circle up their vehicles, front fender to tailgate, get out, and begin conferring. They carry themselves with the confidence of gangsters. Though they are within plain sight of residents living in houses nearby, they are comfortable and unconcerned. They conduct themselves with a swagger, a brazen disregard for anyone who may be watching them. This is their territory.

They gather and begin unloading weapons from some of the trucks: PKCs, RPGs, AKs, small arms. They brandish the weapons, admire them, and pass them from car to car. Not a care in the world is on their faces. Many of them are foreign fighters, professionals. They must have thought of themselves as an all-star team or something—Saladin's warriors defending their caliphate.

The Army acknowledges the report.

The operation was supposed to commence with an appearance of the Iraqi police. An IP unit was supposed to show up, loudly announcing their presence so that the insurgents would begin to disperse. Entering the soccer field from the west, the cops were going to push the Al Qaeda types east, toward a "catcher's mitt" formed by three other sniper positions. Sniper One was located to the west, positioned as backup in case the op didn't go as expected.

Well, it didn't go as expected. When the Iraqi cops made their appearance, they continued driving up the street bounding the soccer field's eastern side. As a result, the insurgents tried to avoid notice by moving to the west—away from the catcher's mitt and right toward Sniper One's hide. It was clear that if a shootout started, the police were going to have their hands full. The other three sniper teams would be in no position to engage.

When you're serving in the teams, you never stop looking for a fight. In Iraq, the fight never stopped looking for us. I guess you could say it was a match made in heaven. The bottom line: you can fight us head-on, or hide and take potshots. Either way works for us. The world would be a safer place if those who meant harm to America simply learned this lesson and conducted themselves accordingly.

On that day, Cowboy and his teammates Jerry and Lars were in place to teach the latest chapter in this lesson book. They knew right away what they had to do.

Cowboy keyed his mike. "This is Sniper One. Requesting permission to engage."

"Wait, One." There was a pause while the operations staff at headquarters conferred. Then the radio crackled again. "Engage."

It was a sniper's paradise.

In BUD/S all of us had to qualify as experts in rifle and pistol. Later, you learn to make up to a five-hundred-yard shot. With a long-barrel and the right optics you should be able to make a seven-hundred-yard shot, but that's pushing it with an ordinary rifle. In sniper school you find out how easy that is when you have the right gear and training. Snipers take the distances out much farther than that. Chris Kyle from Team 3 has scored from sixteen hundred yards with a .300 Win Mag, and from twenty-one hundred with a larger .338 round. Others have done the same, maybe even better. But sniping involves much more than pure marksmanship. Patience, stealth, and a talent for observation are important, too. Everyday psychology is a big part of it. How does a bad guy act? You study body language and behavior for clues to someone's intent. It's a subtle craft. At the end of the day, our snipers are often in the best position to carry out one of Skipper's favorite expressions of our mission in Ramadi: "Rehab who you can; kill those who have forfeited their time on the planet."

That day there were plenty of forfeits. Cowboy, Jerry, and Lars were maintaining concealment within easy range of those seventy or eighty shitheads whose attention was fully occupied by Iraqi police cars arriving along the road to their east. They were completely oblivious to the three snipers on their flank.

Jerry had an M249 squad automatic weapon, our light machine gun of choice. Lars had an M79 grenade launcher. Cowboy had his sniper rifle, a Stoner SR-25. Time to reach out and touch someone.

It was a perfect L ambush. Our guys were on the short leg of the L, enfilading the insurgents from the side. From four stories up, situated on a narrow sundeck, they had a great firing angle. At a range of just about a hundred yards, Cowboy dialed down his scope, and when he and his teammates popped over the wall and went to work, the 9:15 to Seventy-Two Virgin Station hit the express track.

It was a turkey shoot. Cowboy fired his suppressed Stoner as fast as he could, burning through magazine after magazine. Jerry poured out the lead in short, disciplined bursts from his SAW. As some of their cohorts began to fall, the insurgents milled about nervously, then panicked and began running, firing into the air randomly. As some piled into their vehicles, Lars targeted their cars with grenades. Stuck in an open area, they didn't stand a chance. As the vehicles veered and fishtailed, looking to escape, they found themselves trapped by high concrete curbs, impossible to drive over. A scene of carnage and bedlam ensued. Driving over bodies of their fallen comrades, they found themselves enfiladed by Lars's grenade fire. Every car got a dose of lead. Much to their chagrin, a single vehicle—a blue BMW sedan—escaped.

Cowboy went through six or seven magazines. Jerry thought he fired about five hundred rounds with his SAW. With the exception of the idiots in that Bimmer, not a single terrorist survived. A whole cadre of the insurgency's best ringers lay dead in that field. And all the while, as they were dying, they thought it was the Iraqis who were killing them. They never saw what hit them. It was the perfect sniper op.

Their work done, the crew packed up their gear and hit the stairs to the ground floor. From there, they exfilled from their position, running toward the northwest corner of the soccer field, where they had prearranged a rendezvous with

Marine Corps armored vehicles from Combat Outpost Firecracker. Nearby, overjoyed Iraqi police whooped it up, hollering and firing into the air. It was a crushing double victory—a great overwatch op and a win for the counterinsurgency effort as well. We were happy to let the hometown boys take credit.

The Marines who gave Cowboy, Jerry, and Lars the ride back to COP Firecracker were new to Ramadi. Some of them seemed shocked by the bloodshed they saw. Jerry said flatly that if they stuck around the city a little longer, maybe saw a few of their brothers get hit, they'd understand. Cowboy put an exclamation point on it when he spotted that shot-up blue BMW just as he was getting into an armored vehicle. He took a knee and it was over in a hurry.

It was a productive day in the war to destroy Al Qaeda in Iraq. Those three guys effectively closed a whole neighborhood to the insurgency. Not a peep was heard out of the area for the rest of the year. And the surge in morale for the locals could be felt all the way back to Camp Corregidor.

14

Flight to Al Asad

At the end of February, Master Chief directed me and some of my teammates to Camp Ramadi, where a helicopter was waiting. He saw to it that his platoon leadership in Ramadi visited other task units in the area from time to time. It was partly to keep us sharing intel and information on tactics, and, probably, partly to show us how miserable everybody else was so we wouldn't start thinking our leadership was neglecting us. The grass isn't always greener. In Habbaniyah, thirty-five klicks east of us down the highway to Fallujah, we were sent out to link up with some guys from another task unit. They were having a grand old time, getting into shootouts almost every time they hit the streets. In the town of Hit, out west, a good friend of mine from back home, Breg, was serving with a Bradley unit. One night I got to spend a few hours with him. It was really good to see someone from home. We had hung out a lot and trained together as kids to get ready for our military careers. When Morgan and I went off to the SEAL teams, Breg and his brother joined the Army. They're now both Green Berets.

Our destination this time was Al Asad air base. Master Chief wanted to connect me with an old teammate of his, a seasoned frogman who was serving as senior chief of a SEAL troop based there. This little surprise was something he had been working on for me ever since workup. My host was universally known by his nickname, Slab. It turned out to be a great learning experience for me, just as Master Chief knew it would be.

If you've read much about our operations since 9/11, you may already know his name. He's seen and done almost everything there is to see and do in the teams. Years before Operation Redwing happened, Slab had walked the path of tragedy and unwanted notoriety. He had survived disaster, redeemed himself through his courage and fortitude, and returned to work, ever the quiet professional. He and Master Chief had served together on a previous deployment. Master Chief realized during workup that we would be working just down the smuggler's road from Slab. He thought it would be a good idea for our paths to cross. Now that I was doing op plans, after-action reports, and leaving the fun to my teammates, he thought a change of scenery would be good for me. He also thought that circulating someone from the platoon leadership to Slab's operating area would bring valuable insights and lessons that would cross-pollinate with our units.

Only an unlucky handful of us have been in a situation where life and death spun totally out of control, and a mission went "beyond all contingencies," as we say. For Slab, it happened in Afghanistan in March of 2002, on a peak called Takur Ghar. Like Camp Marc Lee, that mountain ridge would later be named for the Navy frogman whose death there marked it in the hearts and minds of everyone whose boots ever touched that ground. Everyone in our community remembers the day that mountain became known as Roberts Ridge.

Neil Roberts was a twelve-year veteran of the teams, a husband, and the father to a young son. He was part of a small team of operators that was dropped onto Takur Ghar to do reconnaissance for a big U.S. push against Taliban and Al Qaeda forces in the Shah-e-Kot Valley, southeast of the city of Gardez. Known as Operation Anaconda, the operation put a large element of a Taliban and Al Qaeda army squarely in the crosshairs. The job given to Slab, Roberts, and their teammates was to locate the enemy in their mountaintop hiding places and direct air strikes against them. Little did they know that their landing zone was one of the best natural fortresses in the whole Middle East. The Afghans had defeated Alexander the Great there, and, more recently, the Soviet Red Army. History had spoken. What would it say to us?

As their MH-47 Chinook flared down and maneuvered to insert the fire team, it came under heavy fire. It was riddled by machine-gun bullets and took hits from several RPGs. Flames and smoke engulfed the crew compartment. Hydraulic fluid and oil sprayed wildly out of the shattered transmission. As the pilot threw on the power, looking to escape, the helo lurched upward and then back down. Neil Roberts, hunched near the open rear ramp, saw a crewman slip on the fluid-soaked deck. As the man slid down the ramp, Roberts went to assist him—only to slip himself. He fell out of the helo and hit the snow about ten feet below. It all happened fast. As Roberts tumbled into the waist-deep drifts, the pilot struggled to save his wounded bird. Electrical power failed, but the engines didn't. The Chinook lifted away, hydraulics leaking, then dove down a steep slope. Only then did the pilot realize that one of his passengers was no longer on board.

Surviving the fall, Roberts appears to have turned on his infrared beacon, marking his position so that airborne rescuers could find him. The pilot of the Chinook wanted to circle back and return for him, but without hydraulics, he had no control of his aircraft. The crew chief opened a quart can of hydraulic fluid and poured it into an emergency scuttle, giving the pilot precious additional seconds of flight control. Spiraling down the mountain slope at nearly a hundred miles an hour, trading altitude for distance toward home, the pilot managed a controlled crash. The helicopter made it about five miles before hitting the ground near the base of the mountain. The pilot ditched hard, breaking his back in the process but saving the lives of everyone on board.

Slab, his teammates, and the helicopter crew regrouped around their crash site and called for assistance. An AC-130 relayed their request to Gardez, where another Chinook was spun up and sent to retrieve them. When the other helo arrived, Slab piled in with the survivors of the first bird and expected to be taken back into the fight. When he asked the pilot whether AC-130 gunships were available to provide preassault fires ahead of their insertion, he was told the commanding general had refused to authorize it. Their bird was directed back to Gardez to offload their gear. Slab made it clear to the pilot that one way or another, despite the wishes of his command, he was going to fly straight back to the mountain and try to save Petty Officer First Class Roberts.

Alone on that mountain, Roberts was in serious trouble. What happened next isn't totally clear. As he scrambled up the mountain slope toward cover, he was soon found and surrounded by enemy fighters. He went down like a warrior, firing his light machine gun till the end. An AC-130 sent back infrared imagery of his last moments. It showed the heat signature of a man holding a weapon. There was a bright flash as he fired toward a figure seated by a tree. Those who saw it in real time would not know what had happened until later. At 4:27 a.m. local time on March 3, 2002, Neil Roberts became the first SEAL to die in the War on Terror.

By the time he found a helicopter to take him back to the mountain, Slab tried to arrange for that preassault bombardment from the aircraft stacked overhead. A minute out, he and his team were told again that the AC-130s would not fire into an area with friendly forces present. Two days earlier, a friendly-fire incident had killed two men and wounded fourteen others. Commanders' nerves were still tight.

With no time to search for an alternate landing zone, the pilot decided to land in the same place where the other helo had gotten hit the first time around. Slab told his five teammates that they had to assume Roberts was still alive. Their professional creed was to leave no man behind. He told them an IR strobe light had been activated and that they were going into a heavily defended, enemy-controlled area. They assumed Roberts was in evasion mode, descending the mountain away from the enemy. Slab also knew there was a good chance this was not a rescue but a recovery mission. Either way, Slab told his teammates, "We're going back up there and killing every last one of those mothers."

As the helo held a low hover, Slab jumped into the snow with his Stoner SR-25 sniper rifle slung around his shoulder, eight fragmentation grenades, and a SIG Sauer 9mm automatic pistol strapped to his leg. His teammates followed, hitting the deep drifts. When that elite team, code-named Mako 30, put its boots on the mountain, it was the beginning of a seventeen-hour ordeal in which they repeatedly assaulted a well-dug-in enemy position in an effort to save or recover their teammate.

Slab is very quiet about his career. Like so many of our best guys, he doesn't stand out in a crowd. Before I met him, I envisioned him as a giant—that's how big his reputation is. On first glance, however, few would suspect the lean, unassuming man of being one of the most effective guys in the spec ops world. But dynamite comes in small packages, and trains run on rails. Thirty-seven years old when I was with him in Anbar Province, Slab was at the peak of his career, a thoroughly tested and seasoned senior frogman, confident and unflappable in the worst of situations. The untold and untellable stories of the many missions he had participated in were written into the wrinkles around his eyes. It was a privilege to hear him talk about it firsthand.

Slab and his teammates were immediately set upon by the enemy. They were Chechens, experienced in mountain fighting. They began surrounding Mako 30, firing at them from three directions. The SEALs were exposed, stuck in the middle of what we call a horseshoe ambush. About seventy-five yards downhill from them, the enemy had two bunkers to use for cover and support. Faced with torrential gunfire, Slab and his radioman, Air Force sergeant John Chapman, laid down covering fire for two teammates, Randy and Turbo, who were moving toward one of the bunkers. Mako 30's other two SEALs, Kyle and Brett, were trying to flank the enemy position, too.

The pilot of the AC-130 saw the action as a light show of infrared lasers poking back and forth on the mountainside. He was surprised by how close the opposing forces were. It was "a firefight in a phone booth," he would say. It must have been like a scene out of *Star Wars,* that big battle scene on the ice planet, with tracer rounds zipping back and forth brightly over the snow. Fighting near the top of a mountain ensures you'll be surrounded. At lower elevations, at least you have somewhere you can go. I don't know what I would have done in Slab's shoes—maybe play dead while holding an unpinned grenade under me. When they neared, I'd release the lever and take them with me.

Slab used his M203 launcher to fire a grenade at the bunker, but its impact was muffled by the deep snow. An enemy round hit Chapman, wounding him badly. Brett was shot through both legs. Then Turbo took a hit that nearly severed his foot above the ankle; he was kept from bleeding out only by the compressive force of his snow-packed boot.

Slab threw a smoke grenade and tried to break contact. The pilot of the AC-130 stayed on station well beyond the safety envelope for his fuel supply. Slab directed him to fire on a cluster of trees just fifty meters from the SEALs' location; he worried about hitting the Americans. Slab told him, "I don't care how close. It's the only chance we got." Circling slowly counterclockwise overhead, with his 105mm howitzer unholstered on its left side, the aircraft began firing. The pucker factor was high, because neither the pilot nor his crew would ever sleep again if they killed the outgunned SEAL operator they had been talking to. With his fuel running critically low and in danger of being exposed to fire by the brightening dawn, the AC-130 rained down about seventy-five heavy rounds on the mountaintop, then the pilot reluctantly decided he had to return to base. His heart was in his throat as he turned toward Bagram, exposing Slab and his boys to renewed ground attack until another aircraft could take station. A pair of F-15E Strike Eagles based in Kuwait were inbound fast. Slab hid out during the interval, praying for their arrival. Additionally, some Army Rangers were on call as a QRF.

When the F-15s arrived, Slab got on the radio and tried to guide them into the right groove to launch their weapons against the enemy, near the top of the mountain. From the pilot's perspective, the SEAL was calling for bombs to be dropped right on top of his own position. The fast-moving plane never put its ordnance on target. After two passes, dropping bombs that fell wide of the mark, the pilot announced, "Bingo"—indicating that he was almost out of fuel—and left to find a tanker aircraft. Slab and his teammates were on their own once again.

The Ranger platoon that was on call as a quick reaction force consisted of twenty men in two Chinooks. Summoned to assist Slab and his team, they planned to fly from Bagram to Gardez, where they would stage for the rescue mission. Only one of the helos got airborne, however. And since they quickly realized time was running out, that bird flew straight into the fight.

As it made its approach just before dawn, the Chinook carrying the Rangers was riddled with gunfire. Somehow, though, the pilot managed to crash-land without killing anybody. Landing in a bowl of snow surrounded by enemy shooters, the Rangers were caught up in a firefight every bit as intense as the one that greeted Mako 30. Under the command of an Army captain from Waco, Texas, Nate Self, the Rangers soon found they needed to be rescued as well.

This is where Slab's story took a personal turn for me. One of the Air Force pararescuemen (or PJs, as the elite combat medics are known) on that bird, Jason Cunningham, had gone to the Army's "18 Delta" medic school with me. He served with the PJ community's elite Twenty-Fourth Special Tactics Squadron. While the Rangers assaulted up the face of the hill, Cunningham turned the crashed helicopter into a casualty collection point, treating several badly wounded men while under heavy fire from an enemy bunker just a hundred yards away. Mortars were landing all around the helo when, at 12:30 p.m., an enemy bullet struck Jason, tearing across his pelvis and inflicting serious internal wounds. He used the last of his energy to tend to wounded soldiers before he bled to death in the snow. Around 8:00 p.m. on the night of March 4, Jason Cunningham became the first Air Force PJ to die in action since Vietnam.

The QRF suffered four killed in action and nine badly wounded before their determined assault, along with heavy support from coalition aircraft, finished off the enemy in the area. Finally a pair of Chinooks came to pick up the battered Ranger unit. The first bird took the living, the second loaded up the dead, and they returned to Bagram.

Slab and his team waited six more hours in the cold. Triangulated by mortars, pinned down and bleeding in the snow, they were saved only by the shelter of the ice-walled ravine in which they hid. Somehow a pilot named Tom Friel, a member of the 160th Special Operations Aviation Regiment, returned well after dark and flew a Chinook toward Slab's position. One of the SEALs flashed the laser designator from his weapon straight up out of the ravine toward the sky, drawing Friel to him. Hovering above the narrow gash in the rocks, the pilot lowered his big tour bus of a helicopter down into the ravine. With his rotors whipping the air just a few feet from the rock, he steadied up well enough, maintaining a hover with an expert hand and enabling the crew chief to drop the ramp. The helo was just low enough to the ground that the three wounded SEALs could be heaved on board. When the aircraft charged up into the sky, the mission was over, leaving Slab and the other survivors to live with its echoes.

I listened to Slab the way a junior frog should: with my mouth shut and my ears open. I'd read the statements and the after-action reports, but hearing the story from him personally made me realize there was no way to come out of a situation like that without having a cross to bear. One thing Slab taught me: it's easy after a disaster to dwell on the experience, to spend too much time with your mind stuck on it, and to let it define you. Slab showed me how to put something like that in a box, and to control how you think about it, and to turn a negative into a positive. It's the people who focus on the positive that will come out on top. Afterward, your dominant thought about a bad experience shouldn't be *I can't get over this;* it should be, *I'm going to better myself because of it.*

I was stunned to learn later that Master Chief could easily have been on that op, too. At the time, he was serving in Slab's squadron, but he was stateside, tasked to a training and support role for his command shortly before 9/11. It simply wasn't his fate to be on that flight line that day. I suppose when your unit gets overrun, it's not much worse to be the lone survivor on the ground than a survivor who had to sit it out far away. Either way, you live the rest of your life knowing you should have been out there in the mix with your men, and having no good answer to the question, What if? Master Chief told me it was some consolation that he was on hand to help handle his fallen teammate's homecoming and burial. He said he knew he was where he needed to be, he accepted the importance of his role back home, comforting the family after his teammate's body was flown home. Sometimes the hardest part of being a SEAL is not being part of the fight.

Slab dealt with his experience by putting it in a box, extracting a few "never agains," and pushing his high-speed career to the next level. He's a thinker, private and introspective, a dedicated hard charger. But he said enough to me in our time together to show me how he continued to operate and why, how bad experiences strengthened his motivation, and how he learned to distinguish fear from the impostor, *being afraid*. Fear is a force that sharpens your senses. Being afraid is a state of paralysis in which you can't do anything. It's critical to understand the difference, but I never fully saw it until I spent time with Slab. You have to use your fear to keep from that deadly state of being afraid. Watching him go about his business, planning missions and dealing with his troop, had the same effect on me as being with JT,

Josh, JJ, and Morgan after I got home from Redwing. He recharged me by his presence and commanded my respect without saying a word.

You don't have to be an Adonis or a giant to accomplish feats of greatness. You have to have drive and commitment—as well as an honest sense of what is and isn't possible. During my time with Slab, I realized there was very little I could have done to change the outcome there in the Hindu Kush. I felt my energy level and motivation surge in his presence—just as Master Chief knew it would. I have found that the best way to get through tough times is to surround myself with positive people. If you spend time around people who are weak or always feel sorry for themselves, it's bound to rub off on you. Always look forward, never back. Thanks, Slab, for all the help.

On February 19, I was still hanging with Slab and his teammates in Al Asad when Al Qaeda in Iraq revealed just how desperate it had become. That morning in Ramadi, a car full of explosives approached an Iraqi police outpost at a place called Tway Village and blew. The guardhouse and the gate were knocked flat, then another vehicle-borne IED—a big dump truck carrying about four tons of explosives and a tank full of liquid chlorine—rolled through the wreckage toward the police station. The extremists no longer cared about influencing the population. With the whole city turning on them, looking to drive them out once and for all, nihilism and murder were all they had left to offer. The truck plowed right through a concrete wall and exploded in the middle of morning muster. Sixteen Iraqi cops were killed and more than sixty were wounded.

"This is the choice that we gave them," said Sheikh Sattar's brother, Sheikh Ahmed. "You can either surrender to us or you can be suicided. They despaired of accomplishing any victories, so now they resort to suicide." If they were chasing an early flight to hell, they caught it, and we were only too happy to help.

When I got back to Camp Marc Lee, my teammates let me know how busy life had gotten. The Army and Marines had been heavily engaged all through the city. Fizbo told me how he had gone out to overwatch a big clearance by the 1/9 infantry out of Camp Corregidor. They inserted into the Ma'laab district around three a.m. and Fiz quickly found a JTAC's paradise. With his faithful eyes in the sky, he could see the enemy on the move almost everywhere he looked.

For once, headquarters had loosened the leash. Fizbo was giddy as he told me about all the nine lines he had gotten approved. Sitting in a sniper hide with a group of operators, including my brother, he steered tons of air-launched ordnance onto enemy positions. The Army, meanwhile, made excellent use of their multiple rocket systems. Apache helicopters strafed and fired Hellfire missiles. And the big Abrams tanks weighed in, too. By the end of that three-day op, many enemy fighters had been killed. More important, after what happened the last time we went into Ma'laab, it was good to see every one of the boys roll through the gate again with a success under their belts.

Around that time, some encouraging news arrived concerning our recent casualties. Johnny Brands was doing well after surgery. The docs thought he might be able to jump back on the horse someday. Elliott's prognosis wasn't as good, but he was finally cleared to fly home from Germany to Texas for treatment of his burns.

Meanwhile, there was a feeling around Task Unit Red Bull that scores had been settled, and that the insurgency in Ramadi was wobbling on its last legs.

15

Blood and Victory

As our time in that hellhole wound down, the rains became heavy and I suppose some part of hell froze over somewhere, too, because the press suddenly seemed to start noticing what had happened during our watch in Anbar Province. With General Petraeus arriving in Baghdad to take command of Multi-National Force–Iraq, reporters seemed newly willing to look at U.S. successes out west (though all too many of them seemed to think it had sprung from the desert unaided by American hands).

Please understand the bitterness I'm spitting here. During the time I'm talking about, my team took more than a dozen wounded—in addition to SEAL Team 3's own heavy casualties, including two killed—and the conventionals serving alongside us had nearly one hundred killed in action, plus innumerable other casualties. U.S. forces inflicted upward of eleven hundred KIA on the insurgency and captured at least that number for interrogation. The success was there for all to see.

Compared to six months before, insurgent attacks

against our forces and local citizens were down from an average of twenty a day to about ten. The total number of mortar and IED attacks fell by two-thirds. The number of insurgents participating in the increasingly rare complex attacks was down by half, from twenty to ten.

The work that remained was to integrate the Sunni people into the Iraqi government at all levels. When Saddam was booted, the removal of his Baath Party from power pushed a lot of Sunnis out of government, so their leaders boycotted elections. With eighteen thousand more Americans arriving in country—five Army brigades to Baghdad, two Marine Corps battalions to Anbar—and with many soldiers' deployment schedules being extended from twelve to fifteen months, President Bush's "surge" was under way, and the presence of all that strength encouraged many terrified Iraqis to come in out of the cold.

In April—the end of our tour—the peace that settled over Ramadi was surreal. There had been about sixty violent incidents a day when we got there in October; that number was down to one or two a week as the two platoons of Task Unit Ramadi got ready to go home.

However, as our EOD commander, Paul Craig, said, "Being a day closer to going home doesn't make you safer on any given day." Our men in Fallujah ran some important but costly operations, too. In early April, a platoon from Team 4 carried out a capture-kill raid in northern Fallujah, targeting an insurgent cell that had reportedly been shooting down our helicopters with SA-7s—Chinese-made shoulder-fired surface-to-air missiles. It was suspected that one such nasty little weapon had shot down a Marine Corps CH-46 cargo helicopter in March. When our intel finally fingered the cell's location and a combined unit of Iraqis and SEALs hit the house, the enemy was ready, bunkered up behind fighting positions inside. In the shootout that developed, one of our men was killed and all his teammates were forced back outside the house.

All his teammates but one, that is. The platoon's chief, a tough frog named Dan, got pushed into the corner of the entry room. A twenty-one-year veteran with seven deployments under his belt, including two in Iraq, Chief Dan was alone with numerous enemy gunmen. They shot him twenty-seven times at close range. Eleven of the bullets were stopped by his body armor. You do the math. As he was falling to the ground, he managed to kill three of the enemy with bursts from his M4. Before they could finish him, his teammates regrouped and assaulted the house again, killing the insurgents and taking Chief Dan to safety. Fortunately, his wounds were to the lower extremities, and none of them were fatal. As for that insurgent cell, all he'll say is, "After that night, they're not shooting down any more helicopters."

Shortly before we went wheels-up, we took another casualty. Studdard, my longtime point man, was walking outside Camp Marc Lee with forty-eight hours to go before punching a ticket to America. After running more than two hundred combat missions without a scratch, something hit him in the ribs. He thought it was a thrown rock at first. Looking around, furious and in pain, he realized his wound was deep and hollered for help. The whole camp emptied and we swept the premises looking for his assailant. What hit him was a 7.62mm round, a lucky Hail Mary that had come arcing in from somewhere across the Euphrates River, nearly a mile away. The bullet burrowed in close to his spine—so close that surgeons wouldn't be able to remove it. By the time they took him away to the hospital, I didn't have the chance to thank him for everything he'd done as our point man. Doing that night after night in a hellhole like Ramadi wasn't good for your life expectancy. But he never complained once. And now he still carries a little piece of the city inside him as a reward.

We all took something home, of course. The biggest thing, probably, was victory. The city had been transformed: not its broken infrastructure, but its daily psychology. When the advance element of SEAL Team 7 showed up to relieve us—their turn to do a turnover op, feel out the dangerous textures of this city, and find their battle rhythm—everything had changed. Tribal cops were in the streets. More than three thousand new recruits had joined their ranks. There was no sanctuary for Al Qaeda when the locals were standing tall in uniform. The police knew their neighborhoods. It was easy for them to spot foreign terrorists, and if a local did something bad, well, there was usually a cop nearby who had gone to high school with the guy's best friend. The fruit of our work could be seen in the new activity by the chamber of commerce to get small businesses working again. Kids played soccer in the side streets. Iraqi women began organizing, aided by some female Marine Corps civil affairs officers who listened to their problems and taught them how to depend on themselves, organize their finances, get jobs, learn to read, and run their households. Most of them were widows, thanks to years of murder and terror in their country. As they began having a greater role in city life, they also served as a bulwark against Al Qaeda's return. When one of their sons came home with a pocketful of cash, saying he was on a holy mission, Mom had the courage to challenge him: "What kind of holy mission? Who is telling you this?"

In September 2007, there was a five-kilometer road race in memory of an Iraqi police officer, Captain Ali, who died trying to stop a suicide bomber who was targeting his police station. It started at the Ramadi Glass Factory, passed Camp Hurricane Point, then turned down Route Michigan—once almost impassable because of IEDs—and ended in the Ma'laab district. More than a hundred Iraqis took part, and onlookers were waving national flags all along Route Michigan. The success went beyond Ramadi. Skipper and Master Chief had used their freedom of movement in a wide area to help integrate our operations with SOF and conventional units in Fallujah, Habbaniyah, the northern Euphrates River Valley, and even all the way out to Al Qaim, near the Syrian border. Army Special Forces were a big part of it. I saw it up close on my trip to the city of Hit. Those Green Berets did great work there and in Haditha, too, allowing us to focus on the Ramadi-to-Fallujah corridor.

From there, the Anbar Awakening spread east toward Baghdad and north into Diyala Province. Sunni sheikhs in those areas signed their young men into service and went after Al Qaeda wherever they found them. Enjoying the goodwill of tribal leaders, our soldiers were welcomed into towns and villages that had never seen Americans before. Together they systematically dismantled the terrorist threat.

The change that overtook Anbar Province was so durable that it survived even the assassination of the Awakening's principal sponsor. On September 13, during the opening days of Ramadan, Sheikh Sattar went to Al Asad air base to be photographed with President Bush. At his home afterward, Sattar was attacked by suicide bombers. He died along with several of his guards. It was a blow to the good guys, but just as you can't kill your way out of an insurgency, Al Qaeda couldn't kill its way back into one, either: Sattar's death had no real impact, because his brother, Sheikh Ahmed Abu Risha, stepped into his shoes, took charge, and kept up the momentum toward reconstruction. Believe me, I understood Ahmed's motivation.

We also saw a different attitude in the Iraqis at the training range. Where once they lived from paycheck to paycheck, caring for little more than getting by, now they seemed interested in something larger than themselves. One time a big argument started between some trainees, and our terps explained what was going on. An Iraqi soldier (a malcontent, one of the lazy ones) was complaining to the others, asking them why they were working so hard. The other trainees responded, "We're going to fight for Iraq. We're going to make this country great someday." The attitude spread. They started training harder, and the next thing we knew, we had a company and then a battalion of Iraqi forces more or less ready for action. We integrated them into our operations and got some great work done straightening out their broken city.

DQ, our operations officer, told me he used to get kidded about the way we were handling the COIN mission. His counterpart in regimental headquarters at Fallujah, a hard-charging Big Army type, liked to say that the SEALs in Ramadi weren't doing much more than handing out soccer balls. But after seeing the change that had come over the city, his tune changed. He said to DQ, "I'm buying what you're selling. It all makes sense."

It was around this time that the majority leader of the U.S. Senate stood on the floor of his chamber and said, "This war is lost and the surge is not accomplishing anything." The president called it "one of the most irresponsible acts I witnessed in my eight years in Washington." Naturally the president's opponents were determined to deny him any credit. The smart people at another media outlet told their readers, "Whatever [President Bush's] cause was, it is lost.... Additional military forces poured into the Baghdad region have failed to change anything." These people's hatred for our commander in chief seemed to overshadow their love of their country. With Anbar Province turning the corner, it looked like they were moving the goalposts to manufacture a defeat. When America got a new president in 2009, the press seemed more willing to credit us for what we did. Eventually *Newsweek* ran a cover story declaring, "Victory at Last: The Emergence of a Democratic Iraq." Better late than never, right? Those of us who were there know how the history really went down. When the guys from the 1/506, the Currahees, got back to Fort Campbell and held their awards ceremony in the Lozada Physical Fitness Center, two hundred soldiers received decorations, including eighty-seven Purple Hearts, fifteen Bronze Stars with a "V" device for valor, and three Silver Stars. Their names stand proudly in the annals of the American military tradition, but they were generally typical of all the men I saw in action in that city.

All of us understand the price we paid for victory.

Something Master Chief said still stands in my mind today as the ultimate expression of what our work is all about, and what it means to serve. When a few of us complained that we were putting ourselves needlessly at risk by letting Iraqis do our work, Master Chief replied, "There are times when you have to put yourself at a disadvantage in order to accomplish a larger mission and secure a longer-term goal." He went on, "You can take the simple view that Iraqis are all corrupt and beneath us. Or you can see it another way—see that they're all human, and even America's been that same way at times during its own history, with innocent people taking fire from both sides in a bloody civil war. There are people who have to live in Ramadi, who can't flee to Syria, America, or Baghdad. They're stuck, just trying to get by. It's complex. And that complexity means you have to understand that everything you do can have a huge effect." We did have a huge effect in Ramadi. I look to American history to measure it. In 1787, after the shooting was over, the meetings that produced the U.S. Constitution had just adjourned and a lady asked Benjamin Franklin what kind of government he had given the American people. "A republic," he said—"if you can keep it." I guess that's what we helped give the people of Anbar.

Once again, it was Master Chief who summed it all up: "We've trained and trained for a reason: to be better at the craft of war than our enemy, to use our skill to perform the mission, and to accept the risks. As American warriors, it's our obligation to protect the innocent. And that means, sometimes, that *we're* the ones who need to be put on the disadvantaged side of the threat cycle."

In other words, it's not about us. I don't think you'll find a better expression of the true nature of service than that.

* * *

During the deployment, I fired my weapon at an enemy probably only four or five times. A chief's job is to put his men in position to handle the gunplay. I took care of my guys and did my best to make sure they had what they needed. There's satisfaction enough in that.

That deployment marked the last time I would carry a rifle with a SEAL team into battle. The time was coming for me to hang up my spurs as an active-duty warfighter and get on with life's next adventure.

At the end of the day, what we did in Iraq wasn't exactly the kind of revenge for Operation Redwing that I thought I had wanted, but as we packed up our gear at Camp Marc Lee and welcomed the advance elements of the SEAL team that was relieving us, I realized I had managed to accomplish my own personal mission as a by-product of the larger, more significant one.

Every now and then, I awake from my dreams thinking of Mikey, Danny, and Axe, and praying that they might be proud.

Part II

How We Live

16

Hitting the Wall

Morgan and I had always meant to become SEAL officers. Our plan was to enlist, work our way up through the ranks, then jump into Officer Candidate School (OCS) or the Navy's Seaman to Admiral program. Officers who come up through the enlisted side, known as mustangs, have a lot more street cred than the ninety-day wonders who take a commission straight out of college. The mustang's path was the one we always planned to walk.

As my teammates and I boarded a C-17 transport at Al Asad and left the country, we counted our successes and tended to our wounds, wondering when the next chance to fly downrange to find bad guys would come our way. Except for me. I was done. After nine years in the Navy, I knew then that it was time for me to retire.

With my book *Lone Survivor* set for June release, I had to separate quickly. The Navy required that I not be operational when it was published. Normally we get a month of leave after coming home from deployment. Back at the Strand, I finished up my medical boards (examinations

that determine your benefit levels), filled out my separation papers, and turned in my military ID and my classifi-
cation card.

The Team 5 area was a ghost town, with everyone gone
on postdeployment leave. Team 7's quarters were nearly
vacant, too, as they were overseas in Anbar Province,
doing the Lord's work. The other odd-numbered teams
were in various stages of workup and deployment. The
sheer anticlimactic feeling of it all wasn't what I expected.
I turned in my gear, picked up my DD214 service record,
and said adios, amigos, to the skipper and the team master chief, finally checking out of my life as an active-duty
SEAL. When the gate slammed shut behind me, it started
to sink in. I'd never get back inside without an escort.

Leaving the Navy was my hardest evolution. I immediately missed having a place in the active-duty fraternity
of men who were forged on that anvil. You learn each
other's habits and quirks, but you share everything in
common in spite of your differences. You pick on each
other relentlessly, but it's the by-product of brotherly love.
Seeing my teammates in situations of great stress (as well
as mind-numbing boredom), I got to know many of them
better than their own families did. The worse things get,
the more you know you can count on men like that to
always have your back. If you really want to know if
someone is a true friend, get yourself into a tight spot with
him or her; everyone has plenty of friends when things
are good, but true friendship is forged in moments of
chaos. It's a sad fact, but it's the truth.

I was scarcely out of uniform when the news came:
Morgan had been accepted to Officer Candidate School;
he was going to Pensacola to cross over to the dark side. I

stood at a fork in the road, too, bound for the book-promotion circuit. Our directions, if not our lives, diverged a little at that point.

Morgan finished his three months in OCS as the "honor man," first in his class, just as he had done in "A" school (where enlisted men go after boot camp), at BUD/S, and at SEAL sniper school. At his graduation ceremony in Pensacola, I swelled with pride to see him in dress whites with an ensign's gold stripe on his sleeve. He was still in the brotherhood.

I know I'm blessed to have survived, and to have served in the company of the best warriors on God's great earth. But survival wasn't necessarily a wonderful thing if it left me stuck wondering every day what I was meant to do with this gift of life, which I would have gladly given a dozen different times under fire for any one of my guys, any time, any place. In combat, you're in a world where things are certain. Even in a counterinsurgency mission, which is filled with so many areas of gray, the enemy is always out there, looking to kill you. That brings energizing clarity to even the most ambiguous situation. At home, the world is far less urgent and clear. When I went back to Texas, I felt like a lost dog looking for a new home. Every time I saw a news story about something the teams had done overseas, I felt some jealousy tainting my pride as I wondered, *What are the boys up to? What's the mood at the team house?* I missed them more than they will ever know.

As a wise man in the Naval Special Warfare community once said, "This thing is not going to last forever, and the flaming Ferris wheel will continue to spin without you." Boy, does it ever.

* * *

You walk a steep and dangerous path from your time in military service back into civilian life, and the warriors in my family haven't always walked it well. All the men on my mother's side served in our armed forces in combat—warfighters from front to rear, right on down the bloodline. There were World War II fighter pilots, infantrymen, Marines, and Civil War riflemen. My mother's cousin traced our line back to the Revolutionary War and a distant relative of Martha Washington. We've been here for a long time. Our menfolk fought wars while the women raised more warriors. My father made sure we got his message. He'd tell my brother and me, "Before you take advantage of this country's opportunities, son, you are going to serve it in some way. Just like all the men in your family before you." When I got out of the Navy, I felt like I'd checked that box. *Now what?* I often wondered.

Many of my teammates drew on powerful military traditions in their lineages. Matt Axelson's grandfather was on board the USS *Pennsylvania* when the Japanese attacked Pearl Harbor in 1941, and his grandmother served in the Marine Corps. His dad was drafted into the Army and served as a radio operator with an infantry company in Vietnam. Danny Dietz's father was in Nam, too, a Navy corpsman attached to a Marine Corps reconnaissance unit. Master Chief, who is a first-generation American from a Czech-German family, said his grandfather was a conscript in the German army. Other teammates of mine were first-generation military and served proudly as pioneers in their bloodlines. Either way is fine by me.

Our family folklore holds that Luttrells are lucky in

war. Based on the experience of Morgan and me, I guess that's true. But we haven't always made a clean transition back to the country we helped defend in the wars that failed to kill us. In the long line of family members who have served this country, Uncle Frank is a cautionary tale.

Though I never met him, he was a huge presence in my life, and the most powerful of the many forces that steered me into military service. He was with General George S. Patton in just about every major U.S. operation in the European theater during World War II, from Africa to southern Europe. He even served as Patton's driver. In combat, he put together a glittering record, earning several Silver Stars and several more Purple Hearts in battles from North Africa up through the boot of Italy and southern France—all the way to Nazi Germany itself. Whenever Morgan or I were downrange, my mother prayed to his spirit to look after us and keep us safe. But Uncle Frank's spirit, powerful as it must have been, took a severe beating during his own time under fire. He never talked about his wartime life. He practiced an almost monastic silence on the subject.

My father described another war veteran who was close to the family, the father of my godfather. Somewhere along the way, something terrible had happened to him, something that must have broken his soul. Dad described him as sitting by the sea, his face in his hands, still and pensive, watching the waves. The root of his haunted feeling may well have come from sheer coincidence: he noticed that almost every time he got close to a young soldier in his unit, that soldier would turn up dead in the next combat action. As his company made its way across Europe toward the German border, he came to believe he was the touch of death to his own men. That superstition became corrosive.

My dad usually glorified military service to us, but as we got older we learned to see the other side of the story. At our house, my mother has an old-fashioned tintype of Uncle Frank. It's a faded photograph, but it shows him at his best. That's the way I'll always remember him, but the image sends conflicting messages: though he looks awfully tough, it's hard to miss the fact that wartime life and the passage of years had reduced him to a shadow on a sheet of iron. When the war was over, Uncle Frank went home to Arkansas a lost soul. He took refuge in drink and before long was living out of railroad cars. He'd show up unannounced at family events and stay until he wore out his welcome with his drinking and sullen moods. Then it was back to the road.

I wondered if I was destined to follow these examples. If, as now seemed likely, I really was going to survive into old age, what kind of old man would I finally become?

R. V. Burgin became a Marine when they were still making dog tags out of brass. Born in 1922, he belonged to the generation that would be called upon to defeat Nazi Germany and imperial Japan in World War II. I met him by virtue of the same force that drew me to so many other frogmen during my career: he is a Texan.

Raised in Jewett, Texas, now living in Lancaster, he served in the Marine Corps during World War II. He saw action in the Pacific at Cape Gloucester, Peleliu, and Okinawa. If you know your history you'll know that those names are shorthand for "hell on earth."

To help him through it, he always kept a short prayer at

the ready: "God, I'm in your hands. Take care of me." At Peleliu, as Mr. Burgin was going ashore in an amphibious tractor with the number 13 painted on its bow, God stretched his hand down from heaven and hung his boat up on a reef, blowing its appointment with a Japanese artillery round arcing down from a howitzer on the beach. Had the amtrac kept going, it would have been blown to pieces.

The mangrove jungle that covered half the island concealed a landscape of nightmares from our reconnaissance planes. The Marines were surprised by the steep ridges of limestone and deep swamps that gave so much perfect cover to the Japanese defenders. It was a rotten place. If you threw a rock into a bush, it produced a cloud of green flies thick enough to cast a shadow. The only clean water to drink was deep behind enemy lines. The corpses teemed with maggots. By September of 1944, the Japanese army had smartened up. They learned to quit banzai-charging. On Peleliu they were stealthy throat slitters whose arrival was announced in the night with scuffles, grunts, and long screams from American foxholes. Their snipers targeted our stretcher bearers. Though the island was just two miles by six, the ferocity of the defenders bogged down Mr. Burgin and his buddies for a month. The Japanese weren't on Peleliu; they were *in* Peleliu. Thousands of them dug caves right into the island. Sometimes the first sign of them was the sound of their voices leaking up from underfoot.

Corporal Burgin was one of the stoutest NCOs in the unit, but even he reached the point where he didn't care if he lived or died. The First Marine Division had more than sixty-five hundred casualties in thirty days, and their

Army replacements took fifteen hundred more. Mr. Burgin's unit, the K/3/5—K Company, Third Battalion, Fifth Marine Regiment—went ashore with 235 men. When the Japanese surrendered, just eighty-five were still standing. There's a photo of the remaining group on Mr. Burgin's living room wall. Most of them are skinny and exhausted. Some of them look like ghosts.

After the war, Mr. Burgin locked his experiences in a box and shoved it into a deep recess within him. He didn't speak of it for thirty-five years. Not a word of the trials of Peleliu, or of wiping out a Japanese machine-gun position in Okinawa, an act that earned him a Bronze Star with Valor. Though he worked in civilian life with four combat Marines, veterans of Tarawa, Guam, and Tinian, they never talked about it, and when the war did come up it was only in the context of funny stories, which mostly served to keep them from thinking about the more troubling ones.

I think it's only when the shooting stops that you realize how war has changed you. You'll be sitting there reading the paper, or doing a household chore, and you'll feel yourself craving something. You may feel like you're ready for action, but there's no action to be had. Your internal wiring is standing by, ready to offer its full capacity to carry the charge of the physical, psychological, and emotional overload you've gotten used to in the war zone. Since those sensations are not generally available in civilian life, you settle for the next best thing—removing all that excess capacity to carry those sensations, just so you can keep the feeling of being fully charged. And so here comes that bottle, turning itself upside down in your mouth. In a few minutes, depending on your metabolism, you're right back in a satisfying—but very temporary—state of equilibrium.

If writing about my experiences in Afghanistan had been a kind of first-phase therapy for me, traveling around the country talking to the public after *Lone Survivor* was published was the next phase, and a pretty startling one at that. Today, when I watch the first television interview I did, I see my skin twitching with nerves still tuned for war. At the time, it had been nearly two years since Operation Redwing went south. Sitting there in the network studio wearing a suit and tie, I spoke haltingly, eyes darting. At the end, I told the interviewer, Matt Lauer, "I died on that mountain, too, sir. I left a part of myself up there." Getting that out in the open on national TV was one step toward dealing with the fact that just because bad things happen in war, your life doesn't have to be over.

My reasons for writing that book were twofold: to honor Mikey, Danny, Axe, and the all the guys in the rescue helo, and to debunk the inaccurate stories that were gaining circulation. My teammates encouraged me to step out from the cover of being a "quiet professional," and our higher-ups did as well. Without their encouragement the story would never have been known to the public. At first I had a real problem with the idea, but now I have a feeling that the story has done more good than I will ever know.

Publishing a book requires you to put yourself out there. Speaking to audiences large and small, I felt like I'd been turned inside out. There were times when that was literally the case. If I told the story in too much detail, I'd feel it in my gut. I'd go to the restroom and give back dinner. No matter how much time goes by, every time I tell the story my body sweats and my heart races uncontrollably. In less than a minute, I'm back on the mountain.

More than a few times, the price I paid for slipping off that path was worth it. When there were other veterans in the audience, they would see my discomfort, our eyes would meet, and then I'd see theirs. A moment like that usually passed silently, never a word spoken. I've shared more than a few of them with older warriors, and after each one I came away feeling that, though I'd never met the man before and though we may be from different service branches, races, creeds, colors, or upbringings, all of us are brothers, once you've boiled all the unimportant stuff away.

Same blood, different mud.

17

Angels on My Shoulder

I'll tell you one story that stays with me, one I wish I could have told when I was working on *Lone Survivor*. It's the story of the U.S. Air Force combat search and rescue (CSAR) pilots who flew high into the mountains of Kunar Province, searching for us near the summit of the mountain known as Sawtalo Sar. One of them, a hell of a good helicopter pilot they call Spanky, finally came down and picked my sorry ass off a mountainside in the Hindu Kush late one night. Some of his brave aviator teammates had the honor, finally, of bringing my fallen teammates home.

Of all the guys who put on flight suits and take a seat behind the stick, none are closer to the special operations community than the helicopter pilots. Most of our operations rely on them. They risk their lives with us, and take us into and out of the rabbit holes where we do our work. The news headlines you see are often a testament to the price they pay. I think of the pilots and aircrews who served in the "Black Hawk Down" incident in Somalia in 1993, and over Roberts Ridge during Operation Anaconda in 2002. Sixteen men made the ultimate sacrifice on June 28, 2005, trying to deliver the rest of my platoon to assist Mikey, Danny, Axe, and me. For every mission gone wrong, of course, there are a hundred good ones you never hear about. And the story I'm going to tell now is one of them.

I will always owe a debt to the pilot and crew of the helicopter that finally found me five days after it all went south, and also to the pilots of the A-10 Warthogs who cleared their path to the landing zone. It's a heroic tale, one that ranks with any I've ever heard for the gallantry of the aviators involved.

With nineteen of our dead in several locations, Operation Redwing produced a whirlwind of confusion. While I was still fighting for my life with my team, most of the A-10 pilots who would play a large role in helping Spanky Peterson reach me during the search and rescue mission were focused on a big firefight taking place down south, near the city of Khost, between U.S. forces and Al Qaeda and Taliban forces coming across the border from Pakistan. When their daily intel briefing mentioned an operation known as Redwing, they didn't know anything about it. My team was under a different command. A pair of A-10s was scrambled from Bagram as soon as we alerted our command that we were in contact with enemy forces. The planes arrived overhead just in time to witness Turbine 33—the call sign of the ill-fated helicopter carrying our sixteen would-be rescuers—rolling down the mountainside, a ball of fire. From that moment on, chaos reigned, and the priority was to search for survivors near that black smear on the rocks.

A huge CSAR effort ensued. Dozens of aircraft of various types were vectored into the area from all over Afghanistan. Part of the reason things got so confused was that nearly everyone from my command who had all the details about Operation Redwing was on board Turbine 33 when it went down. The secrecy of our mission meant that we hadn't filed an evasion plan with the Air Force. Special operations forces sometimes work in that independent way, but when things go wrong it can complicate and slow a response, and in this case overlapping and conflicting command responsibilities definitely made life difficult for our rescuers.

Though the CSAR mission that eventually took shape to find me was epic in scale, I could see very little of it from my vantage point on the ground. When I was hunkered down on the mountainside, all fragged up and with several broken bones, an A-10 flew over my position, fast and low. It was so close I felt I could have hit it with a rock.

If an airplane ever went through BUD/S, it would finish Hell Week as an A-10 Thunderbolt II, better known as a Warthog. When you see it fly by, it just looks like a knuckle-dragging brawler, knees bent, hands on its holsters, with a fast and nasty turbofan swagger. Highly versatile, it flies missions that encompass the yin and yang of life and death in wartime. Close air support is a rough business that the A-10, armed with an assortment of potent weapons, excels at. Few sights from the ground are sweeter than a Warthog playing with us overhead, throwing storms of lead at our enemy with its 30mm Gatling gun. CSAR is the Warthog's other calling. With good low-altitude flight characteristics, a sturdy, survivable airframe, and an ability to remain on station for a long time at slow speeds, it's excellent at saving lives, too. It's a guardian angel and an angel of death, all at the same time.

Though I could see the back of the pilot's helmet as he passed through the narrow slice of sky a few hundred feet above me, I couldn't talk to him without a radio, and he had no way of seeing me, wedged down there in that crevice. This aircraft was part of an airborne armada that had been specially trained to locate and rescue missing personnel on the ground. The discipline of Air Force CSAR was first established in Vietnam. Pilots who undergo advanced training can earn the special designation "Sandy." That call sign reflects their incredible skill and dedication to a unique mission and carries a lot of weight in their community.

The CSAR team was focused on Turbine 33's crash site when commanders realized that somebody needed to search for the four-man SEAL recon team whose bad day on a mountaintop started the whole mess in the first place.

On the run in the hornet's nest, I was what combat search and rescue guys call an evader—the focal-point objective of everyone on the CSAR team. In such circumstances, the rescuers will do whatever it takes to find and save that man. If he can manage it, the evader can do a few things to make their job easier. Standard procedure is to turn on an emergency beacon that pilots can see and triangulate a position on with their direction-finding gear. An evader can also signal them by toggling his radio button, revealing his presence to friendly forces in a way that doesn't betray him to the enemy, as voice comms would.

As I later learned, in addition to the A-10s, there were several Air Force HH-60 helos out there that night looking for signs of me, as well as a Navy command and control plane. "This is Air Force rescue," they announced on the emergency frequency, which all our radios monitored. "Please show yourself." Hiding deep in a crevice, with enemy all around, I had a radio but was unable to speak because my mouth was so dry and full of dirt. In any event, the enemy was so close it would have been crazy to try. That would have been like putting a big neon sign above my head: BUSTED-UP REDNECK LYING HERE WITH A ROCK JAMMED UP HIS WAYHOO. I settled for turning on my survival beacon—and praying extra hard.

In spite of bad weather and low cloud deck, one of the A-10 pilots, Captain Barry "Sluf" Coggins, spotted an infrared strobe north of Turbine 33's crash site while moving away from it along a ridgeline. Technicians in an AC-130 Spectre gunship, using better sensors, verified that they had heard radio clicks. The pilot flying in the lead position that night, the rescue mission commander, was Captain Brett "Zero" Waring. He directed Sluf to return to Bagram to refuel while he explored whether the helicopters could make a pickup in the event that the mysterious signal could be authenticated. Finally, the worsening weather—a huge towering thunderstorm, dragging cloud cover along with it—got in the way. As a result, the helos that were standing by to grab me couldn't search the coordinates that had been given to them. All aircraft were soon forced to return to base. The SOF ground commander wasn't at all happy that everybody had to go home. It was a frustrating first night for the Air Force, too.

Turning in for the night at Bagram, Zero went to the cramped phone booth in the ops center and called his wife. "How are you?" she asked. When he failed to answer with enough positive energy, she followed up. "Are you all right? What happened?"

He couldn't give her any details; he just needed to hear her voice. All he could say was, "Today was a bad day. A really bad day. Something bad happened. A lot of good men died today."

"Will it be on the news?"

"I'm sure it will be. You'll know it when you see it."

It's incredible, the power of the sound of a loved one's voice when times really get tough. I've seen the hardest of men break down in tears over it. It bothered Zero that everyone who needed him most was so far away. More than anything else, though, he wanted to scream to the heavens, *Why couldn't we get a helicopter in there?*

"Be safe," his wife told him.

"I will," he said, by which he meant, *I'm sorry, I can't.* A dangerous job awaited him over enemy-controlled territory. He thought about the Taliban who were out there, competing to be the first to find us and maybe bring down another aircraft or two along the way. Zero vowed, *I'll be back out there shortly. Make me a liar to my wife. Let's dance, assholes.*

I know now that it was Zero who banked that A-10 Warthog right over my hidey-hole on Sawtalo Sar that afternoon. Visible for only a moment, he offered me a thread of hope before dashing out of my line of sight. He was just one cog in the huge combat search and rescue operation the Air Force was to carry out in the coming days.

My best chance at making it came, ironically enough, with my capture. A pair of Afghan men found me. One of them was a medicine man named Sarawa, from the nearby village of Sabray, which was where I met Gulab.

Without a working radio, I was hard-pressed to make contact with American forces. Now and then, when I suspected planes were up there, I'd struggle to my feet and start swinging, like a lasso, a radio wire to which I'd tied a bunch of infrared ChemLights, trying to get their attention. An A-10 pilot reported seeing my covert signal, but couldn't lock his sensors onto it through the broken layer of low clouds. His fix on my position was accurate only to within a mile, and the hour quickly got late.

It was finally the pride of the Pashtun villagers that saved me. Shortly after my arrival in their custody, the elder from the village, Gulab's father, walked several miles to a Marine Corps firebase near the town of Nangalam in the Pech River Valley, carrying a note I had written explaining my location. In spite of all the airpower overhead, it still took an individual act of bravery to give the Air Force the location they needed to recover me. In delivering that information, as required by his culture's ancient tradition, the old man was living up to his own notion of service, and it helped save me.

On the night of July 1, I felt and heard massive explosions in the valley surrounding the village. In *Lone Survivor,* I mentioned that the Air Force "had had it up to their eyeballs" with Ben Sharmak and his militia. After drones provided detailed overhead imagery of the Taliban leader's compound in the Korengal Valley, a B-52 Stratofortress was vectored in from Naval Support Facility Diego Garcia, an island base far away in the Indian Ocean. After the huge bomber unloaded six short tons of iron onto that little patch of earth, not much was left standing of the Taliban's local HQ. On a tough night, here was reason for celebration. A small cheer went up on the TOC back at Bagram. I felt a nice rush a few ridgelines away in Sabray, too.

For the CSAR team, the first definitive word that I was alive reached them around dawn on July 2. A twenty-man team of Army Rangers and Green Berets was quickly dispatched on a fast march to the village. I wouldn't have gotten out of there had it not been for their never-say-quit attitude, skill, and courage—or that of those dedicated Air Force rescue pilots and their crews.

CSAR pilots have a legacy that goes all the way back to World War I. It was during Vietnam that the dangerous rescue and casevac missions got the nickname "dustoff" flights—I guess for all the dust those Hueys tossed around when they reached a landing zone full of wounded men. Today the pilots are more capable than ever—network-linked, satellite-guided, flying better aircraft, and trained to an unheard-of level of skill. Even with all this technology, the character and preparation of the man in the cockpit is still the key to everything.

Major Jeff Peterson, with the call sign Spanky, flew with the 305th Rescue Squadron, part of the 943rd Rescue Group, based at Davis-Monthan Air Force Base in Tucson, Arizona. When it was my turn to get off that mountain, I was lucky that the call went out to an outfit like them.

Spanky was thirty-eight at the time, married to a woman named Penny, raising four sons back home in Tucson. Originally from Utah, he attended Brigham Young University for a year before leaving to serve for two years as a Mormon missionary—white shirt, dark tie, engraved black name tag, the whole nine yards. Afterward, he transferred to Arizona State University, where he entered the Reserve Officer Training Corps (ROTC) program. He took his commission as an Air Force second lieutenant in 1991. A reservist, Spanky had an expert touch flying a Sikorsky HH-60G Pave Hawk (basically a souped-up Black Hawk). Most reservists are older guys who've logged a lot of hours in the air. By the time he came looking for me, he had fourteen years in uniform and had flown more than a hundred missions in Afghanistan, not to mention quite a few here in the States, rescuing stranded mountain climbers, sailors, firefighters, and victims of different types of accidents. He's helped save scores of people, and his squadron as a whole has saved thousands. He had worked with special operations forces before, too. On the night of July 2–3, 2005, I became one more notch on his harness.

For Spanky, it was a long journey to a small rocky ledge high in the Hindu Kush that would serve as his landing zone. Shortly after Turbine 33 went down, with the search and rescue plan in its earliest stages, he was summoned with his team to the flight line at Bagram Airfield, north of Kabul. His copilot, Dave Gonzales, who had flown with the Border Patrol and the U.S. Customs Service, had more than four thousand hours in helicopters. Spanky's flight engineer had done two tours in. These men weren't "weekend warriors"—the term often used to describe reservists. They were full-time, experienced professionals. Their talent far exceeded their reputations. Nevertheless, when two crews from the 305th were summoned to Bagram from Kandahar and invited to submit a rescue plan to the Joint Special Operations

Command leadership, they saw that a bias in the special operations community against reservists remained.

At their briefing, two helicopter crews, one led by Spanky Peterson and another led by Lieutenant Colonel Jeffrey Macrander, known as Skinny, were read into Operation Redwing—that is, they were given the details on everything that had taken place. With my note in hand, delivered by the village elder from Sabray, they had the name of the village I was in. As it turned out, one of my saving graces was the decision I had made, while things were heating up in the mountains, to activate my emergency radio beacon. Its battery was dying, but I turned it on and placed it on the windowsill of my hut. Drawing the last of the battery's strength, the signal was heard by a pilot monitoring the emergency frequencies. He authenticated the survival code, and "interrogated" the unit electronically to provide a GPS location. That verified the information they had from my note and made those soldiers more determined than ever to reach my village.

Studying overhead imagery of the area, the rescuers identified an LZ that looked large enough for their aircraft to touch down on, then got busy with mission prep. The platoon of Rangers and Green Berets would secure the LZ and bring me to the village.

When Spanky and his team looked at the coordinates for my estimated position, they realized it was not far from where Turbine 33 had crashed a few days earlier. Clearly the pickup itself was the most dangerous part of the mission. They knew the area was full of Taliban fighters, and feared what every rescue pilot fears most: that the operation would reveal itself as a trap, one set by the enemy to lure another American aircraft to its doom. The enemy

Major Brett "Zero" Waring was part of the Redwing rescue team. *(Jim Hornfischer)*

Zero with his Hog. *(Courtesy of Brett Waring)*

Major Jeff "Spanky" Peterson flew his helo through hell to reach me. *(Courtesy of Jeff Peterson)*

(TucsonCitizen.com/ Gannett)

These two crews from the 305th Rescue Squadron pulled me off that mountain. L to R: Master Sgt. Mike Cusick, Staff Sgt. Chris Piercecchi, Staff Sgt. Ben Peterson, Staff Sgt. Joshua Donnelly, Master Sgt. Josh Appel, Tech. Sgt. John Davis, Tech. Sgt. Jason Burger, Lt. David Gonzales, Lt. Col. Jeff "Skinny" Macrander, Master Sgt. Brett Konczal, Maj. Jeff "Spanky" Peterson, and Maj. John Phalon. *(Courtesy of Josh Appel)*

USAF pararescuemen Josh Appel and Chris Piercecchi. *(Courtesy of Chris Piercecchi)*

That's "Checky," somewhere over the Sandbox. *(Josh Appel)*

R. V. Burgin at the First Marine Division reunion, San Antonio, August 2010. *(Jim Hornfischer)*

Mr. Burgin at his home near Dallas. *(Jim Hornfischer)*

Aaron "Trey" Vaughn and his wife, Kimberly. *(Courtesy of Kimberly Vaughn.)*

Jon (JT) Tumilson
on the day he
graduated BUD/S.
(author's collection)

We will never
forget JT.

Boss eulogizes his teammate, Rockford, Iowa. *(Jim Hornfischer)*

Hawkeye and JT, August 19, 2011. *(Lisa Pembleton)*

The SEAL brotherhood and friends circle around JT's family, August 19, 2011, Rockford, Iowa. *(Jim Hornfischer)*

had proven its ability to take down our birds. (Hell, we later learned it was a twelve-year-old kid who had shot down Turbine 33.) Failure could easily mean putting another helicopter into the mountain, adding its pilots and crew to the roster of people needing rescue or recovery.

Seeing how the terrain offered cover for hostiles, Skinny proposed a maneuver known as a trailer spooky, a carefully choreographed dance that allows two helos to support each other at the landing zone. The lead bird flies in, buzzes the LZ, then climbs to orbit overhead, watching for threats. Then, as an AC-130 Spectre shines its powerful infrared spotlight down on the LZ from ten thousand feet, and as A-10 Warthogs strafe nearby ridges, the second helo—the trailer—flies in, flares, lands, and makes the pickup.

When Skinny finished his proposal, Spanky felt his heart jump. Since he was flying trailer, it was his helicopter that would touch down to grab me off the ridge. He knew that Skinny, as his senior officer, could have saved that honor for himself. But Skinny thought the mission more important than the glory, and the odds of success would be better if his subordinate handled the touchdown and pickup while he flew lead.

As the helo pilots and crews worked through their part of it, the commanders of the Close Air Support (CAS) aircraft, including a pair of A-10s and an AC-130, drew up plans to use their heavy firepower to cover the pickup—or, as the Hog drivers say, to "put a bubble of lead" around the LZ. The skies over Sawtalo Sar were filling quickly—some twenty aircraft were on the case.

Then Skinny asked his PJs to design not only a rescue plan but an evasion plan for us in case the worst happened and we all ended up stranded and in need of rescue ourselves. The PJs prepped their kits, working with the flight engineer to make sure their gear didn't exceed weight restrictions. For starters, they decided not to fly with their body armor on. This was a significant self-sacrifice—par for the course in the rescue community.

The seeds of a mission's failure usually sprout from confident expectations that things will be simple. Before their deployment, the rescuers had rehearsed missions like this one in the mountains around Albuquerque and elsewhere in the Rockies in conditions far more severe than those they expected to find in a combat theater. But as they would soon discover, grabbing me off that mountain ledge was going to be no easy night's work.

Skinny and Spanky had a few moments to collect their thoughts before gathering with their copilots and four-man flight crews—a flight engineer, a gunner, and two PJs—to go over the pending operation. For a while, they listened to the busy radio chatter, with A-10 and AC-130 pilots talking about their fire missions and sightings of suspected enemy forces in the area. The LZ was way too hot, and it became clear to many that the mission would have to be scrubbed. With one Chinook already down and sixteen men lost, it was thought reckless to risk another bird in the same area. But the crews also knew that the window for my rescue was bound to be short.

The JSOC commander, a SEAL captain, listened to Skinny make his case, then heard a different plan from the Night Stalkers. Reasoning that Skinny's nimbler, smaller HH-60s had a greater chance of success than the Night Stalkers' larger Chinooks, the commander decided that the 305th Rescue Squadron would make the pickup.

One reason for his decision was the fact that some Rangers at Turbine 33's crash site, preparing for a recovery, were in need of extract, too. Some of them fast-roped in too high and heavy, burning their hands on the rope and suffering broken ankles upon hitting the ground. Unfortunately, their needs contributed to the shortage of available rescue airlift.

The senior frog called a briefing at the ops center, and told all the pilots and crew, "The mission tonight is to bring home our men. Nothing else has priority, and we will not fail." Without any further fanfare, the pilots were dismissed and jogged to the flight line. Skinny and Spanky, their copilots, and four-man crews boarded the two HH-60s, fully fueled and ready, and fastened their harnesses.

For the Rangers and Green Berets searching for me, marching across the Hindu Kush at nine thousand feet was much easier said than done. Though they were continuously overwatched by a pair of A-10s, they needed most of a day to get there, and by the time they arrived, some of them were totally smoke-checked from dehydration. Trust me, those mountains were brutal. Through hard terrain and thin air, these men never gave up.

Come to find out, the soldiers thought all along that I was being held hostage in that village. Thinking that heavily armed insurgents were holding me, they had spent much of the first day after their arrival in the area making a plan to rescue me via direct assault. Attacking a well-defended compound where a hostage's exact location is unknown is tough work, even for our best operators. But they were ready to go in hard and fight for me, even knowing that some of them were likely to die in the effort. Damn good men.

That night a thunderstorm moved in, tossing monsoon-like rains. With the Taliban rattling their swords and making new threats, Gulab decided to move me to a neighboring village. We were set to go before midnight, but the rain didn't quit. We scrubbed the plan. It was too dangerous to move. As Gulab stood watch over me, I settled in and rested for the first time in days.

When morning broke, the Taliban encircling Sabray were still in a tense standoff with the locals. The enemy leader had delivered an ultimatum to Gulab—"Hand over the American, or every member of your family will be killed." With eight kids, Gulab had a lot to lose. But there was nothing about him that suggested he would back down.

I had no idea what was going to happen next. Lying around while Gulab and his men figured it out, I didn't know what the plan was. I guess my new Afghan family had just made contact with U.S. forces, because they soon pointed me toward a steep forested escarpment. We hadn't gone far when all of a sudden I saw an Afghan with a rifle standing in the distance. As we drew closer, I saw he was a government commando. He was wearing a cap that was printed with the slogan BUSH FOR PRESIDENT. Of all the things I expected to see in the mountains of Afghanistan, believe me, *that* did not make my short list.

Before I knew it, Gulab was running toward a group of about twenty men, yelling, "Dr. Marcus, two-two-eight!" He was authenticating my identity with my BUD/S class number, which he had seen tattooed on my back. As the villagers took me to meet my rescuers, I got my first up-close look at friendly forces in more than five days.

"Marcus?" one of the Rangers asked.

Just hearing English spoken for the first time in almost a week felt liberating. I said, "Hey, bro. It's good to see you."

He turned his head to the rear and shouted, "We got him, down here!" I grabbed hold of that guy and hugged him as though we'd been friends our whole lives. (I'd never hugged a man that way before; I hope he didn't think it was weird.)

The Rangers and Green Berets marched me to higher ground and put me in what I figured was a goat pen, judging by all the manure. Their medic, T.O., began dressing my wounds. We were far from out of the woods, of course. Outnumbered in an area crawling with the enemy, we were all in the same boat and the sea state was rough.

The soldiers set security around the settlement while T.O. doctored me up. When they tried to post a watch outside my hut, the Afghans stepped in firmly and said they wouldn't have Americans doing any such thing, not while their tribal law required them to protect my life with their own. The doctrine of *lokhay warkawal,* a precept of hospitality that is part of their ancient tribal code, *Pashtunwalai,* had gotten me this far. They weren't about to be relieved of that ancient obligation now. It turned out pretty well for everyone—the soldiers got some rest while the villagers took the watch.

I was talking with T.O., joking around a little to lighten the mood, when he leaned over and dosed me with a gunshot cocktail—basically a big shot of antibiotics with a morphine chaser. Preferring to keep my mind clear, I wanted to decline it. As a medic, though, I knew better than that, and the Ranger, sizing up my weakness and my wounds, gave me no choice. Soon afterward I started throwing up. I was seriously sick, infected with a parasitic bug of some kind that wouldn't let go of my stomach. "This isn't good, dude," he said. "We have to get you out of here."

Those helos needed to show up, and fast.

As I lay down to rest again, the commander and his platoon sergeant came in to say hello. They were followed by some of the Rangers. As they took turns walking over to shake my hand, I could see how rough they had had it. They were heavily loaded, with full body armor, kits, and weapons that seemed out of place in steep, high terrain. "Man, you look like hammered shit," I said to one of them. "Did you come down the mountain the same way I did?"

I knew that if I were in their shoes, I'd be cussing the stump-headed Navy cowboy who'd gotten his ass stuck this far out on a ledge. (They confirmed for me that, yes, they had done just that.) I apologized to each of them. They were at the limit of their endurance, and now their survival depended, as mine did, on the rescue helicopters getting in and taking us home. All that was left to do was recite our most heartfelt prayers that nothing would stand in their way.

18

"You Might Want to Pray Now"

As Skinny and Spanky flew through the night toward us, they were dismayed to see storms socking in the entire area. They had been praying that the monsoon weather would stand off to the east. No such luck. Clouds blanketed the earth and rains scoured it clean. Worse, the overcast blocked the sources of ambient light that their NVGs needed to work properly. Still, they pushed on.

Having studied their route using drone imagery, the pilots knew they would have to "lighten ship" to reach the LZ. This meant dumping precious fuel to reduce weight. Spanky hesitated to release the kerosene-based JP-8 jet fuel over a populated area, but knew he had no other choice. A short stretch outside Asadabad, he pulled the safety wire, saying quietly, "This is for Penny and the boys." As his tanks opened, five hundred pounds of fuel showered the earth. With less fuel on board, he would have less margin of error maneuvering into and out of the landing zone, but at least with a lighter aircraft, he now stood a decent chance of reaching it in the first place.

Dave Gonzales, the copilot, said over the intercom, "If you guys are praying guys, you might want to pray now."

Finding the LZ was going to be their biggest problem. The coordinates they had put them in the ballpark, but to touch down safely they needed a good visual sense of the ground. And that required lights.

As I was led over mountain paths toward the LZ, we occasionally took fire from Taliban fighters sneaking around the surrounding mountains. Now and then I pitched in, lasing targets for the aircraft covering us using the laser designator the Afghans in the village had detached from my rifle. At one point, I saw one of the guys open a laptop computer. As the bright white light bathed his face in the dark, Gulab quickly conveyed the idea that he needed to shut it down. We were sitting ducks already, and any light could have given away our position. It was important to observe strict discipline regarding light. Just a few nights before, Gulab had torn me a new one for activating the light on my G-Shock watch, just to check the time.

It took us maybe twenty minutes to reach the landing zone. Hunkering down underneath a stucco-and-rock wall that bounded its cliffside edge, we sipped the dregs of our canteens and waited for salvation to descend from heaven.

It was just before midnight. Spanky Peterson and Skinny Macrander had turned away from the dry riverbed they had been tracking through the valley and began to climb. The chatter of a whole airborne cavalry filled their headsets on five frequencies. Tight and crisp, the voices announced their positions and confirmed their movements—and, as always, there were some (a few of them located more than a hemisphere away) that were constantly demanding to know the status of this and the status of that. Spanky could feel his own status through the soles of his boots. When his altitude reached seven thousand feet, his two General Electric T701 turboshaft engines registered their distress by trembling and shaking, which Spanky picked up through vibration in the floor pedals.

The plan called for the Rangers to toss an IR strobe into the middle of the LZ to mark it for the pilots. But that plan went south fast: once those Warthogs started strafing their targets, our troops were quick to make their positions known. Each man carried a strobe for just such a purpose, and quickly the entire mountainside came alive in a constellation of blinking IR. Speeding uphill at high speed, surveying the terrain ahead, Spanky had no idea which one of the dozens of flickering phosphorescent green lights was his landing zone. The place was like a 1970s disco. And, two minutes from touchdown, he had little fuel to waste on delays.

At this point, all hope rested in the AC-130 Spectre gunship orbiting the LZ. The mission plan called for the plane to shine its powerful infrared spotlight on the landing zone thirty seconds prior to landing. The IR device carried by the Spectres is huge, but its output is invisible to anyone not wearing NVGs. Properly equipped, however, what you see is a bright flood of light illuminating the LZ. The aviators refer to it as an artificial sun.

Throttles maxed, the two Sikorsky-built angels took on the ancient mountain, rising toward us, higher and higher, through thinning air. The twelve souls on board were soon to confront the most dangerous stage of their mission. The ultimate test of their training was almost upon them.

When Spanky was about ten minutes out, Mercury, the A-10 pilot flying as Sandy 1, the mission commander, announced, "All players: execute, execute, execute." The AC-130 Spectre rocked sideways as its belly-mounted 105mm howitzer opened up on suspected Taliban positions. The A-10s ripped out short bursts of 30mm cannon fire at a rate of seventy rounds a second, sounding across the ridges with a distinctive, throaty *urrrrp*. The gunship's 40mm Bofors cannon joined in, too, and soon the mountains were a killing field. Anyone in the way would have been cut down by high explosives. The smallest of these shells had the hitting power of a hand grenade.

In the hills around my village, I had seen the fires of the Taliban encampments and the bobbing lights of their lanterns as they moved around. Now the enemy, if they had managed to survive, either had gone to ground or died. I felt my heart move to my throat.

Through his helmet-mounted night-vision goggles, Spanky could see the clouds saddling the mountain peaks flicker and flash with sudden pulses of light from all around. The A-10s made several strafing passes not far from us, and several additional runs on ridges farther away, to divert the enemy's attention from the actual landing zone. The hellacious racket also masked the sound of rotors as the two helicopters approached.

Rushing upward over that stark terrain, Spanky still could not actually see the LZ. Less than a minute out, he was still counting on the AC-130 to bathe the landing zone in infrared light. He was wondering where his spotlight was when he heard a voice on his radio, cool and professional, slightly urgent, but scarcely betraying the desperation of the moment. It was the pilot of the AC-130 gunship high above.

"Halos: negative burn, negative burn."

"Halos" was the call sign for the two helicopters. "Negative burn" meant the AC-130 was unable to illuminate the landing zone. Cloud cover was total. When the technician in the plane turned on the IR spotlight, it couldn't penetrate the vast blanket of white. Without it, there was no way Spanky would be able to land.

Sometimes you have to let a tough situation develop before you can finally find a way through. As I know from my career as a SEAL, the right solution never comes from panic or despair. And what happened next is a perfect example of how a professional handles adversity: he lets the situation develop.

After Spanky got the bad news from the AC-130, he radioed Skinny, and the pilots went back and forth:

"Which strobe is the LZ?"

"You got it?"

"I don't see it...."

The A-10 flight lead, Mercury, must have heard the rapid-fire exchange. Like the rest of them, he was well aware that the weather was getting thick. The thunderstorms were swelling through every altitude. There had to be another way of illuminating the landing zone. There would be no second chances.

Mercury couldn't do it himself. His armament control panel, which he used to operate the laser in his targeting pod, had had a system failure and was not working. This left him with no way to shine his targeting laser on the

264 of MARCUS LUTTRELL

landing zone. But his number two might be in position to pull it off. Sandy 2 (Mercury's exec, in effect) was a Warthog pilot known as Wookie for his unusual height and gentle nature. Seeing what might be the mission's only chance, Mercury toggled his radio and said, "Sandy Two, mark the LZ."

Wookie copied Mercury's order while he was making a gun run on a Taliban fighting position. Focused on the target in front of him, he alerted his flight lead as a matter of course: "Two's in hot"—meaning that he was about to open fire. This news put Mercury into a minor panic. He was expecting a simple acknowledgment. Thinking that Wookie had heard him wrong and was preparing to blast the landing zone with high explosives instead, Mercury shouted, "Negative! Abort! Use your laser marker, not the gun!"

Recognizing the harmless confusion, Wookie smiled. Coolly finishing his strafing run, he pulled his aircraft into a climb and turned it sharply onto its right wing. Then he activated his targeting pod and slaved it to the coordinates for the LZ. Even in his elite peer group, Wookie's touch at the stick was exceptional, but a divine hand must have guided him, too. The mass of low-level clouds down on the deck was still substantial, but there was an opening in that thick carpet, right where we needed it to be. When Wookie triggered his targeting laser, that small patch of open sky was passing right between his aircraft and the landing zone. Luckily for me, the critical window stayed open for about twelve seconds and his beam hit it dead center.

Still hovering, Spanky saw the beam shine down through the hole in the clouds. As his copilot, Dave Gonzales, would say, it was like the finger of God marking the landing zone with infrared light.

The two helo crews had gotten the idea from aerial photography that the LZ was about the size of a football field—an easy mark for an experienced HH-60 driver. However, owing to the optical illusions created by the satellite camera's angle, they had no idea how steep and tight it really was—a small shelf in the mountain near a cluster of gingerbread huts. Spanky knew that no sane pilot would ever try landing there, even by day. It was nearly midnight. As he made his final approach, a warning came over his headset: "Known enemy one hundred meters south of your position." The back of his neck prickled— the LZ was just as hot as they feared it would be. But there was no backing out now.

This close to landing, a pilot and crew have to work as a team. The pilot has his hands on the stick, controlling the helicopter's three axes of movement. The copilot is on the throttles, ready to pull emergency power and get out of Dodge. The flight engineer monitors the engines and other systems, while the gunner and the PJs in back stay alert for any obstacles and follow the aircraft's progress toward touchdown, talking to the pilot all the way. If, for example, the gunner says, "Stop left," the pilot knows he has to correct his leftward drift immediately. This is tough to do by day, much harder at night, and just about impossible when the helicopter, as it did at that moment, starts kicking up a storm of sand and dirt with the downwash of its rotors. Spanky was lost in a brownout, flying totally blind.

It was after 11:30 p.m. when I saw the helo approaching the ledge, descending, descending, then holding, and holding, and holding...Just above the brownout, I could locate Spanky's main rotor by the luminescent disk it sparked in the sky, fifty-four feet in diameter—a disk made by the friction of the titanium blade tips striking particles of sand and dirt. Seen through NVGs, it was a floating green halo, standing in the night.

The danger meter was pegged all the way to the right. If Spanky touched one of his tires down on the ground while the bird had any sideways drift, it would roll over into the mountain. If it drifted too far left, it would pile into the cliff's stony face, burying its rotors and balling up in flames on the ledge. If it rolled right, it would fall straight off the precipice, plunging to the rocks fifteen hundred feet below—or falling right down on top of us.

Huddled with T.O., Gulab, and the rest of the Army team just below the landing zone, on the other side of that low stucco-and-rock wall, we pulled as much of the prayer load as we could. Let me tell you, I've never taken such a bath of flying crud in all my life. The helicopter's twin engines, producing more than three thousand shaft horse-power between them, made an unending metallic scream, loud enough to drown out all thought. If the darkest place in the world was that Persian Gulf sewer pipe that Master Chief had explored, the loudest place in the world is right in the dust-choked footprint of a landing helicopter.

Even all these years later, some of the events that night remain a bit of a blur. I think there were troops in contact not far away from us. I believe the LZ itself—that is, we—may even have been taking some fire, though it was hard to tell in all the noise and dust. The Air Force was still working a few ridgelines nearby. And right there above us, in the middle of it all, the helicopter's crew was keeping calm and collected as they called adjustments to Spanky over the radio headset. The space they occupied between life and death was narrow. But I guess their legacy was assured. If they died here on this mountain, they would go out as heroes, pushing a daring mission to the limit. And if they lived, well, the result would speak for itself. Heroes all around.

As the calls of "Stop left" and "Stop right" became increasingly urgent, several of the crew in back lay down flat on the deck of the crew compartment—standard aviation fieldcraft for anyone looking to avoid a fractured spine. Though as calm as he could be, Spanky couldn't prevent thoughts of his wife, Penny, and his four sons from pushing through.

Though the finger of God—also known as Wookie's targeting laser—had shown Spanky the way, yet another heavenly sign arrived. Through the cyclonic vortex, Spanky suddenly saw something ahead and to the side: the trembling branches of a shrub of some kind. I think his rotors must have washed half the dirt off that mountainside before it was possible for him to see it. But there it fluttered, fixed in space and calling to him like a sign from the Old Testament. As I said, sometimes you have to let a situation develop. With the shrub as a visual reference, Spanky adjusted to a steady hover and eased nineteen thousand pounds of steel to the earth. The two Air Force PJs bounded out of the helicopter's right-side door as soon as it landed.

Time for us to move, too. As T.O. slapped me on the leg, I rose to my feet, knowing in the back of my mind that if there were any enemy nearby, they would be sure to send an RPG downrange and blow us all to kingdom come. As Gulab and I came over the stucco wall and began walking toward the helo from behind, the more immediate danger, of course, was getting our heads split in half by the spinning tail rotor. It was hard to figure out where the aircraft even was.

Looking for their prize, the PJs saw us approaching them, about fifty meters away. I was dressed in a pair of Gulab's "man jammies"—traditional local garb—just like a mujahideen. Gulab was looking a little bit fierce, too, I'm sure. Both of the pararescuemen, Chris Piercecchi and Josh Appel, were based in Arizona. When 9/11 happened, Chris (known as "Checky") had retired from a 1990s stint in the PJs and was working as a paramedic with the Albuquerque fire department. Then the crumbling towers in New York called him back to full-time service in the reserves. Josh had just finished medical school at the University of Arizona en route to becoming an emergency-room doctor. When the war started getting hot, he had the same feeling Checky did: there were greater challenges out there, and more valuable ways for him to serve. That was Josh's route into the elite pararescue community.

I was glad to see them—except that they almost killed me before they saved me. Suspecting we were hostiles, Checky and Josh dropped the Stokes litter they were carrying and drew their M4s. Through the monocular night-vision scope mounted on his helmet over his left eye, Checky studied our hazy green figures hobbling toward him and put the infrared dot of his laser sight on my chest. He saw I was armed, but the way I was holding my rifle—stock in hand, barrel pointing toward the ground—gave him the small margin of comfort he needed to keep from blowing me away in an instant. They didn't shoot. They let the situation develop.

When I stumbled and fell while approaching them, they noticed a third figure behind us. One of the PJs fixed his laser on this new presence—producing bright glare off the IR-reflective American flag on the figure's chest. It was T.O.'s Old Glory patch, glowing green in Checky's NVGs, that saved us. The PJs knew in that instant that he was one of theirs. The state of alarm downshifted from red to orange, so to speak.

Checky rushed toward us, raising his forearm and stiff-arming us to keep us from blundering into the tail rotor. (Now *that* would have made for a hell of an ending to the Redwing story, though you can bet it never would've made the papers.) He grabbed T.O. by his harness, pulled him close, and above the whine of turboshaft engines yelled, "Where's the package?"

The Ranger medic pointed at me. "Here's your valuable cargo!"

Checky turned to me and asked, "Who's your favorite superhero?"

Both PJs had memorized my ISOPREP form, the compilation of personal data that's kept on file for all special operations personnel and is used to authenticate our identities.

My reply—Spider-Man—matched my ISOPREP form and ensured my passage to safety. Thanks, Spidey.

Checky brought Gulab and me to the side door of the helo. I saw that about a dozen crates of bottled water and MREs were in the compartment with us. (No vodka. Still, it was full-service rescue.) There was no room for twenty soldiers in a small HH-60, of course, so the Rangers and

Green Berets were going to stay behind. The helo's crew pushed those crates out the side door and hoped they could make do till a larger Chinook could come get them.

As we took off, I never shook loose the fear that we were all soon going to get hit by an RPG. But we had angels on our shoulder: a two-ship element of A-10 Warthogs in a holding pattern to our west, ready to light up the mountainside again should the enemy make a move, and an AC-130, playing quarterback from on high. All were listening for news that the pilot had been successful. Finally confirming that he had rescued us, Spanky broadcast, "Popcorn plus two," indicating that the rescue bird was taking off—popping like corn—along with two additional passengers. Panic flared over the number of people Spanky took aboard. Some were expecting just me ("Popcorn plus one") and feared that the extra passenger might have been a muj wearing a suicide vest. Finally it was straightened out—Gulab was legit—and the A-10 flight lead announced to everyone: "All players, this is Sandy One. Home run! Home run!"

Checky leaned over and asked me if I needed anything. He checked my vital signs. Then he let out a deep breath and looked at me closely for a moment. We both registered the intensity of the hours just passed. He grasped my hand and shook it. His eyes still fixed on mine, he said, "Welcome home, brother."

A skeleton version of this story appeared in *Lone Survivor,* but I wanted to revisit it here because, when I was working on that book, I didn't know the men who had saved me and didn't understand what a close-run thing it had been for them to pull it off. Wrapped up in our busy lives since that night, we haven't spent much time together. I can't claim to know them as well as I do my teammates. But they have a story that deserves to be told. I consider them members of my extended family, a family of warfighters brought together by tragic circumstances. They belong proudly to the larger family of those who have served their country by putting themselves in harm's way. This story is my small tribute to all who wear Air Force blue.

During the short flight to Asadabad, I held Gulab as though he were my own son. We were sitting on the deck of the helo right behind Spanky, with my head leaning against the skin of the aircraft. Gulab was seated between my legs with his arms wrapped around my calves. My left arm was wrapped around his head, my right hand on my rifle. I was overcome with gratitude and sorrow, and Gulab was scared nearly to death. During this, his first ride in a helicopter, the dynamic between us had switched 180 degrees. He had been my protector in his world. Now, in mine, I was his. He had been a tower of strength in my time of need. Now he cowered at my feet. I held him tight. I told him, "It will be okay. I promise." That was when Checky turned to me and shouted above the engine noise, "We have to stop and drop off Gulab."

What? I was shocked that the man who had saved me was to be taken from my company. The military had different plans for us.

When we landed at A-bad and the door opened, Checky took Gulab and they stepped out of the helicopter. Gulab hesitated and tried to make his way back toward me, but the door was slid shut in his face. I never was able to say good-bye to him. I yelled at Checky through the door, "Take good care of him." He shouted back, "I will. Like my own family."

At the time, Checky didn't know much more than I did about the Afghan people. He certainly didn't know Gulab. I think he considered him dangerous. Leaving the flight line, the PJ grabbed him by the upper arm, took control of him, and directed him toward the ops center. Passing through the gate in the nearly pitch-dark night, Checky tripped on some rocks. Feeling Gulab pull away from him, he became alarmed. Was the strange Afghan making a move? As Checky lost his balance, the Afghan reached down, grabbed his hand, and pulled him back to his feet. It turned out all Gulab wanted to do was save him from a hard fall. It's exactly what the rescue team had just done for me.

The emotions of the rescue's endgame were overwhelming for everyone involved, but as is so often the case, there was no time to sit back and reflect on what had happened. With hardly a pause, everyone piled back on board the helicopter for a short flight to Jalalabad air base. When they landed, Spanky's helo had just five minutes of fuel left. I was transloaded to an MC-130 for the flight back to Bagram, where the odyssey of Operation Redwing had begun more than a week earlier.

When they strapped me down, the docs went to work. I remember how calming it was to hear a woman's voice asking me if I was in a lot of pain. After I nodded my head, she said, "I will fix that, sweetie." It reminded me of how my mother would take care of me when I was sick. I never learned her name or had a chance to thank her, but if she reads this, I hope this belated thank-you will do.

Another doc leaned over and told me how proud he

was of me. He took off his cap and placed it on my head. It had an American flag on the front of it. He said, "You did our country proud." I still have the hat. Every so often I'll take it out and put it on to remind me that no matter how bad things get, if you keep getting up and moving forward, you can accomplish anything.

The reunion with my squadron from SEAL Team 10 was happy and heartbreaking at the same time. I tried to joke around with them a little—"The Army guys came and saved me; where were y'all at, man?" I was out of it, and hardly had any idea what to say, but that didn't go over well. The air was still heavy with the fact that three of our brothers were still on that mountain.

After some time with my teammates, I spent a couple of days in the hospital, was debriefed, and was given over to a medical trauma team with orders to fly out to Germany.

Spanky Peterson's experience following the mission was revealing. At Jalalabad, he went to the ops center and called Tucson. Penny was relieved to learn he was safe. Though he wasn't able to give her details of what he'd been part of, she intuited that it had been dangerous, exhausting, and big. She knew she couldn't ask him for details, so she went straight to the bottom line of it all.

She asked her husband, "Did you just do what you've been training for ten years to do?"

At this, Spanky got emotional. Choking back tears, he said that yes, he had done exactly that, but he couldn't say much more about it not only for reasons of security but also because some guys nearby were waiting to make a call, and he didn't want them to see him cry.

The idea that Penny hit on—that our professional

military men and women train for years without knowing whether they will ever have to actually carry out their missions to the fullest extent of their abilities—is the very heart of what service is all about. Heroes aren't designated in advance. Everyone must always be ready to execute.

In my experience, it's always our greatest heroes who claim they never did anything beyond what any of their buddies would have done in the same situation. Our training and our culture breed that response into us all, no matter what war we were part of. You train yourself to a standard and thereby make yourself interchangeable with others who share the same standard. And that gives everyone an equal claim to the pride that goes with having served your country.

19

That Others May Live

In the air ops center at Bagram, which occupies the first deck of the old Soviet tower, there was muted celebration over cigars and near beer. In the suite of plywood huts known as the Hog Drivers' Pen—quarters for the junior A-10 pilots—the pilots watched eight-millimeter footage of Wookie turning his plane on its right wingtip and landing his targeting laser bull's-eye on the landing zone. But their celebration didn't last long. Operation Redwing wasn't over for anyone until all of us were found.

On July 4, 2005, the sixteen men who died on Turbine 33 were recovered from the mountain. The Night Stalkers went in and did the honors, treating that duty as a matter of pride and redemption. As a pair of MH-47 Chinooks prepared to land, Zero and Sluf, joined by an AC-130, flew cover, lighting up the mountainsides, keeping trouble at bay. When the shooting stopped, all was quiet in the alpine forest.

When the two helos brought the men home to Bagram, Zero thought "the aircraft seemed to bow a little that evening in deference to their masters, who had come home on their shields." The entire complement of the base turned out along the flight line and its access road to witness the ramp ceremony. They stood stiffly at attention as the remains were carried home. Chaplains read scripture, and the pallbearers took the caskets one by one from the Chinooks. It was a dignified procession of heroes. And they deserved nothing less.

Now all the focus was on recovering Mikey, Danny, and Axe. The most solemn part of the Air Force CSAR team's mission remained: bringing home my three teammates, missing on Sawtalo Sar.

Details from my debriefing had enabled our teams to locate Mikey and Danny. A team of Rangers secured the area. Since the Night Stalkers were standing down for one night to remember their fallen, it was up to the HH-60s to pick them up. Zero was Sandy 1, with a young pilot, Fudd, on his wing. Skinny flew the lead helo with Checky and Josh as his PJs. The thunderstorms stood off that night, allowing them to fly in without hindrance. As Sandy 1, Zero played quarterback and delivered the instructions that specified how each pilot was to do his job.

"All players, stand by for a fifteen line." The mission script.

"Line one: Poison one-five has LZ control." That was the call sign of a JTAC on the ground.

"Line two: Two-by-KIA." The two fallen SEALs were their objectives. Zero regretted immediately he didn't use their real names. He realized he should have said, "Michael P. Murphy and Daniel P. Dietz, coming home."

"Line three: Location, current as of oh-four July at fourteen hundred hours Zulu, updated at nineteen-ten,

Papa Alpha seven niner seven five eight, six one two zero three." The site of their incredible last stand.

"Line four: Condition—deceased." Zero had to pause and regain his composure after that one.

"Line five: Infrared strobe." That was how the LZ would be located. Rangers were on the ground, marking it for the helos.

"Line six: Authentication complete. Threats in the area include RPGs, small arms. LZ is secure at this time." The Warthogs and the gunship were going to light it up anyway.

"Line seven: Elevation is eight-three-niner-two feet. LZ is a ravine. Initial Point is Papa Alpha eight three three, six eight one. Jolly ingress down the valley, call ten and three nautical miles, egress is reverse routing to Asadabad. Covering ordnance is one-oh-five and forty-millimeter from Shooter, thirty-millimeter from Boar, and fifty-cal on Jolly. Shooter has the LZ, Boar is diversionary strikes and escort, recovery is hoist."

So went the script, the dialogue terse and efficient, covering everything the aviators on the mission needed to know without attempting to explain what could never be fully explained.

Having finished the sequence, Zero asked, "Any questions?" With silence as his answer, he hit the mike again and said, "All players, time stamp twenty-one fifty-two, execute, execute, execute." And with this the mountain began to explode.

Over the steep terrain, the trailing helo entered a hover and two JSOC PJs fast-roped to the ground and guided the hoist from the HH-60 down to the ground. They collected Mikey and Danny's last earthly remains and placed them into a litter. Zero and Fudd circled out of their gun runs and flew cover overhead. Zero turned on his running lights and flew as low as possible, to distract any enemy warriors looking to make trouble for the recovery. Then Mikey and Danny were lifted heavenward with a winch— reverent thoughts foremost in everyone's mind—taken aboard the helo with dignity, and flown back to Bagram for their own ramp ceremony.

At that point, only one task remained for the CSAR team: find Axe.

In the very best case he was badly wounded and still missing. In the SEAL community we never presume one of ours is dead until we actually find his body. These pilots work that way, too. The Air Force Sandy pilots who flew day after day searching for our last missing teammate impressed me with their dedication. In the old Soviet control tower at Bagram, Zero looked east, toward the objective area. He was thankful to see the thunderstorms breaking. He said quietly, "We're coming, Axe. Let us know you're out there, brother, and we'll bring you home."

Zero was one of three pilots rotating in the role of Sandy 1 during the operations to find me and the bodies of my teammates. From Los Angeles, he served with the Seventy-Fourth Fighter Squadron, based at Moody Air Force Base in Georgia, a unit whose lineage goes back to World War II's Flying Tigers—the First American Volunteer Group—which tormented the Japanese from bases all over China. His A-10 was painted with the same characteristic shark's mouth that graced General Claire Chennault's Curtiss P-40 Warhawks back in the day. The aircraft of the Seventy-Fourth, Seventy-Fifth, and Seventy-

Sixth Fighter Squadrons are the only ones authorized by the Air Force to wear that distinctive mark today.

A 1996 graduate of the United States Air Force Academy, Zero had been scared to death of fast amusement-park rides when he was a kid, but in training he found himself hooked on low-altitude flight. It gave him a rush to fly just a few yards above the treetops, with a map spread out just below his field of vision. Throttle pushed to the firewall, he looked back and forth between his map and the world blurring by below, tracking his progress by visual reference. He made his career in A-10 Warthogs, and while serving in Korea asked his squadron weapons officer to help him earn a Sandy upgrade—a coveted certification as a combat search and rescue pilot.

With Axe unaccounted for, the A-10 pilots knew they had some long nights of work ahead of them. SEALs never quit, and that's the Sandy pilots' creed as well.

"Do you think it's possible that this guy is still alive out there?" Zero's wingman, Clap, asked.

"We have to assume he's still alive," Zero replied. "Because if we were to assume anything else, we'd go with less than a full effort. And if we're wrong in that respect, we will have failed a man who's out there with *everything* on the line." But after the first day, all their radios brought them was the static of empty airwaves. Then one night, flying over the mountainscape, monitoring the emergency frequency, Sluf and his wingman, Butters, registered the sound of microphone clicks on their radio.

Sluf keyed his mike and said, "Evader, if you can hear me, click your radio twice." Two clicks came in reply.

Somebody's out there listening to me, he thought.

Sluf instructed his wingman to separate from him, fly

north, and listen again from another position in order to triangulate the signal with his direction-finding equipment. Doing so enabled the pilots to place the source of the signal south and east of the Turbine 33 crash site. They had a man, but was he *their* man?

You'd think a guy could just make voice contact and speak over the radio. But for an evader on the ground, sometimes it's impossible to talk. The enemy may be near enough to hear you. More likely, if he's smart enough, he can intercept your transmissions and use direction-finding techniques to locate his quarry. For this reason, evaders will often simply click their transmit key to communicate with the CSAR team. Sometimes they're too badly hurt to do anything else. That night, receiving no further responses, Sluf and Butters were unable to authenticate the source and were forced to return to base.

Zero flew the next day. Shortly after he arrived on station, he, too, began receiving mike clicks on the guard frequency. To authenticate the sender and determine whether it was Axe, he went into his call-and-exchange mode, knowing all the while that he might well be hearing an enemy with a stolen radio looking to set up a trap.

Authenticating a lone evader on the ground may be the most intellectually demanding part of CSAR work. The game of call-and-response the pilot plays is a matter of life and death, requiring the utmost in professionalism and care. Taliban fighters were known to take the emergency radios from those they killed and play games with the rescue pilots, sometimes trying to lure them into a trap. This was known as spoofing. A pilot had to distinguish the signals of a real evader from spoofing attempts by the enemy.

"Evader, we copy your signal. If you can hear my

voice, I want you to give me the number of mike clicks equal to the second-to-last digit of your Social Security number." That piece of data was included on Axe's ISO-PREP form, which Zero had right there in his cockpit. He desperately wanted to hear the correct number of clicks, but heard only silence. He repeated the call.

Now an answer came. Just two clicks. He needed to hear five.

Zero wondered, *Could he be hearing me wrong?* He decided to dispense with numbers and get more personal. "Axe, we need to know that we're talking to you—the enemy is listening and trying to keep us away from you.

"You're going to hear a series of names. When you hear the name of your tan Labrador retriever, I want you to give me four to five distinct mike clicks. If you understand, give me two clicks now."

When the radio returned two clicks, Zero thought he might be onto something. To his wingman, Clap, flying as Sandy 2, he said, "Here goes nothing."

"Axe, here come the names. Hank...Hank..."—no reply.

"Bobby...Bobby..."—no reply.

Keep going. Give nothing away to the enemy.

"Boomhauer...Boomhauer..." This was the name of Axe's dog—

Nothing.

The pilot's heart sank, but he continued with one more name. "Redcorn...Redcorn..."

This returned a flurry of mike clicks. He asked Barnyard, a Navy command and control plane listening high above, for confirmation.

"Barnyard confirms, two clicks heard after Redcorn only."

Zero suspected he was being fooled with—Redcorn did sound a little like the name of a dog—but he could also imagine that a badly wounded man, dehydrated and slipping in and out of consciousness, might not always respond reliably to prompts over a shaky radio link.

"Axe," Zero continued, "I'm going to ask you yes-or-no questions. If the answer you want to give me is yes, give me two clicks. If it's no, give me a quick four or five clicks. Do you understand?"

"Barnyard reports two clicks."

The signals were too weak for even our best listening technologies to take a directional fix on, so Zero figured he'd see if Axe was well enough equipped to make it for a while. "Axe, I'm going to list items of survival equipment. If you have it and can use it, give me two clicks. If you do not have it, do not make any clicks."

He started with a list of gear that Axe might be able to use to signal us: signal mirror. IR strobe. MRE heater. Wristwatch with illumination. Pen flares. Matches or other means to start a fire.

Barnyard reported receiving two clicks in response to both the strobe and the MRE heater.

"Axe, I want you to activate your IR strobe."

"Barnyard has six clicks."

Damn it, what on earth does that mean? Zero thought. *Is Axe unable to activate the light? Or is the enemy spoofing me?*

Zero checked his fuel. Very low. As he bingoed out to rendezvous with a tanker, he asked Barnyard to stay on scene and find a way to triangulate the evader's position on the ground.

During the twenty-minute diversion to refuel, Zero

reflected on his exchange with this phantom. He realized time was not his friend; he needed to be more overt with his covert instructions. If it was Axe, he needed to give him information more clearly, even though the enemy may be listening. When he had taken his fill from the tanker, he returned to the missing SEAL's suspected location and picked up where he left off.

"Axe, buddy, go ahead and activate your strobe light."

Immediately Clap's voice was loud in Zero's helmet: "Sandy Two has an IR strobe that just came on!"

And there it was, right below, a flashing light in a wavelength only detectable with NVGs. *We've got something!* Zero locked his targeting pod onto the strobe and studied the four-inch screen in his cockpit. Very clearly he saw two individuals on the ground, near the flashing infrared beacon.

"I have two individuals with an IR strobe, location north thirty-four, fifty-two point zero three...east zero-seven-zero, fifty-seven point niner-three," Zero called. Clap turned his sensors to the same location and confirmed it.

Zero wondered why there would be two people down there—was it a pair of bad guys spoofing him, or could it be someone like Sarawa, offering assistance to an American? He passed the coordinates back to headquarters and waited. His soaring hopes made the eventual news even more shattering.

"Barnyard has word from higher up: that's a U.S. Marine Corps sniper team. Coordinates and location confirmed."

Zero's helmet suddenly felt like it was made of lead. Even so, he kept thinking creatively.

What's the one thing a SEAL would never be able to forget, even under severe duress? Then it hit him: as anyone who had gone through BUD/S would remember till his last days, all you had to do to end the brutal selection process was to walk over to a big dinner bell that the instructors always kept handy and give it three hard whacks. That's how you quit—what they called a DOR, for "drop on request." Nobody got through BUD/S without feeling the temptation to ring out. The path to freedom was always kept open, with fresh coffee and doughnuts standing by. By the time you made it through, you would have heard the bell ring for four out of five of the men who started with you. The sharp brass cadence of surrender—*clang, clang, clang!*—was something Axe would know even in extremis.

Zero said, "Axe, if you had decided to DOR out of BUD/S, how many times would you have rung the bell?"

The reply was instantaneous, and so loud in his cockpit—*CLICK, CLICK, CLICK*—that he dropped his pencil and his flight log. The pilot queried his wingman and Barnyard: "How many clicks did you hear?" They all heard three clicks.

Holy shit, do we finally have him? Zero thought.

"Axe, brother, let's keep this ball going. Let us know it's you and we'll bring you home tonight!"

Nothing but static filled his headset.

"Axe, let's get a hack on your position. Give me a five-second hold-down."

Zero hoped a transmission with a longer duration would be easier to triangulate. Sure enough, Barnyard confirmed a faint signal, a "squelch break," lasting five seconds.

"Come on, guys, we've got to be able to triangulate that," Zero said. But Barnyard reported the signal was too weak.

"Axe, give me a twenty-second hold-down."

"Barnyard has two five-second holds, and two eight-second holds."

Somebody down there was listening, and judging by the pattern, he might well be injured. Knowing there was little time left for games, Zero went for broke. No more beating around the Taliban's bush.

We need to know if this is Axe and we need to know now, he thought.

"Axe, tell me your first name, and tell me now. I need to know who I'm talking to."

Static.

"Axe, tell me your first or middle name."

Static.

"Axe, give me mike clicks when you hear your initials: Juliet Papa Whiskey…Bravo Alpha Delta…Juliet Lima Sierra…Mike Golf Alpha…Sierra Mike Alpha…Juliet Charlie Tango…"

No reaction to any of it.

In a helpless rage at eight thousand feet, Zero pounded his fists against the bulletproof canopy. *We had something! We were there!* Now he was done. He noticed a new front of heavy electrical storms encroaching from the west. He saw that his fuel tanks were rapidly draining, too. Given no choice by these inescapable limitations, Zero instructed his primary players to return to base. As a new two-ship of A-10s and another AC-130 arrived to relieve him, he used the secure radio connection to give the newcomers a recap of the past five hours, including details of his transmissions and responses. He felt defeated, but refused to betray it when he toggled his mike again with a parting message to the evader on the ground.

"Axe, buddy, I'm heading back to fill this pig up. She's about as thirsty as a sailor in the Big Apple during Fleet Week. But my brothers are here. They'll keep talking to you. We aren't going anywhere. You aren't alone, and you're coming home with us soon."

Back at the air ops center at Bagram, for the benefit of skeptics, Zero played a recording of the exchange he had had with his mystery man on the ground.

"Somebody's out there," he said, "and we're gonna keep authenticating him until we know for sure one way or the other."

Shortly thereafter, he learned of a news report on the American Forces Network that a Taliban spokesman in Pakistan was boasting of capturing an American service-man in the mountains near Asadabad. Efforts to recover him would be useless, the Taliban said, and unless certain demands were met, the captive would be executed and left in the wilderness.

Zero's spirits sank. He took a walk to the SOF com-mand tent to see what the latest word was, and his morale took another hit. A contractor who worked as a signals analyst told him that, according to his advanced computer-based processing and analysis equipment, the radio clicks he had heard were just atmospheric noise.

Zero gaped. "Look, I may just be a dumb fighter pilot, but I know that atmospheric anomalies don't respond to questions asked by human beings. Your computer tells you one thing, but my ears tell me another. I trust my ears."

"No one was trying to signal you," the analyst said. "We have a very unstable atmosphere out there tonight. Those thunderstorms are playing havoc with our frequencies."

"You telling me we should give up?" Zero noticed that both his hands had clenched into fists. His hopes were threatening to cartwheel down a mountain, but he knew what he had heard and kept hope in his heart.

Leaving the SOF compound, he encountered an Air Force sergeant. "Hey, what the hell's up with these shit-heads out there, saying they've got Axe?"

"They don't have Axe," the sergeant said.

"Say again?"

"They don't have him."

"And we know this how?"

"Because *we've* got Axe."

At this, Zero's knees went wobbly. He was speechless.

"One of our patrols hit the canyons again based on Marcus's debrief, and they found his body about an hour ago. Those assholes never got their hands on him."

"We're sure about that?"

"They never touched him after the battle. They're just trying to jack around with us because they knew we were close to a recovery. We bring him home tomorrow night. You're Sandy One, Zero. You've got the recovery."

The men on the ground who finally located Axe were his own SEAL brothers. The rest of the guys from his troop in SDVT-1 had flown in from Iraq to join some operators from SEAL Team 10 in scouring the mountains. These guys stayed out there without a break for more than a week, tracing and retracing the likely routes leading away from the battlefield on Sawtalo Sar, and developing leads with the locals.

The reason the enemy never laid hands on Axe had a lot to do with what happened in the village where those frogs finally found him. The Afghans there were willing to talk, but seemed nervous about what had happened. Finally they admitted that they had taken Axe and buried him in order to keep his body out of the Taliban's hands. They had done him this final honor out of respect for who he was: word had gotten around fast about the savage fight he had put up till the bitter end. They wanted to deprive the hated radicals of a war prize that they could use to boost their stature. Though the courageous villagers feared that the SEALs would be outraged that they had taken this liberty, they received nothing from them but gratitude.

On the night of July 10, a pair of Army MH-47 Chinooks took off from Bagram after sunset and turned east toward the Korengal Valley. Zero led the pair of A-10s covering them. As winds out of the south held the thunderstorms at bay, keeping the LZ clear, the recovery aircraft reached the slopes near that village. One Chinook lowered a pair of PJs from an Air Force reserve unit out of Florida. Fast-roping down to the slope, the pararescuemen linked up with the frogmen and went to Axe. Laying their hands gently on him, they took him aboard for the return flight to Bagram. As the second Chinook landed to pick up the SEALs, Zero thought how sadly common these missions had become. But when he landed at Bagram, he felt a strong sense of satisfaction that he'd made good on the promise he had made at the start of the operation. He had brought Axe home with every honor due him.

The flight line was full of personnel from all four service branches standing rigidly at attention. Joining the crowd, the A-10 pilots found themselves struggling to hold their composure and keep their shoulders square. And now, as a final ramp ceremony began, the chaplains and pallbearers approached the Chinook bearing Axe's remains and reunited him with the eighteen other heroes of Operation Redwing.

In the center of the flight line, a C-17 Globemaster cargo plane was parked, its rear ramp open, with two ranks of men from the Night Stalkers and SEAL Team 10 standing on either side of the approach to the ramp.

Then they appeared. One by one, the nineteen dead, each in a separate truck, one following another in procession. Their steel caskets were each covered with an American flag. As the crowd snapped to attention, rendering salutes, a U.S. serviceman playing bagpipes groaned out "Amazing Grace." The chaplains read scripture as pallbearers carried the caskets up the ramp and into the C-17's hold. When the last one reached the top, the SEALs and Night Stalkers filed in behind it and the ramp closed. The plane would be airborne soon, but not until the men on board had time to conduct a private ceremony of their own.

The professionalism and care that the Air Force rescue team brought to the mission to recover my teammate still moves me deeply. It means as much to me as my own rescue did.

I'm telling this story here because stories like it fill warriors everywhere—from special operations and conventional forces alike—with gratitude and comfort. The rescue guys seldom get much attention, but what they do makes a huge difference to their brothers in uniform. The slogan of the PJ community is THESE THINGS WE DO THAT

OTHERS MAY LIVE. Without exception, that selfless spirit applies to the whole lot of them. And, in a deep sense, that motto is lived out by all who serve with their lives on the line. Why do we do it? We do it for others, so that they may carry out their duties, serve their missions, serve their comrades, serve their nation, and go on to live the good lives they deserve. And along that path, some of our very best people lose their own lives. It's the ultimate price that some pay to serve. And in serving in that way—laying everything they have on the line, live or die—all of them stand as heroes. Imagine our world if everyone lived by their creed.

20

Stir-Crazy

Those who serve experience something that people who don't wear a uniform seldom do: the feeling of being tightly part of something larger than themselves. In the company of those who set their priorities the same way, we form powerful bonds of fraternity. (And never forget: there are many devoted women in the military, too, from EOD techs to A-10 Warthog pilots to support elements of all sorts, including in the special operations community.) The relationships you build tend to be permanent. The bond I have with Morgan is a degree stronger than those I have with my other teammates only by virtue of blood. And when you wear a uniform, the way you think about your country changes a little, too.

But how do you come home from it? What do we do with the skills we've acquired and the stories we have? Who outside the fraternity will relate?

Among my goals in life now is to become one of the old men Morgan and I never thought we'd become. Our pledge to each other—"womb to the tomb"—was never very clear about duration. As I said earlier, we both had our doubts that we'd make it past forty. But now when we talk about it, we picture ourselves ending up like Robert Duvall in *Secondhand Lions,* or Clint Eastwood in *Gran Torino.* We want to cut our lawns wearing sneakers and black socks, and holler at the neighbor's kids when they hit baseballs into our yards, hiding smiles behind the backs of our hands. More than anything else, we want our experiences to grow into wisdom.

I would settle right now for becoming the kind of man R. V. Burgin is. I look at him, at home in that small town south of Dallas, and see honor, integrity, love, and peace. Any of us should be so fortunate. Though we met late in his life, I relate to him as though he were part of my own family because of the important, uncommon things that we share: we've taken heavy fire and been wounded. We know the vacant feeling you get in the soul when you lose a great friend in action, and the feeling of awe you get in the presence of strong leadership. We know the thrill of having good air support; he thinks of Marine Corps F4U Corsairs much as I do A-10 Warthogs. We know the ache of thirst—the wringing-your-socks-out-in-your-mouth kind, so deep you can feel it in your feet. We have witnessed up close the finality of death as well as almost surreal moments of unexpected peace. In 2003, on a recon mission in the Shatt al-Arab waterway, my team was hunkered down in a ruined Iraqi bunker, keeping watch on the wreck of a big tanker that had run aground. The reports said that the enemy was running drugs out of it. On day six, a storm rolled in. It didn't bother us, but it did stir up some hogs who were living in some brush nearby. It didn't take long before one of our snipers put one on the ground, and about fifteen minutes later I was field-dressing it for dinner, skewering it on rebar and roasting it with hot sauce taken from our MRE kits. We were happy.

It's exciting to chase the dragon. Combat is like a drug. There's nothing like the rush of fast-roping out of a helo, or walking down a street that everyone knows might be planted with an IED. Down there on the ground, life can get so intense you simply don't have time to be scared or impressed by anything. When I was out there alone during Operation Redwing, doing my best not to get killed, I always had an immediate goal to focus on. I'd pick out a big rock or a tree in the middle distance, and that would be my objective, my only concern—to traverse those hundred meters to reach that point. I always had a problem to work through. In fact, having been reared in the forests of East Texas, I found that there were a couple of times when I felt strangely at home up there. Bad as it was, part of me misses the hostile mountain, and the small rewards of surviving its challenges.

Master Chief retired from the teams in 2008, turning down a six-figure reenlistment bonus after twenty-one years. He had given the teams everything he had, and now it was enough. He had other plans. After he finished a graduate degree in global leadership, he took his special operations skill set to the corporate world. He's doing some work for a top-line sports equipment and apparel company, advising them on product development—lightweight outdoor boots and other gear for serious athletes—and strategy. He still crosses paths with his teammates once in a while, but he's a civilian now. The work isn't demanding in the same way as combat, but he's challenged and happy, and lucky to have some involvement with some of his brothers in the teams. I still can't get over the stories he told me of meeting corporate human resources people who questioned his fitness for a job because of his lack of experience in their particular industry. Not enough people appreciate what a guy like that brings to the table in terms of leadership, adaptability, and a hundred other skills and intangibles. Industry skill sets can be taught. The capabilities you have after more than two decades in the teams almost can't be measured. If a SEAL command master chief runs into that kind of nonsense, imagine how bad it can be for everyone else.

The boys from Task Unit Ramadi came home and continued taking on the world. Johnny Brands, who Morgan and Dozer carried out of a house in the Papa sector with both his feet nearly severed, is back in the game, a chief in a West Coast team, and still one of the fastest runners in the Naval Special Warfare community. Studdard came out of a long stay in the hospital to serve—as he had before joining the teams—as a firefighter in Colorado. He's laying his life on the line, helping other people, while also raising a family.

Our brotherhood closes up around its wounded. After the docs amputated Elliott Miller's left leg at the knee, he faced a hard climb in rehab. Dozer and some others who were in San Diego virtually moved in with him. For four months, in addition to their platoon duties, they tended to him, mending him in their team guy way, tending to his every need. Being frogs, they did a whole lot more than that, too: they hammered on him when he needed it, and he responded. Though the powers that be in the Navy sometimes thought the boys were going a little too hard on him, he gained strength fast under their care. Though they mean no harm, doctors are often professionally inclined to tell you what you can't do and outline in detail why. But where we come from, you do everything you can to prove them wrong. We take away our reasons not to try. So Dozer and the guys started helping him learn to speak again. Lesson by lesson, day by day, it was like going back to grade school. I don't think a brother can ask for more than that. But the point is that he never had to ask.

Elliott will be in a wheelchair for the rest of his life, but his courage changed his course in more ways than one. He impressed his physical therapist so much that she married him. Though he has great difficulty speaking, he still has plenty of game: as I write this, she's pregnant with their first child. With such courage, he lives out the saying Never Quit.

Many of my teammates from Task Unit Ramadi are still out there, bringing hell to our enemies: Commander Leonard, Senior Chief Steffen, Slab, Wink, Marty Robbins, and Jerry have moved on into deeper waters, doing things that would make all of us proud.

My friend Chris Kyle, the Team 3 sniper, is out of the Navy now. At Sadr City, he was in a hairy firefight during which, in the space of about two minutes, he took a bullet in the head and another in the back. Though his helmet and rear plate protected him from serious wounds, those bullets delivered a message he hadn't seemed to hear before: *I can die.* His wife, Taya, didn't mind having him follow that newly recognized logic to a family-friendly conclusion: *That was two too many close calls, and it's time for me to hang up my guns.* No one should ever think he's bulletproof, not even a tough redneck from Texas.

On a bitterly cold morning in early January of 2009, the war, in a sense, found Chris again. What happened to him not far from his home outside Dallas never made the news, since the town involved didn't want the publicity, but the incident would certainly have made national headlines had a reporter ever gotten a tip about it.

Chris was minding his own business, fueling his pickup truck at a gas station, when he found himself at gunpoint. Two men holding pistols demanded his truck. Law enforcement will usually advise you to give in to the criminal in a situation like this. And that's good advice. But Chris took another route. Very calmly and coolly, he sized up which of the two was handling his pistol more comfortably. He put his hands up and told them he was going to reach into the truck to get his keys. Then his hand went under his coat. From a waistband holster, he pulled his Colt 1911. Swinging the pistol under his left armpit, he gave each robber two .45-caliber Hydra-Shok hollow-points to the chest. By the time the cops responded to the 911 call from the terrified lady who had locked herself in a car behind Chris's truck, the matter was settled. Elapsed time: about ten seconds. The service station's security cameras caught the whole thing.

I pray for anyone whose life gets so desperate that he or she chooses to resort to a life of crime, but it's hard to resist a little cold laughter all the same: I mean, how unlucky a dumbass do you have to be to target a random guy for felony armed assault and find out he's killed more people than smallpox?

Incidents like Chris's can interrupt a veteran's best-laid plans to readjust to civilian life. I know, because war came for me a few months later.

It was April 1, 2009. The night started out like any

other. Recovering from surgery, I wasn't sleeping very much. Of course, I never do, but so much of life is the attitude you bring to it, and so much of your attitude depends on how you think and talk about what you do. The next sunrise always holds the promise of new possibilities—keep that front and center and it becomes a little easier to deal with the bags under your eyes.

That was my frame of mind as I was tooling around the family ranch near Huntsville one night—and was suddenly startled to hear the ring of a gunshot outside the house.

My first instinct was to check on my mother. Grabbing a pistol, I hurried to her room and got eyes on her. Satisfied that she was okay, I swept through the rest of the house, then ran outdoors.

I found her near the road. DASY, my four-year-old yellow Lab, was lying in a puddle of blood. She had been shot, and then beaten. A trail of blood ran back toward the street, marking her path to the place where she died.

Beyond the fence dividing our land from the dirt road, I noticed a suspicious car stopped, and four men inside. From where DASY was lying, I crawled across the grass and under the fence, crabbed through the culvert, and snuck up on the guys in the car. They had no idea I was there, less then thirty feet away from them. I had them dead to rights, but couldn't get a clear shot. As the driver put the car into gear and started onto the road, I ran to my truck, jumped in, cranked the engine, and peeled out after them. When they saw me in the rearview mirror, the chase was on.

As the pursuit began across the back roads of East Texas, I called 911 and told the operator what was happening, adding, "You need to get somebody out here, because if I catch them I'm going to kill them"—all four of them.

I believe in forgiveness, but these guys had gone too far. It was time to apply the old code: an eye for an eye, blood for blood.

The chase covered forty miles across three counties, sometimes at speeds in excess of a hundred miles an hour. It felt like business as usual.

The pursuit ended when we reached a roadblock set up by the Onalaska police department. With law enforcement on hand, I was able to hold back my rage and stop short of the inevitable. As the cops cuffed the men, I approached them and asked, "Which one of you killed my dog?" One of the guys started running his mouth about what he was going to do to me. He had no idea. I was silently running my mouth at myself, too, trying to talk myself out of putting another notch in my gun.

I'd seen human depravity at work in places much worse off than Walker County, Texas, but this came close to the worst of it for gratuitous cruelty. When I learned the details of what they had done—one of the guys beat DASY with a baseball bat before another guy shot her—I found myself craving ten minutes in a locked room with them. I'd spot them the baseball bat and the gun, and it wouldn't have mattered. What kind of trash beats a helpless dog with a baseball bat then shoots her? Believe me, it took everything I had not to engage. But I knew I wouldn't be much of a warrior if I failed to uphold the law I was sworn to protect, no matter how much the criminals deserved a penalty beyond the one spelled out in the statutes.

And their time will come. God sees everything. He saw me with tears in my eyes as I took DASY and buried her under a tree by a lake.

*   *   *

On September 24, 2009, the entire spec ops community took another blow that no one saw coming. Two days after undergoing successful reconstructive surgery, Ryan Job, the Team 3 gunner who had been hit in the face in Ramadi in the summer of '06, died of complications from his procedure in Arizona.

It was not considered a combat-related death. It was referred to in his medical records as a "hospital-acquired injury." Ryan had recovered well enough to climb Mount Rainier after coming home. He trained for a triathlon, and married his girlfriend, Kelly. We lost a brave soul and fine warrior who survived horrendous wounds and deserved to live a long, fulfilling life. Kelly was three months pregnant with their daughter when Ryan passed. He never met his child. Being a new father myself, I can't imagine the pain Kelly has gone through. She will always have a family in the teams. God bless her.

We all have our crosses to bear. We carry them heavily, out of love for our brothers in arms. But sometimes you have to let go of the idea that anyone down here is in control.

21

Family Ties

In October 2009, after Morgan was injured in that helicopter crash during the training exercise off Virginia Beach, he tackled rehab as I always did: pissed off that his body had broken down and willing to push himself like a madman to get back to his team.

After he joined me in Pensacola for rehab, he needed just five months to get back to his fighting weight. When he finally checked out of Athletes' Performance, the docs couldn't believe it. He finished the program a lot faster than anyone expected.

In April 2010, he linked up with his team again as they deployed to the Middle East. While he was over there, wouldn't you know it, he flew several missions with the same aircrew who had crashed on that ship with him that night.

Back home, as I traveled around the country as a keynote speaker, I never would have thought that my story would have the power to motivate others. When I met the people who had come to hear me, I saw that my career was just the tip of an iceberg that reached deep into the ocean beneath me, far out of my sight. It was natural to feel kinship with my SEAL teammates. But there were so many other military men and women, including those from different service branches and periods of history, without whose service nothing we do would be possible today.

My experience getting healed up ultimately helped give me the vision to launch a foundation dedicated to caring for those who sacrificed part of themselves in service to America. I established the Lone Survivor Foundation as a nonprofit entity in February 2010, and set to work raising money to develop programs to restore, empower, and renew hope for wounded service members and their families using therapeutic support, health, and wellness tools, with an emphasis on the kind of outdoor experiences that have helped get me right after coming home.

We worked to bring on an excellent medical staff— volunteers who specialize in the types of injuries that combat vets often have—to work directly with the soldiers and schedule retreats. And as we got our nonprofit designation, we put together a board that has a high level of motivation and understands the community of wounded warriors they serve. They see that a warrior's wounds affect not only the veteran but his or her family, too.

Shortly after the Lone Survivor Foundation was put together, I met Sherri Reuland, an orthodontist from Tyler, Texas, who was so moved by *Lone Survivor* that she came up with a creative idea to give back to the men and women who protect this country. Sherri and four of her friends started the Boot Campaign, an awareness campaign based on selling official "Give Back" combat boots.

The group tries to honor those in uniform while using the net proceeds to support veterans' charities such as the LSF and others.

My destiny took another turn in June 2010, as the Lone Survivor Foundation was preparing to host its inaugural fund-raising gala in Houston. A gracious man from Houston, Brad Juneau, became involved in supporting the foundation, thanks to his friendship with an old college fraternity brother of mine, Danny Cortez. Danny knew Brad had a passion for helping military men and women, so he and Andy McGee, another lifelong friend of mine, talked me into going to visit Brad's ranch one weekend. It wasn't far from where I lived. Around that time, I got introduced via e-mail to his daughter, Melanie. Long story short, Mel was on a long vacation in Belize, so we e-mailed and texted each other while I was having a guy's weekend at her father's ranch. Then we started talking on the phone—often for five to eight hours—every night. (I never did have the heart to tell Brad that I was talking to his daughter while I was hanging out with him during the day.)

After about five thousand dollars' worth of international cell phone charges, I knew I had to meet her as soon as she got home. We had a date planned for Friday, three days after she got back. But I decided not to wait that long. While she was still in flight to Houston, I texted her and said, "There is no way we're going to be in the same state together and we're not going to meet." We met that night at a restaurant in the Woodlands. The moment I laid eyes on her, I knew she was the one. We sat at the bar and talked until the place closed down. Then I walked her to her car, gave her a kiss good-night, got in my truck, and sent her a text saying, "This is the last time you will ever leave without me." And it was. The day after that, we officially started our life together.

I would have married her in a heartbeat if it weren't for one small complication: I had to wait for Morgan's blessing. And Morgan was in Iraq. I understood quickly that my personal life couldn't go far before Morgan got loose of the war.

Team guys look after each other, but some need the help more than others do. Take JT, for example. He would get so quickly smitten with one woman after another that we were constantly having to save him from himself. His next girl was always the One. He was so easily swept away that the guys in his platoon nicknamed him True Love. His heart was always out there, looking for Mrs. Right. In a case like that, it was a team guy's duty to protect his brother, to keep him whole, healthy, and focused. If he was going to get serious, his girl had to go through us. JT knew how to love and he knew how to serve. But it was always a team effort to keep love and service in practical harmony. With JT it was a full-time job.

A few months after Mel and I started dating, we entertained a visitor who had had a profound impact on me, to say the least. The last I'd seen of Gulab was the night he was taken, terrified, off Spanky's helicopter at Asadabad. He was debriefed by our intel guys, then returned to Sabray. The military eventually repaid his friendship by having some engineers build roads and establish an electrical infrastructure in his village. Because of the danger posed by the Taliban, Gulab and his family were moved, for their protection, to an undisclosed location. But after he saved my life, I never had the chance to thank him personally. I was able to get in touch with him through some special friends in Afghanistan, a Green Beret named Joe, and an Army civil affairs officer, Major Clint Hanna. With these capable guys working their channels, I had been hoping to get him Stateside in time for the Lone Survivor Foundation gala, but a delay in paperwork kept that from happening.

By the time his flight finally reached Houston in late September, the only agenda I had was the one that really mattered: personal gratitude. When we met Gulab at the Houston airport, he was carrying a single backpack for luggage and was in the company of two men: an interpreter and a military friend who had greased the wheels for his visit. Gulab was exactly as I remembered him: dark, sure on his feet, with chiseled facial features that even his heavy black beard could not conceal. I felt his serenity and his courage, too—the same qualities that had enabled him to refuse that Taliban commander who demanded that Gulab allow him to take me from the village.

Being reunited with Gulab brought me a feeling of comfort and ease similar to what I had felt with Morgan, JT, Josh, and JJ and my family after coming home from Afghanistan. Gulab was my teammate, just as they were, and I drew strength from his presence. He took care of me at his home; now it was my turn to take care of him.

He stayed with us for more than two weeks. Mel and I took him to places he wouldn't be likely to see in his part of Afghanistan. At the Museum of Natural Science, he didn't know what to make of the Tyrannosaurus rex skeleton. The look on his face was priceless as he asked the interpreter whether something like that could really have walked the earth.

We found an Afghan restaurant that he seemed to like. (The only American food he really enjoyed was glazed doughnuts. He also knocked down bottle after bottle of antacid tablets.) Later, Mel and I took him to dinner at the Petroleum Club of Houston. I'll never forget Gulab standing by the floor-to-ceiling windows in the forty-third-floor dining room, gazing out at the city's sea of lights. He couldn't believe the freedom we enjoyed in America, where you could get into a car and drive as far as the eye could see. Such liberty was as alien to him as the T. rex.

A few months before his arrival, he and one of his cousins were driving home when they were ambushed by some militia. During the fight, Gulab was hit in the hip and his cousin was killed. Just a normal day—that's how he described it to me. Since our time together his house has been burned down, his car blown up, and he's been shot. After I picked him up at the airport, I asked him what he wanted to do first. He replied, "Blow up your car, burn down your house, and then shoot you in the hip." Of course he was joking, but it really hit home just how much he had sacrificed to save my life. He is a true hero.

Throughout his stay, we sensed his anxiety over his family. He still had family living in Sabray, as far as we could learn. He remained in contact with them, and what they told him didn't always bring him peace. There were always firefights and explosions from IED attacks in the area.

On the last day of September, Morgan returned from his deployment and we all linked up with him in Washington. Mel and I thought it was pretty hilarious to see the expression on Gulab's face when he saw how much my brother and I resembled each other. When Gulab and he embraced, I felt a circle becoming complete.

We visited the White House, got a tour of the Pentagon, and went to Arlington National Cemetery. At the Newseum, a news museum on Pennsylvania Avenue, there's an exhibit devoted to 9/11. It features a huge wall displaying coverage of the attacks from the front pages of newspapers around the world. Seeing it brought home the reasons that I had been started down the path that brought me crashing into Gulab's world.

He told us that he never wanted any gratitude—no money, nothing—for simply doing something Allah wanted him to do. He said he couldn't believe anyone could have survived what I had gone through. If the overwhelming force of militia didn't kill me, the terrain should have, he said. He added that when he first saw me in his village, he saw mercy in my eyes and felt called by Allah to protect me to the end.

In Washington, Melanie was finally able to spend some time with Morgan. Thus began her audition, if you will, to join the family as his sister-in-law (or outlaw, as we like to say in Texas). It didn't go well. Maybe because he felt that our relationship had gone too far while he was out of the loop overseas, he put up the wall and didn't let her in, remaining as cold as bare steel. Hell, he'd only been home from Iraq for a few days—his nerves were still tuned for fast-roping out of helos on midnight raids, not dealing with his brother's new girlfriend.

It was only later, when Morgan and Mel got back to Texas, that my brother finally thawed out. They spent some time alone together and got to know each other. It went great. It was all just a formality as far as I was concerned, but with the visit complete, I could breathe deeply. I was in the clear to propose to her, and with Morgan in tow, we got it done. Now that I think about it, I can't remember if I asked her or if Morgan did. I remember being on a knee with the ring and then it was over. Either way, mission complete.

After I posted news of Gulab's visit on Facebook, several hundred of the folks who keep up with me there sent greeting cards to him. I was glad to see the outpouring of love and respect. When we hauled the cards home from the Lone Survivor Foundation office and showed them to Gulab, he, too, was touched.

To further break the ice, Mel picked up some Rosetta Stone language-teaching software so that she could learn Pashto. Gulab thought it was the funniest thing ever. As she played with it, trying to familiarize herself with his language, he teased us, revealing a sarcastic, even smart-ass side to his personality that I hadn't seen before. But when Brad asked him what he and his friends could do to help him and his village, Gulab became earnest and serious. Educational and medical supplies were urgent needs, he said. We shipped a couple of boxes of bandages, wraps, and antiseptic cream, and put word out on Facebook, where people responded generously, as they always do.

As Gulab's visit ended, Mel and I began preparing for our wedding, and Morgan returned to Virginia. He was in a place similar to where I was when I returned from Iraq in 2006. After eight deployments and a training accident that he was lucky to survive, he'd put a whole lot of mileage on his chassis. Having earned the rank of lieutenant, junior grade, he decided it was time to hang up his fins. He accepted a transfer from his team to a headquarters at "the Creek" in Virginia Beach. His plan to was endure a year of riding a desk, then make the transition out of the Navy.

We all had our transitions to make. The last week of November, Mel and I tied the knot at her dad's ranch, where our late-night talks had begun. In front of three hundred friends and family seated on the long slope behind the main house, we said our vows as the sun set behind the lake. It was a perfect night, pure magic. I couldn't be more proud to call her my wife. Though the late autumn air was damn cold, my heart was warm and full. Marrying Melanie was the greatest accomplishment of my life. It took me a long time to find her, and I wasn't going to waste another second more without her as my wife.

Part III

How We Die

22

Heroes of the Day

Unless Morgan is overseas, I almost always keep my cell phone turned off after ten o'clock. For some reason that night in Washington, D.C., in the first week of August 2011, I left it on. After midnight, it began ringing on my hotel room desk, vibrating on a room-service menu. I didn't answer. A few seconds later, it started a second time. I left it alone. When the phone rang again, I walked over to it and saw that the name on the display belonged to Boe, a former teammate of ours. Given the hour, I knew this was no social call.

I grabbed the phone, swiped my finger across the glass, and said, "Who did we lose?"

When he told me he didn't know, but that things didn't look good for some buddies of ours who had been in a helicopter that went down, my inability to sleep suddenly became convenient. I was going to be up for a while.

When I checked in with Boss, who was home in Virginia Beach, it turned out that he had sensed something had happened even before I gave him the news. Early every evening, when it was oh-dark-hundred in the Middle East, Boss thought of his teammates downrange, doing their thing. Knowing their work made the world a slightly safer place each night, he always swelled with quiet pride. All of us do this. We try to keep up with who's home and who's overseas, who they're with and what they might be doing. But that Friday night, Boss was sitting on the couch, chilling with his wife, Amy, and their curly-dark-haired baby daughter, Lulu, when something unusual happened. Suddenly he felt ill, a sickening, dehydrated sensation. He went upstairs to lie down for a while, stopping in the bathroom along the way. His urine was clear—this told him that, physically, he should have been good to go. He drank a glass of water and tried to rest, but couldn't shake the unsettled feeling. He said to Amy, "I think JT might be involved in something. Something's happened." He tooled around the house a little, still never feeling quite right, then turned in around eleven thirty. About an hour later I buzzed him from D.C.

When Boss picked up the phone, I figured he had already gotten the news, so I said, "Hey bro, you got any updates?"

"Updates? On what?"

"On JT."

There was silence on the other end of the line. JT and Morgan were his best friends in the world.

"His bird went down. We're waiting for more news."

Details were hard to confirm, but with each call, the magnitude of the loss was revealed in grim increments.

At first, the death toll was put at five. Though it was known that a troop from JT's squadron was involved, no one knew anything more. A subsequent call raised the number of dead to eleven. Then seventeen, twenty-one, twenty-seven, and then the final tally: thirty-eight souls. Everyone on board that bird was gone: thirty Americans, eight Afghans, and a dog.

Twenty-two of the U.S. KIA were SEALs. There was a pair of Air Force PJs and a combat controller, five soldiers from the Chinook's aircrew, and a brilliant Belgian Malinois attached to the unit as a military working dog.

When someone texted Boss the list of fatalities, he said out loud to no one, "This can't be true." He knew every one of those guys. They were some of the finest talent in the SEAL community and, more than that, friends: Aaron "Trey" Vaughn, Matt Mills, JT.... "There's no way we've lost every single man," he said.

But it was no mistake. As the phone lines continued to burn, we eventually confirmed the death toll. Proportionally speaking, the losses on that helo were to that team what losing a nuclear-powered aircraft carrier would be to the Navy at large—almost 10 percent of its fighting strength. And Boss, for one, felt it happen from seven thousand miles away. The loss of those three men hit our circle hard. Morgan and Trey Vaughn were very close. They had shared space at our house in Virginia Beach. Matt was a great guy, a Texas boy from Dallas who I'd known my whole career. Our community is so small that any death will always make you feel the ripple. But JT's loss stabbed us deepest of all.

After a sleepless night in my Washington hotel, I had little spirit left for the speech I was supposed to give later that day. It was a big event and I had to show. Before I went on stage, my hosts played a short video recounting Operation Redwing. It said that the losses we took— nineteen men—were the worst ever in the history of the

SEALs. When I went on stage, the first thing I had to do was update the record.

"It's been a crappy day," I said. "And I'm sorry to say that video is now incorrect. The teams have had a mass casualty. We've lost a lot of our teammates. Twenty-two SEALs died in Afghanistan last night."

The news shocked the audience. In May, after SEAL operators killed Osama bin Laden on a midnight air-assault raid into Pakistan, the teams—and especially the one JT served with—became a popular obsession all over again. The simultaneous loss of so many of our best operators became a big story. (Some reports suggested that some of the frogmen who helped take out bin Laden died in the August shootdown. It wasn't true.)

A lady in the front row put her face into her hands. There was stirring, nervous murmuring, and some sobs. All that the news media had reported so far was that a NATO helicopter had gone down in Afghanistan. I didn't relish my role as the messenger, but I had to tell the audience that I was simply in no condition to continue talking. I rambled a little and finally said, "I'm sorry, ladies and gentlemen, but my mind's on something else." As my voice choked up, I broke it off. I nodded apologetically to everybody and walked off the stage. The only thing I knew to do was make flank speed to Norfolk. I had to be with my brother and our teammates. The wreckage of the helo was still smoldering on the ground when I was en route to join them in their grief.

The last that was ever heard from JT's helo was a simple announcement of its ETA. "Three minutes out," the co-pilot said.

About sixty miles west of Kabul, they were inbound to a hot LZ in the Tangi Valley in Wardak Province, where a platoon of Rangers was shooting it out with Taliban forces. What started as a snatch-and-grab of a high-value target turned into a sustained firefight after the enemy detected the ground forces' approach. As the tracers began to fly, the Rangers' target, a warlord who controlled Taliban forces in the valley, tried to hightail it out of the area with several of his lieutenants. They took off like rabbits scrambling for the brush.

The Rangers, tied down under fire, couldn't pursue. Seeing his prize slipping away, the U.S. commander called for help in cutting off the escape route of the squirters. Our boys were the handiest rifles available. That night they didn't have their own op to run, so they were standing by as a quick reaction force, or what we call a spin-up team. When the Rangers called, they went. JT and his brothers piled into a fueled, loaded, and ready CH-47D Chinook flown by Army reservists from Bravo Company of Task Force Knighthawk, part of the Tenth Combat Aviation Brigade. That bird had thirty-three seats, and it took off full.

The Chinook, call sign Extortion 17, was inbound fast, tracing the floor of a valley at an altitude of about three hundred feet, when enemy fighters on the slopes took it under fire. From the tower of a two-story mud-brick building about two hundred meters to the helo's south, Taliban fighters fired two or three RPGs in rapid succession. The first rocket missed, but the second hit the aft rotor assembly and exploded, slicing away ten feet of a fiberglass blade.

The helo jerked violently and lost altitude fast. Inside,

anyone who wasn't thrown out the open rear ramp was shaken so hard that he couldn't have been conscious when the Chinook finally burst into flames. It was about three a.m. when Extortion 17 hit the deck.

The Rangers rushed to secure the crash site. No extended Air Force CSAR mission, no long march by a ground team, would be needed to bring these fallen warriors home. But the Taliban commander got away, and the men who shot down the Chinook were soon on the run, too, reportedly trying to escape into Pakistan.

JT. Everyone knew him by his initials. He was also called JT Money, inspired by the pep talk Vince Vaughn gave to his down-and-out friend in the movie *Swingers*. His unit worked in the shadows, but in death—as long as we live well—we all come into heaven's light. So, too, with our fallen brother. Now we can honor him by the name his parents, George and Kathy, of Rockford, Iowa, gave him: Jon Thomas Tumilson. He was money.

It had been JT who had kept watch over Morgan when my brother was in the hospital and whose way with the nurses had given us the smoke screen necessary to evacuate Morgan from the premises. And now...

Boss and Morgan greeted me at the airport in Norfolk. Boss was in BUD/S with me and had gotten tight with JT during a Team 1 deployment to Baghdad. Both were hugely outgoing nonconformists with strong moral codes. In 2009, right before JT went to the East Coast, he and Morgan served as best men at Boss's wedding. Boss's bride, Amy, became like a sister to us in the teams. She understood us, was strong enough to stand up to us, and was therefore the ideal partner for a hard-driving guy like

Boss. Along the way, she became as close to JT as his sisters, Joy and Kristie, were.

Family was important to JT. One Christmas, when his parents weren't expecting him to be home, he surprised them by jumping out of a large wrapped box. (Stealth— that's how our best guys roll.)

Soon Mel joined up with us, as did our friends Scott, Andy McGee, and some others, too. We circled up and leaned on each other for strength.

The Tumilson family asked the crew to bring JT's personal belongings to Iowa. It was an honor to be asked, and as more of our friends and teammates rolled into town, we had enough strength in numbers to handle the pain of going to his house in Virginia Beach and breaking it down.

We loaded anything the family might want, including his Honda CBR1000RR sport bike and several mountain bikes, into the bed of our pickup trucks for the drive home to Iowa. As we rummaged through JT's closets, attic, and storage containers, we tried to wrap our minds around what had been lost. Sorting through his familiar collection of crazy, offensive T-shirts, outdoor gear, weapons, plaques and awards, and a number of things we hadn't seen before—shoe boxes full of photos of friends and family, and other personal things he held close—we saw a great patriot's life scroll before us like a history lesson.

JT had a chocolate Lab named Hawkeye, who he loved like a son. Scott inherited Hawkeye, as per JT's will. The neighbors were great, bringing food and standing by to help. No one seemed to know what to say. Really, there were no words: "I'm sorry"—that was all you could offer.

The final culmination of JT's quest to become a Texan was his pickup truck, a Chevy Silverado 2500HD. As he pursued his quest, Morgan and I treated him as though he were a student in the Lone Star State version of BUD/S every step of the way. When he first visited us in Huntsville, driving some other brand, we gave him a hard time. When he got smart and bought that Chevy, then jacked up the suspension with a six-inch lift kit, we said he was driving a "low rider." (If you're going Texas-style, you've gotta have at least fourteen inches of lift.) JT spent hours poring over accessories catalogs, only to decide on Baja fenders. But in Texas, you need a full-on Ranch Hand replacement kit, strong enough to brush aside a cow. (Or at least that's what we told him.) When he brought around his latest model, we asked him why anyone living in urban Virginia needed a Duramax diesel 4x4 with twenty-two-inch BMF Novakane Death Metal eight-lug rims (six hundred bucks apiece). It was almost a respectable vehicle for Walker County, but *Norfolk?* We also had to point out to him that no self-respecting rancher would drive a truck painted that awful metallic blue. "With that rig, you're on a road to nowhere, bro." The one-upmanship twisted him in knots, but it kept him hustling.

Now, looking at that metallic blue Silverado in the driveway, all we could do was smile and love him for the dedication and passion he brought to everything. True Love was one of a kind.

We soon learned that on the morning JT died, he had sent the people closest to him some very emotional e-mails. He had told more than a few of us he didn't think he'd come home from this deployment. When he'd said that to Morgan and me when he was visiting Texas on leave, we didn't think much of it—all of us say that kind of thing from time to time. But we don't say it *much.* Yet now, every time anyone mentioned JT speaking this way, somebody else would pipe up with, "Yeah, he said that to me, too." So JT knew. And Boss felt it happen. Considering this in light of my own experiences, I do believe these spooky feelings mean something.

After our work at JT's place was done, we went to see the widow of another frogman who died on that helo, Chief Matt Mills. We knew him from way back in 2002, having met at SEAL Qualification Training. He was an Arlington, Texas, guy who we all liked and respected. We did what we could for his wife, Keri, and their children, taking care of the trash and cleaning house. We told Keri stories about Matt and held her close.

The following day, August 9, I parted company with the gang for a quick trip to Chicago. That night, Boss, Morgan, Scott, Justin, Sean, and Andy finished loading up and hit the road for Iowa. Boss was at the wheel of JT's Silverado with Scott, Sean, and Hawkeye riding along. Morgan drove his own rig, hauling Justin and McGee. With a playlist of JT's favorite music cycling through— "Fallen Angel" by Poison, "Back Down South" by Kings of Leon, "Hero of the Day" by Metallica, Toby Keith's "American Soldier," "Chicken Fried" by the Zac Brown Band, on and on—they cruised through the Shenandoah Valley into West Virginia and Ohio, keeping up a ninety-mile-an-hour pace. Soon, the cops were onto them—not with their radar guns, but to provide an escort. And when word got around about what was happening, people turned out in a big way, rendezvousing with my brothers in Indiana and taking them to the border of the next jurisdiction, each patrol handing off to their colleagues across the city limits or county line.

Boss and Morgan could have taken any exit between Norfolk and Des Moines and been less than a morning's drive from someone who was ready to lend a hand. Offers of places to stay, home-cooked meals, support, and friendship came from South Carolina, Pennsylvania, Maryland, Oklahoma, South Dakota, Indiana, Wisconsin, Georgia, Ohio, California, Tennessee, New Mexico, Kentucky, and Arizona. That reads like lyrics from a Johnny Cash song. Each time they crossed a state line, they stopped for a group photo with JT's Gadsden flag—the yellow one from colonial times, with the rattlesnake and the slogan, "Don't Tread on Me." Volunteers donated gift certificates for gas and food. Melanie followed through diligently, responding to all the generous offers and helping all the chaotic goodwill that was stirred up online materialize as the guys continued their trip.

Whenever I get down, I always try to remember: this is the kind of country we live in, a country of decent, caring people who stand by to help a good cause.

Late on the first night, they reached Louisville. Thanks to the Facebook family, they got not only good advice on a place to stay but also rounded up some volunteers who stood watch in the hotel parking lot, keeping an eye on their precious cargo overnight. The next day, the mayor of Indianapolis met them. With a police escort, they visited Lucas Oil Stadium, home of the Indianapolis Colts. At the Indianapolis Motor Speedway, they kissed the bricks. Then they toured the Congressional Medal of Honor Memorial, where there's a tribute to Mikey Murphy, among other great heroes.

Meanwhile, downrange, in the world's dangerous places, our teammates had stayed busy, as they always do. On the night of August 9, news broke that a U.S. special operations team had tracked the men who had shot down that Chinook as they tried to flee into Pakistan. The insurgents were all killed in an air strike. We knew it would happen eventually, and those headlines produced some quiet satisfaction, but that's the most that can be said for it.

And when the media got wind of the journey of the blue pickup and showed up shoving microphones in people's faces, Boss, Morgan, and the guys had to go undercover. Several hundred people converged on them at a gas station, thanks to a tip that some reporters had found them there. Boss escaped detection by telling the interviewer there had been a misunderstanding: he was just another ordinary American patriot, looking to catch a glimpse of the road-trippers.

Speeding through Illinois and reaching the Iowa state line, they stopped for another photo op. The sheriff from Rockford—one of George's close friends, who had known JT since he was a kid—took over escort duty. In Davenport, they linked up with some Patriot Guard Riders. A Good Samaritan paid for their hotel room.

On Friday afternoon, after three full days on the road, they finally reached Rockford. Over the next few days, the brotherhood showed up in force. At least thirty-five of JT's teammates rolled into town. Mel and I flew into Minneapolis and joined them with our new baby, Axe, and spent several days getting the family ready for JT.

The following Thursday, JT's body was flown in from Dover to Mason City. The white hearse carrying his casket was the centerpiece of a procession that included a dozen police cars and about five hundred bikers from the Patriot Guard Riders. When JT reached Rockford, both sides of Highway 122 outside town were lined with people holding American flags. Many of them were small kids. In town, the Avenue of the Saints was jammed as JT came home. Red, white, and blue was everywhere: bunting, shirts, and flags of every size. It was a patriotic town honoring its fallen son and his family, and it did them proud.

The governor of Iowa and one of its U.S. senators were among the fifteen hundred people who gathered in the gym at the Rudd–Rockford–Marble Rock Community School for the memorial service. Display cases in the foyer showed his valor awards. His citation for a Bronze Star with a "V" was a snapshot of his work as a frogman. It read:

For heroic achievement in connection with combat operations against the enemy as task unit communicator and sniper for Naval Special Warfare Task Unit–Habbaniyah in direct support of Operation Iraqi Freedom from 17 October 2005 to 21 April 2006. Petty Officer Tumilson trained eighty Iraqi soldiers and advised them during the execution of over sixty combat operations. On 4 April 2006, he performed exceptionally under fire while providing critical precision fire on enemy forces to break up an ambush and allow his fellow soldiers to egress to safety. By his extraordinary guidance, zealous initiative, and total dedication to duty, Petty Officer Tumilson reflected great credit upon himself and upheld the highest traditions of the United States Naval Service.

A day in the life.

In front of the stage, the pallbearers and the rest of the

SEALs were seated on the front row to the right. Hawkeye lay down on the floor in front of Scott.

JT's "final message to the world" was played: a fast-moving Irish song by Flogging Molly, "If I Ever Leave This World Alive." His sisters spoke tearfully of his love for his family, his zest for life, and his lasting influence on them and their children. We all stood up and shared stories, animated by turns with love, anger, and humor, each one a different shade of loss. Boe said he never met another man who could match JT's combination of size, speed, and power. "He was unafraid and loved the work. If JT had known his helo would be shot down while going to the aid of others, he would have chosen to go anyway. If you knew JT, you would know that."

At one point Scott let go of Hawkeye's leash, and damn if the dog didn't wander over to the center aisle, approach the casket, and lie down on the gymnasium floor in front of JT. He stayed there for a while, and nobody wanted to move him. Photos of that moment went viral and got a lot of attention on cable news. It was a powerful moment, one I know I will never forget.

At Riverside Cemetery, north of town, the crowd re-assembled, encircled by Patriot Guard Riders and police. All the SEALs lined up and filed past the coffin, performing our traditional ritual. As each frogman passed JT, he stopped, placed his Trident on the coffin, and pounded in its steel spike with a blow of his fist. This signifies that when a SEAL dies, a part of each of us goes with him. When he reaches the afterlife, he still has them by his side. In death as in life, we stand together, always a family, always a team. The brotherhood never dies.

Almost all frogmen have had the experience of burying

a brother in arms. There's nothing you can do to erase the pain of loss. But you can spread it around and dull its sting. We told every story we could think about this great warrior's days on earth. We helped the family take care of business. All I can say about JT that squares his no-limits personality with the finality of his death is this: he went to heaven for the climb, and for the company.

In his all-too-brief life, JT had summited every peak put before him and cleared every hurdle, had become a SEAL, a champion triathlete, and a chosen member of our most elite unit. One thing he never achieved was taken care of as soon as the news of his death reached Rick Perry: the governor of Texas made JT an honorary Texan. The family has the officially stamped certificate to prove it. It may have come a little late here on Mother Earth, but don't worry, brother, I hear the good Lord has a special place in heaven for good ol' Texas boys.

On September 21, about a month after we all got home from Iowa, the Taliban commander who was the original target of that raid in the Tangi Valley was killed in an air strike. As with the August 9 strike that took out his henchman, the one who had downed the bird, it was small comfort to the families of the fallen, and to our community.

Only when a mission goes wrong or spectacularly right do our most elite warriors come out of the shadows. A hundred other strikes on high-value targets in the months prior to August 9 had netted gains bigger than that one. But somewhere JT, Trey, and Matt, along with all the others, had to be proud to know that their brothers had delivered some payback. Never forgive. Never forget.

The hero of *The Count of Monte Cristo* saw grief and

happiness as relative things. "There is neither happiness nor misery in the world; there is only the comparison of one state with another, nothing more," Alexandre Dumas wrote. He continued, "He who has felt the deepest grief is best able to experience supreme happiness." I think that's why most of us understood that our heavy hearts weren't the end of everything. The sadness we still feel opens us to an even greater joy with our loved ones. In that way, the men we lose truly become immortal.

23

The Warrior Queens

Throughout my time in the military I have had the privilege of serving with or knowing some of the finest people in the world, people who would give up everything for our flag and what it stands for, no matter what the cost.

In this chapter, I would like to bring to light a group of people who more often than not go overlooked, a group that never seeks the spotlight but undoubtedly deserves it more than our most decorated warfighters do. Through good times and bad, they hold the line, usually with no formal training and certainly with no benefit of rank or pay. Still, I think the spouses of our men and women in uniform are one of our nation's most valuable assets for how they support the war effort, without ever firing a shot. It's their ability to remain steadfast under a thousand types of pressure that enables us to go out and do what needs to be done downrange. On the bad days, we need them most. We lean hard on the ones who are closest to us yet also sometimes the farthest away.

Some of the best frogmen I've ever seen work are family men. Part of the hidden reason for their success was the strength and character of their wives back home. While they were gone, they couldn't afford to worry about the particular issues their wives were dealing with. But they did know their wives were strong enough to take care of themselves and the kids, and hold down the fort while they were on deployment.

A lot of women don't make it, and I don't blame them. I was never married when I was in the teams, and I don't know that I could have been. This career is hard on relationships; the divorce rate in SEAL marriages is said to be around 80 percent.

But here are a few stories of some really strong women who held it together for their men. You will read about Amy, Diane, Kristy, and Kimberly. Each in her own way is a warrior in her own right. You've met Amy already. She's on her second pregnancy at the moment, with her husband serving in Afghanistan (and recently extended). Diane is known as "Momma Shipley"; she is married to one of the toughest old frogs out there and has a son in the teams to boot. Kristy is a pseudonym for the widow of one of our fallen but never-forgotten teammates who died in Afghanistan on August 6, 2011. Kimberly is the widow of Trey Vaughn, KIA 8/6/11. She is left behind taking care of two beautiful children.

Here are their stories.

By Amy

Being married to a Navy SEAL is no joke. It's so much harder than people realize.

I have known my husband for twelve years. We met as

friends; I was in a serious relationship and so was he. Like many SEALs, Boss (yes, I call my husband by his nickname and I love it) was married once before. It was what we call a "starter marriage" (a typical situation: young and naive, wrong combo from the start). He was a new SEAL, dedicated and not sure how to balance family and work life, and she just couldn't, or wouldn't, handle just how hard this life can be.

Years later, when both of us were single, life eventually brought us together. After another deployment, he called me up and said, "I'll be in the U.S. in a few hours. Let's hang out." He showed up on my doorstep...and never left. We've been together ever since.

And my life has never been the same.

For most of our relationship, he's been away more than he's been home. The first deployment, I thought I was prepared. After all, I had known him for years and he was away plenty of times before. Well, I wasn't prepared. Nothing can truly prepare you. You just have to live it. The first deployment I turned into a bit of a crazy person—my man and all of my buddies were gone in Iraq, and I had no idea how to cope. But I learned quickly the most valuable asset to a wife in our community: support. Support from family, friends, other wives, neighbors, hell, you'll accept favors from strangers. You have no choice. I once asked a total stranger off the street to come into my house and kill what was I swear the world's biggest, most terrifying cockroach; it was the size of a small dog, and I just couldn't do it that day. I rely on so many people, and that is the key for me; that is literally what keeps me going while he's gone. Well, that and many good bottles of wine.

A few years later, Boss proposed. The story of our engagement pretty much illustrates the character of our marriage. For years, Boss has called me his Warrior Queen. We traveled to Greece for a much needed, long-overdue vacation (I'm Greek and wanted to visit my homeland). The last day of an incredible two-week trip, we drove from Athens to the original site of the Battle of Thermopylae. Today it's nothing more than a pit stop off the side of the highway. Tour buses cruise by, stop for photo ops, and drive off. It's not particularly picturesque. Over the course of time, the coastline has extended several miles, so it no longer borders the water. To us, however, the site was awe inspiring. Across the highway, up a small dusty hill, where the final battle occurred, the Spartans, including King Leonidas, are said to be buried. There lies a simple bronze tablet with an epitaph to them that reads: "Go and tell the Spartans, stranger passing by / That here, obedient to their laws, we lie."

On this spot and on one knee, Boss proposed to me. "We have a great love. I'll always treat you with respect and honor, until the end of my days." After a moment of disbelief, I whispered a sobbing yes.

He never promised it would be easy, he never promised he'd be home when I needed him, he never promised they'd all come home alive. He almost should have said, "I'll be mentally and physically gone, *a lot.* I'll be in danger, I can't always tell you details, money will always be tight, you'll have to become the rock in the family and hold everything together by yourself, you'll likely have to leave your friends and family and career and move to another city across the country, you'll spend a lot of nights alone, oh, and you'll never be able to afford those fancy shoes that you want, but you'll have a new family, you'll be stronger than you ever imagined, and you'll never regret it."

Unlike some wives, I don't watch the news when he's overseas. We have developed our own basic code for the phone—random words and sayings in order to discern where he is, if he's "working," how long he'll be gone, and so on. We usually can't communicate anything substantive, so I wait. I wait for a journal, which he keeps and sends home several months in. I wait for a phone convo or e-mail with some of our lingo to clue me in a little. And I wait for him to walk in the door and, one day, tell me everything he's been through.

Being the wife of a SEAL you have to be flexible. Boss refused to get married without his closest friends (most of whom are also SEALs, all on different schedules). Needless to say, we had four wedding dates and lost three deposits! We had eleven groomsmen! But I had a whole pack of new brothers.

And to me, they are my brothers. His teammates are all special to me and have made this life so damn fun. JT, Morgan, Marcus, and so many men are my brothers. We are a family. And when we unexpectedly lost JT, I finally understood the old SEAL saying: The only easy day was yesterday. Like many wives in this community, my husband's teammates are my family, too. They have taken care of me, and I them, so many times over the years that their presence in my marriage is indispensible. JT would call and e-mail on deployments when he knew Boss couldn't. If they were out partying all night on a work trip, JT would send reassuring updates and text me. The guys always took me out to dinner, to concerts, came over for movies, for breakfast, called me to check in and make sure I was okay. I cooked for them and gave tons of rides to the airport. We went out drinking more times than I can count. When I was pregnant, Morgan, Marcus, JT, and so many others, even guys who were no longer in the military, totally took care of me. They took me out to dinner, exercised my dog, set up movie dates, you name it. All I had to do was call and they were there. One night, I was seven months pregnant while Boss was in Afghanistan, and being particularly lonely and overly hormonal, I called JT up for a dinner date. "Hell yes, pick you up in an hour. Oh, is it okay if Andrea joins us? She's pregnant, too, and I don't want her to be alone." We all went out and he had us carefree and laughing in no time.

At one point, while Boss was out of town, JT and I went to the local watering hole, spent the entire night at the bar drinking and laughing. Boss got a call from someone the next day, reporting that I was brazenly out with another guy. Without hesitation or question, Boss replied, "Yeah, she was partying with my brother. It's all good." JT was one of our third wheels (we had a few—lots of single guys in the teams). He was close like this with so many other couples and supportive of so many other wives. I was only one of many women he was there to support. And, like so many others, I too loved him deeply.

When I lost JT, for the first time in my adult life, I truly fell apart. I didn't cry. Not one tear for well over a week (not a tear until I went to Iowa and saw his bedroom; untouched since high school, it was innocent and hopeful). But when I heard the news, at first I simply said to Boss, "No, he's fine. I don't feel anything." And I literally went back to sleep for almost two hours. When I woke up, Boss was calm and catatonic. And I knew. I collapsed on my bedroom floor and stopped breathing. And then, suddenly, something in me terrifyingly woke up. In my mind I always knew I could lose one of them, even my husband, but only now did it feel real. JT was a crucial part of my marriage, and when he died, that part of my marriage died as well. Boss and I, all of JT's friends and so many wives, will never get over losing these guys, but, strangely, now that several months have passed and the shock has worn off, I have never been more sad and more grateful. I now look at the widows, women who are indescribably, almost unbelievably strong, and I beg God to bring my husband home.

At JT's gravesite the day of his funeral, a beautiful young new widow whom I had never met graciously approached me and said, "I am so sorry." Stunned, I looked at her and responded, "JT was my good friend; he wasn't my husband." With a gorgeous smile she looked at me intently straight in the eye, squeezed my hand tightly, and said, "He was your friend and brother, and I'm so very sorry for your loss."* I will never forget how deeply her words affected me. This widow was comforting me? I was floored by her humble graciousness and selfless kindness. I looked around at all of the wives, female friends, and ex-girlfriends who had traveled so far to attend JT's service, and I couldn't help but think: *We were all married to him, in a way.*

When something can go wrong, most of the time, it will go wrong when your husband is away. After a day, for

---

* That widow, I later discovered, was Kimberly Vaughn.

instance, where I sprained my neck, spent three hours at the doctor's office with a sick baby, locked my keys in the car during a rainstorm, then got a speeding ticket and almost had my car impounded (yes, it was my fault—I was driving like a typical insane Southern Californian person on a Virginia country road), and then, to top it all off, stepped in a massive pile of dog shit while holding a screaming baby in the rain looking for my wallet that mysteriously fell out of my pocket. That night I wanted to curl in a ball and cry myself to sleep. And I did just that. Then I remembered something Boss said to me during a particularly painful time: "We can't have a Great Love without going through hell and back." And I had a revelation: so many other wives have, quite frankly, been through *way more* than I ever have. So many wives have been through more frequent and much longer deployments. So many wives' husbands never came home. I consider myself a relatively new wife, and there is always another woman who's had it way worse than me. So, even on the hardest days, like the one above, I just try to suck it up. I am one of the lucky ones and I'll never forget that. The fact is, all military wives are Warriors, too—they're strong as hell, formidable, tenacious, take-charge women who learn to be resilient, brave, independently capable, who possess more daily courage than the average American. I believe that very few women are born to be military wives. I certainly wasn't. I cry at commercials and hate being alone. I sleep with the lights on and a gun next to my pillow. I believe we're *forged*. With our blood, sweat, and tears—lots of tears—we're continually molded and evolve into this life. And, after losing so many guys over the years, after witnessing so many close friends' marriages end in bitter, painful, messy divorces, after watching the stress deployments put on families, especially our babies and children, my heart tears open again and again, and it takes so much work to keep it together. I know a lot of women, including me, who sleep on their husband's side of the bed when he's gone. I am not sure why; maybe it's just a way to be closer to him? I started doing it automatically and discovered that almost all of my friends do it as well. But we keep it all together. Somehow, we do. We have to. We are the backbone of this community and we take care of *everything* at home so they can leave, do their job focused and confident.

One night at a dinner party in San Diego a kind woman said to me, "I don't know how you do it, being alone all of the time, your husband always in danger. I could never do that." I sat silent, not sure how to respond. Sometimes, I am honestly not sure how I do it, either. I gazed at him from across the room, this tall, incredibly handsome, vivacious man, charismatic and intense, a man who loves me passionately, who would do anything for me and his family, a man who would willingly give his life for his brothers and this great country. At that moment, Boss caught my gaze, and, grinning from ear to ear, he winked at me. I finally replied: "I do it for Boss. I'd give up everything I own, crawl to the ends of the earth and back on my hands and knees. I'd do anything for my handsome husband. Look at him; wouldn't you?"

I wish I could say I am a Navy wife simply because I am patriotic and want to support our country...and yes, a part of me is. I am damn proud of our military and their families. But when times get painfully, unbearably difficult, the only thing that keeps me in the game is my immeasurable pride in and unrelenting love for my husband. I believe in him and always will. I am an American, a Warrior Queen. I will somehow keep it all together—preferably with a nice glass of wine and no giant cockroaches to deal with.

At the end of the day, I'd do it all over again. I love this community. I love my brothers and I admire so many women who are stronger than I'll ever be. We've had so many damn good times it has made the sacrifices worthwhile. I love this life with a zealous passion. It has given me purpose and profound pride. I wouldn't give it up... although if Boss came home tomorrow and told me, "I won the lottery. Maybe it's time I retire and we go shopping," of course I'd happily oblige him.

By C. Kimberly Vaughn

I knew it while we were dating, but it was even more apparent after marriage that being a team wife was amazingly special. Deployments were difficult. Our first was his seven-month deployment to Iraq. We were newly engaged and we decided that I would plan our wedding to keep me occupied while he was away. His second deployment was a four-month augment to Afghanistan and started four weeks after our son was born. I moved back home to Virginia to get help from my parents. Luckily, with technologies like Skype and e-mail, we were able to keep in touch fairly often. We shared our son Reagan's milestones via the webcam and I took tons of pictures. Then for Aaron's third and final deployment he was back to Afghanistan. Yet again, he left just three weeks after our second child, a daughter, Chamberlyn, was born. (He sure had good timing when it came to changing diapers, didn't he?)

How quickly my fairy-tale life would come to an end. Team wife was one of the most special titles I have ever earned and one of the most challenging and excruciating to lose. I learned all that life in the teams had to offer... the good and bad. I knew that Aaron being a SEAL presented opportunities for danger, but our strong faith in God aided in the ongoing worries about the dangers of his career. We truly believed that God had a plan for each of us and if His plan was to take Aaron early, then that was what it was. We didn't go on worrying daily about dying or becoming injured. We lived life to the fullest, took pleasure in the time we did have together, and focused on our future—together. However, "together" was not a part of God's plan for us. On August 6, 2011, while the world learned via television of the Chinook helicopter crash carrying thirty men in the Wardack Province, I was learning that Aaron was on board and that there were no survivors.

Being a Navy SEAL was in his blood; it was just who he was. He loved it—everything about it, even the parts that are uncomfortable or painful: the days, weeks, and months spent away from family, the broken bones and pulled muscles, strained backs, and blisters. To Aaron, all the pain and difficulty just made being a SEAL all the more worthwhile. In my eyes, the fact that so few can endure what these men do is a testament to the type of men who become SEALs. These elite warriors can do what is unfathomable to so many. Their devotion, desire, and mental and physical strength are amazing. I also learned through my years of marriage to Aaron that these same attributes are found in most of the wives as well.

What made us so successful and happy in our marriage was simple. We loved each other. Aaron's career in the teams was a huge priority and it was for me as well. I knew all that Aaron had gone through to earn that Trident, and I admired him for it. The key for me was that I knew I was Aaron's foremost priority. Even though we were apart a lot, I knew I was his first priority and because of that, I knew I could support him in all his endeavors related to the teams; therefore I could make sure that I wasn't placing any undue stress upon him. He needed to have a clear and focused mind, and that included having no issues at home. Don't get me wrong; we argued and yelled, too, but if you don't have some of that in your marriage I'd think it would be pretty boring. And team guys—they are anything but.

By Diane Shipley

October 1984, Navy SEAL Training Compound,
Coronado, California
Basic Underwater Demolition Training Class 131
Secures from Hell Week

I quickly answered the phone on a Friday afternoon and barely recognized the hoarse, gravelly voice on the other end. "I made it. Come get me, honey," was all he said. I raced to Coronado.

Driving around the BUD/S compound looking for Don, I found the sidewalk littered with sleeping, beaten men who survived Hell Week, and I drove right past without recognizing him. Lips split and face swollen, he looked nothing like he had the week before when I dropped him off; he stumbled into the car and fell fast asleep.

During the ride home I nudged him out of his sleep and said, "I'm pregnant." A small, slight smile crossed his face, acknowledging what I had said, and his head went slowly back to the comfort of the passenger-side window.

Unknown to us, the baby I carried would become our next SEAL legacy, and seventeen years later, almost to the day, I would again drive into the BUD/S compound when my son's Hell Week secured to pick him up, 115 SEAL training classes after his father's Hell Week secured.

From a small Tennessee town, I joined the Navy and met Don while serving on board the second ship in the Navy that allowed females as crew, the USS *McKee* (AS-41), and Don and I were married by the ship's chaplain in a small ceremony.

It's a sad fact that most SEAL marriages end in divorce, most stemming from the incredible amount of time SEALs spend away from home on training trips and deployments overseas. It also stems from resentment of leaking pipes and flat tires with a child on each hip while Daddy has a great time traveling the world with a machine gun.

The age of the Internet has made it slightly easier on wives, with e-mail and Skype. In my day as a SEAL wife, we wrote letters to stay in touch and made the occasional phone call, which often did more harm than good. During our first SEAL deployment, Don left within days of our son being born. He called me from a nightclub in the Philippines, drunk. I could hear the hookers' "Me love you long time" chatter in the background.

Coming home, he deployed again in short order for six

months and then again for another six months after that. I'm sure every team wife imagines just how "special" it will be after a long separation. A new hairstyle, a new dress, you'll run into his arms for that first welcome-home kiss, and he'll hoist his son over his head and the tears will flow!

Well, it didn't turn out that way for me.

Don arrived from his first deployment with a black eye, and from his second facing charges for assault. His third was uneventful—until, having just put our son to bed, I lit some candles and dressed for some Don and Diane time, only to find his platoon buddies (bachelors all) forcing the door open, each one carrying a case of beer. And they had just gotten off the damn airplane a few hours earlier.

My son never really knew who daddy was for several years. And I realized then what my life would be like married to a SEAL.

All SEALs mature after a while. The many years of separation with missed Christmases and birthdays harden SEAL families and bind them together. Separations become second nature, but they do become harder as the years go on and more is expected of the SEALs as they promote in rank and take on bigger responsibilities. They become platoon chiefs entrusted with keeping their men safe, while we are entrusted with keeping the home front intact and caring for the children the men have left behind. It's a huge responsibility and we're doing it 100 percent alone.

Alone, except for the greatest support system I found— the other team wives.

We truly became a team of our own. We helped with each other's kids; we changed flat tires with ease. When the holidays rolled around, we helped each other keep our homes as normal as possible for the kids. SEAL wives, and kids, take on the courage and warrior spirit of the men we married.

Wives, mothers, sisters, and children are the unsung heroes behind the scenes of these brave fighting men and go without any medals, ribbons, or glory. We provide a safe haven for them to return home to. We are the constant in their lives and we are why they fight.

I am very proud to have kept my marriage together for over thirty-three years now, and I can tell you that the day my husband graduated SEAL training is still one of the proudest of my life. The only thing to top that was the day my husband stood next to the commanding officer of BUD/S training at our son's graduation and with a warm hug welcomed him to the teams.

By Kristy

Honor, courage, and commitment—those are a few words I've heard used to describe the elite men who fight for our freedom. As a Navy SEAL widow, I never thought they would be used to describe me.

My husband was as humble as they come. He never let on, outside of our tightly knit community, that he was a special operator of any kind. I respected him for being so passionate about his career choice, and for being smart about keeping a sense of normalcy in our lives, safely and discreetly. As I started my new life, in a new place, with new people and a new and very different kind of community, I began to learn that as a SEAL wife, you are three different women.

Person one is what I would consider your average wife. Planning BBQs and play dates for the kids. Packing in a full day of work, making dinner, going to the gym, and spending quality time with the family.

Person two is a SEAL wife—basically a single parent, head of household, counselor, confidante, and ball-buster. I wasn't really a single parent, but with my husband out of town 65 to 70 percent of the time, usually unable to be reached, I got a taste of what it would be like. I always knew I was lucky to have him come home—and just long enough to get the schedule that we were on, a finely tuned machine, totally out of whack. I mean that in the best way; I'd rather be a little unorganized and have my man home than be sleeping with my cell phone on. I always knew I could never keep him from that rodeo. It's just what they do and how they are wired. So you roll with it.

When I say "head of household," I don't mean for tax purposes. I mean running the house. The schedule isn't easy, and if there's a hiccup somewhere along the way, it can all fall apart.

I actually enjoyed being the counselor. If he trusted me enough to share his thoughts on a topic, be it something about bills due, children, or this year's presidential campaign, I had to be rock solid. If you've accepted the role of a team wife, that's exactly what you have to be, a rock.

Person three is the worrywart. I have never been a "sit by the phone" type of gal. Before I met my husband, if I was busy and I missed a guy's call, it was no big deal. I'd call him back. But once I met my husband, that changed. I had never in my life thought that a phone call could be so important. Since becoming part of this community and having seen loss and heartbreak, I never wanted to miss what could very well be the last call. We spoke every day. Often it was about nothing, but nothing was so much more—it was how we loved. We really had to rely on our ability to communicate with each other. That's how we survived the long absences.

Sleeping with your phone isn't ideal, but some of my best memories are those 3 a.m. wake-up calls. We were dreamers; we would talk about what we could, especially when he was deployed. When I asked him how his day was, I would get one of two answers: "Good" or "Same old same old." The rest of the time, which could be as long as an hour, we dreamed of what we were going to do after he retired. From career choices to having a garage full of motorcycles, camping trips, and a huge home for the family to visit, built just the way we wanted. I'd have a perfect kitchen so I could cook my heart out, and he'd have an outrageous man cave that was far enough away that he didn't wake me up when the boys came to visit.

I still have every e-mail my husband ever sent me, and ten or fifteen saved voice mails, just random ones, so I can go back to hear him say "I love you." I came into this relationship knowing that there could be a happy ending and hoping that there would be, but not naive. Who knew that saving these silly things would be so important one day? I had always just put them in a folder, not knowing that one day they would be like a journal of our life together.

When that hollow knock on the door came at 6:30 one morning, the e-mail saving came to a screeching halt and being a single parent became a reality. His death shattered all of those dreams that we had together. I have never said, "Oh, that will never happen to me" and I have never asked, "Why did this happen to me?" Even knowing that, statistically speaking, the more times you roll the dice, the larger the risk. The risk is great, but these men chose to sign on the dotted line; therefore, so did we. That being said, we wives serve our country, too.

They say that you can't choose who you fall in love with, but you can most definitely choose your path. I chose to follow the path my heart led me to. I still stand behind him with honor, courage, and commitment.

Rest in peace, my love. I hope I served you well.

24

Links in the Chain

If you do anything for fun, doing it professionally in the military may ruin it for you for life. After my nine years in the teams, I no longer scuba dive. As a veteran of the SDV teams, I see no point going polar-bear swimming or even exploring the reefs at Hanauma Bay or Truk Lagoon. Not when there's a perfectly good barbecue joint just down the coast road a stretch. I don't rock climb or go to the beach. Mel thinks I'm crazy for refusing to take cold showers, but anyone who's gone through BUD/S will understand.

Though I haven't discussed it much publicly, diving was a huge part of my time in uniform. In the SDV teams, we took it to the bottom. Normal dives in the numbered teams are just a few hours long. Some of ours in the SDV teams took eight hours or more, in total darkness. My longest dive was over ten hours long. I actually have fallen asleep under water twice. And there's nothing else like it. Locking out of a submerged submarine, we'd swim in from offshore, go over the beach, change into our dry gear, do a snatch-and-grab or a recon mission, and return the way we came, back into the arms of Mother Ocean. Nobody else can do it as well as SDV guys. It's the womb we are born from and the home we always return to. It's also the truest definition of *suck*.

With all that said, I knew I had to find something to keep the adrenaline pumping after I got out, so I started hunting to get that rush again. I know it's probably the frogman in me, but I especially like to hunt dangerous game, an animal that's capable of killing me if I screw up.

In 2011 I had an opportunity to travel to South Africa to hunt Cape buffalo. Long story short, when the moment of truth came, I was in the savanna, standing exposed in tall grass near the top of a hill, with one of those monsters just thirty meters away from me. My first shot didn't do much to him, ripping his shoulder with a slug that would have penetrated an engine block. All it did was piss him off. He just shook it off as though it were a hailstone, then turned and started running away. Nineteen hundred pounds of fury went charging down the hill and into the thorns.

We set after him into the dense thicket of the valley below. He made such a huge swath in the grass that we felt like we were following a truck. But we couldn't count on the idea that he'd always keep running away from us. Cape buffalo are known for drawing their pursuers into heavy brush, getting them hung up on thorns and briars, then charging back on them fast.

Once we were out of the high grass, the tracking got more difficult. The professional Zulu tribesman with our party was the best tracker I've ever seen. When we found the wounded buffalo the first time, I was impressed by his patience. I lifted my .416 Rigby to my shoulder and stayed on glass for twenty minutes, waiting for him to come into the open. When he finally did, I shot him again. This time the 10.57mm slug dropped him—for a few seconds, at least. Then he was on his feet—and a bad feeling swept over me.

For a moment, I was afraid he'd charge. If he did, I'd probably have time for only a single shot before he reached yours truly. Even a perfect head shot might still allow his momentum to carry him into me. And if I missed, it was all over. A lion will kill you by raking you with his hind claws and biting your neck once. He'll get it over with and go about his business. A Cape buffalo is different. He'll mash you with the crown of his horns and keep pounding until he can't feel you anymore. Your body will be jelly before he stops. There's something exciting about that ferocity. That fear can get into your head and put a tremble into your scope.

Fortunately, this one had a different plan and we kept up the chase. As we closed in on him, I shot him four more times before he finally let out a death bellow. When the Zulu tracker went to make sure he was dead, he tapped his rifle barrel a few times on the animal's eyeball. Even from a prone position these animals can be up and on top of you before you know it.

As we took our trophy picture, I tried to lift the Cape buffalo's head for a better photo, but managed to get that giant skull off the ground only a few inches. It took a dozen men and a pretty big winch to lift his dead weight into the truck. Worn out by the adrenaline surge and torn up by thorns, I came away humbled by the power and stamina of this great creature. The feeling was indescribable.

This is what we live for, in the teams. Choose whatever quarry you like: the pursuit generates the fear, and the fear gives you the rush. And even after you come home, it's hard to kick that addiction. Domestic life isn't anything like what you find in uniform. That's one reason we try to vet our teammates' girlfriends so carefully. We need to know they're up to the challenge.

My mother says she gave two boys to the Navy and it gave her back men. When Morgan and I were first in the teams, life was simple. Our leaders would take us somewhere and point us in a direction, our only purpose in life being to hit the target we were shooting at. If the chief or LPO said, "Okay, point man, we need to get from this outpost to this house," well, roger that, sir. We had a straightforward job to do.

After a couple of deployments and a couple of promotions, it was a different deal. We learned to see the big picture. We understood our missions in detail and also in context. When we went after someone, we knew not only who we were going after and what his location was but also who his associates were, who his wife and kids were, how many rings his wife wore, what kind of car he drove, where he worked, and where he used to work. We knew who his daddy, his momma, and his sisters, brothers, friends, and friends' friends were. We knew what questions to ask him to get where we needed to go. Knowing all that, we could turn him in circles with our terp in the interrogation room.

By the time you retire and slow down, you may wonder what you're supposed to do with those capabilities. They don't have a lot of use in civilian life. You need to find other challenges. But when you look around, you may find that the world doesn't offer them. The world doesn't understand who you are, what you've been doing, or what you can do. I wrote earlier about Master Chief's job interviews, in which the interviewers clearly had no idea what kind of man they were talking to. Morgan knew the score and didn't like the thought of making the transition, either. Working that desk job in Virginia Beach prior to retirement was miserable, mind-numbing duty.

There were days when I wished my body would whip itself back into fighting shape so I could get back on line and reengage with the guys. But that wasn't my destiny. When I came home, I was blessed to have a course of action set before me: bring the actions of a few to the attention of many. Too many of us who leave military service come home to a life without enough direction in it. I found mine thanks to the Naval Special Warfare community, my friends, my foundation, and my wife and kids.

It's funny how serving your nation makes you part of something larger than yourself but also sets you apart. You realize this when you come home and find so many people who know what you've done but can't personally relate to any part of it.

The military now stands apart from average Americans' lives as it never has before. About 1.4 million people are on active duty in our armed forces today—about half the number that were on active duty fifty years ago. About 2.4 million have served in the Global War on Terror, as it's known. That last number sounds pretty big but it's just 0.77 percent of America's population of 313 million—a truly shocking instance of the "1 percent versus 99 percent" problem. In Congress, where our political decisions are made (or not), only 21.8 percent of our representatives have served in the military. That's down from 74 percent in 1971, when the numbers were pushed up by the draft. That was also a time when you didn't need to be wealthy to run for elected office and most congressmen understood that the term "enemy" referred to someone with a gun on the other side of a demilitarized zone, not someone in the opposing political party.

Today, we don't need to be trivializing war when we've had about 6,200 men and women killed in Iraq and Afghanistan over the past ten years. Overall, we've lost 391 special operations personnel, and at least 1,820 more have been wounded, according to SOCOM (Special Operations Command) and the Department of Defense.

Military life and culture seem to be foreign territory for many of the people who write for national magazines and newspapers today. Every time they refer to Navy SEALs and other SOF outfits as "Special Forces," which only describes the Army's Green Berets, they reveal themselves to be as ignorant as someone who doesn't know, say, a Shia Muslim from a Sunni. Recently, in a well-attended forum at a public university, a prominent journalist referred to the Joint Special Operations Command, the elite command that carried out the bin Laden operation, as "an executive assassination ring, essentially" for Vice President Dick Cheney. The fact that the guy who said this has a Pulitzer Prize might confirm your worst fears about those who write "news" for a living. (Naturally, in the same presentation, he also referred to special operations units as "Special Forces.")

Those who serve in the military are the best of us. They're capable, honorable, and less likely to be hung up on material belongings or themselves. An Iraqi military officer doing training at a U.S. base was asked by a journalist recently what he thought about Americans nine years after Saddam was taken down. "You are a better people than your movies say," he said.

Yet for all the interest in the stories of our heroes at war, as reflected in Hollywood grosses and the bestseller lists, the military still seems to be more isolated from most Americans than ever before. The Army was basically a citizens' militia when our nation broke free of England's tyranny. Today we have a thoroughly professional volunteer force. It's also a caste that stands mostly apart from civilian life. I've heard it said that the members of our military are like sheepdogs in a world full of wolves. If that's the case, not enough people have direct experience in the pasture. Most people don't pay much attention to the sheepdogs until the wolves come calling.

People who don't know our military very well sometimes seem amazed whenever men like Jordan Haerter and Jonathan Yale make the headlines. On April 22, 2008, those two enlisted Marines were standing watch at a checkpoint outside a joint U.S.-Iraqi barracks in Ramadi when a large truck began accelerating toward their position. Their checkpoint controlled entry to a barracks in the Sufiyah district that housed fifty Marines from the newly arrived First Battalion, Ninth Regiment. They were alert to the VBIED threat and quickly and accurately assessed the situation before them—all the more impressive given that the level of violence in the city generally wasn't what it had been a few years earlier. Both Marines opened fire immediately, Haerter with an M4 and Yale with a machine gun. Still the truck rushed toward them. Nearby, dozens of

Iraqi police fired on the truck as well—but only briefly before their instincts for survival kicked in. Expecting a huge blast, they fled the area. But those two Marines stood their ground, pouring fire into the truck until it coasted to a halt in front of them—and exploded.

Later estimates pegged the size of that IED at two thousand pounds or more. The blast damaged or destroyed two dozen houses and knocked down the walls of a mosque a hundred yards away. An Iraqi who witnessed the attack, interviewed by a Marine general afterward, choked back a sob and said, "Sir, in the name of God, no sane man would have stood there and done what they did. No sane man. They saved us all." Lieutenant General John F. Kelly, who investigated the incident to document the Navy Crosses they were to receive, said, "In all of the instantaneous violence Yale and Haerter never hesitated. By all reports and by the recording [of a security camera nearby], they never stepped back. They never even started to step aside. They never even shifted their weight. With their feet spread shoulder-width apart, they leaned into the danger, firing as fast as they could work their weapons." Yale, from Burkeville, Virginia, and Haerter, from Sag Harbor, New York, were decorated in 2009 for their steady nerves and heroism in the last six seconds of their lives, saving at least fifty people living in those barracks in the process.

Our officer candidates today face the challenge of preparing themselves to lead men like Jordan and Jonathan. Fortunately, they're beginning their careers better prepared than ever before, in part because we've been at war for ten years now. At West Point, the Army is doing it right.

You can't go far, in that beautiful stretch of forest over-looking the Hudson River, without hearing about morals and ethics as they apply to leadership. Both a strong body and a right mind are needed to ensure that we have the kind of commanders who make the right decisions where things really matter: down at the platoon level.

The influence of ten years of war on West Point's pipe-line is nowhere more evident than in the summer field-training program that seniors (or "firsties," as they're known) have to complete before they take a second lieu-tenant's commission. West Point began shaking it up in 2007 to make it fit the realities the cadets will run into downrange. "We found that the product we were creating was not what battalion commanders were looking for," an instructor told me. "They weren't adaptive." So West Point brought in the leadership from Fort Benning to take a look at the curriculum.

Now upperclassmen have to go through Cadet Leadership Development Training, a nineteen-day role-playing scenario designed to put them through their paces prior to deployment, much as our special operations selection courses do. In the woods of the Hudson River Valley, they run air-assault operations, simulate cordon and search missions, and deal with Arabic-speaking sheikhs, imams, and other tribal leaders. The program is constantly changing to stay current with what's happening on the battlefield. In the old days, during the seventies and eighties, cadets ran through highly structured "approved-solution" scenarios. Now their decisions mean something, just as they will downrange. It's hard to find an instructor in the Depart-ment of Military Instruction who doesn't have several combat tours under his belt.

There's also a new department at West Point, the Center for the Advancement of Leader Development and Organizational Learning, which uses the Internet to connect company-level officers (captains and below) with each other and with cadets, bringing the lessons of the battlefield into the classroom. Like so many ideas whose time has come, the peer-to-peer approach to learning has caught on. The *Harvard Business Review* chose it as one of its top twenty business ideas of 2006.

Cadets are prepared physically, both outdoors and in the six-floor, 455,000-square-foot shrine to physical fitness on the post, the Arvin Cadet Physical Development Center. The man who was in charge of that facility when I toured it in 2010, Colonel Greg Daniels, holds the title Master of the Sword (the title is a legacy of the 1800s, when swordsmanship was still part of the curriculum). Responsible for the physical fitness and development of the entire cadet population, he presides over a program that includes rooms for boxing, judo, fencing, and so on, as well as the modern Combat Water Survival Swim Lab, fitted with smoke generators, wave machines, and other equipment that produces effects the cadets will likely encounter in the field. The old-school indoor obstacle course test (the infamous IOCT, an acronym that all cadets learn to dread) has eleven stations that test balance, coordination, agility, power, and strength—including rope climbs, medicine balls, and an eight-foot-high shelf, onto which cadets have to hurdle themselves from a standing position. That crushing physical gauntlet has to be passed through twice a year by every cadet, and it hasn't changed much since it was established in 1944.

As a result of all of this forward thinking, new Army

second lieutenants are much more likely to be effective when they take over their first platoons. (The really smart ones will still listen closely to what their sergeants have to say.) When your business is war, you don't miss the distraction of having to break in new draftees all the time. When you volunteer today, you'll serve with other volunteers, which means everyone has a certain level of motivation.

Of course, a Navy guy like me doesn't need to tell you how special Annapolis is. Some of my best friends in the teams went to the United States Naval Academy. The Navy's never-quit motto, "Don't give up the ship," hangs proudly in Bancroft Hall, and the USNA has a long tradition of sending naval and Marine Corps leaders to the battlefield. But West Point's mandatory field-training program is something that any frogman has to respect. I don't know what West Point was like in 1998, when I was entering the Navy, but if I had to do it over again, it would be tempting to heed its call. I had always thought of West Point as a cold, sterile place, a gray-walled castle on a hill. But it's more modern, dynamic, and gritty than that, and its emphasis on preparing young warriors for ground combat will warm any special operator's heart.

No matter what route you follow into service, whether it's the Naval Service Training Command in Great Lakes, Illinois (my route), or another boot camp, from San Diego's Marine Corps Recruit Depot to Cape May, New Jersey, where Coast Guardsmen are made, a military career will test you like nothing ever has. Then, if you're lucky, you'll have a long career and come out of the experience stronger, deeper, and wiser.

Morgan, who served on several deployments after I left

the service, eventually had his own brush with death and faced a crossroads. I took a licking, too, and came out with a broader view than I'd had before. Chris Kyle confronted his mortality at Sadr City, and again back home at the service station, filling his truck.

At some point, you find that you recognize a certain look in a combat veteran's eyes, the reflection of experiences he or she will never forget. You also may start feeling the mileage you've put on your body, and you're left to face the rest of your days. Eventually you slow down, your thinking sharpens, your view broadens, and you find yourself becoming an old man.

May everyone be as blessed as I've been, to have a close family and loved ones who help ease the transition out of the fight.

At a reunion of Marines in South Carolina recently, R. V. Burgin gave the main address at the memorial service. He used the occasion to tell a story of the old days. The year was 1775, when the Marine Corps was founded. The call to form the new service's first two battalions was given by the Continental Congress at a pub in Philadelphia. The first man to come forward did so on the spot. He was given a mug of beer and told to sit down at a table at the back of the room. The second man to volunteer was given two mugs of beer and directed to join the same table. Sizing up the newcomer, the first guy asked, "What gives? They only gave me one mug of beer." The second guy shrugged and said, "I'm just following instructions. They gave me these two mugs of beer and told me to come over here and sit down with you." The first guy considered this for a few seconds, then said, "Well, that's fine, but I'll tell

you one damn thing: things weren't that way in the *old*
Corps."

I give the same kind of grief to my brother, because he
became a SEAL just fifteen months after me. In truth,
because my sins preceded him there, he had a harder time
at Coronado than I did. When he showed up to begin
BUD/S, he was standing on the sidewalk when a black
Chevy Suburban screeched to a halt next to him. A bunch
of instructors piled out, and one of them asked, "Are you
the other Luttrell?" His affirmative reply brought dark
promises of misery and hellfire ahead, and they pretty
much made good on them during his twenty-one weeks
on the Strand.

No matter how good a SEAL might become, there's
always someone with more seniority, experience, or skill
nearby to bring him back to earth. At the SEAL reunions
I go to, the World War II UDT swimmers will tell the
Korean War veterans, "Hey, new guy, go get me a beer."
The Korean War guys say the same to the Vietnam guys,
all the way down the line. Once I was pushing through a
crowded hospitality room when I bumped into a frog who
was a lot shorter than me—because he was seated in a
wheelchair. The first two syllables of an apology weren't
out of my mouth before he was laying into me with *You
mother* this and *I'll whip your sorry* that. I noticed he was
wearing a T-shirt printed with the words BUD/S CLASS 1.
This man was nobody's pushover. He was having a load of
fun with me. Everyone around him was howling in appre-
ciation. In the teams, you're always a new guy to somebody. That's how we keep each other honest. And if you
stick around the teams long enough, well, you're asking
for a lesson in humility, because at some point, in some

school, or a new command you're going to be nobody all over again.

On Flag Day of 2011, I visited Mr. Burgin at his house in Lancaster, south of Dallas. The town's tree-shaded streets were lined with red, white, and blue. He greeted me at the door of the home he's occupied since 1965. On the wall of his living room, he showed me a photo of his brother, J. D., killed by German artillery fire in Alsace-Lorraine in 1944, when he was eighteen. There was that photo from Peleliu, too, showing eighty-five weathered veterans of that battle, including Mr. Burgin, shirtless and forty pounds lighter than when he arrived. He shook his last bout of malaria in 1947, after he came home, and was happy never to talk about it again. The media in his day had little interest in Peleliu. Everyone expected it to be a sideshow, so it took a while for history to give it its due. That suited Mr. Burgin. He was strong and silent about it, kind of like his hero, John Wayne, who has a photographic shrine of his own farther down the hallway.

Mr. Burgin didn't talk about his service until 1980, when his First Marine Division buddies found him and made sure he went to Indianapolis that year. Twenty men from the K/3/5 were there. He knew them all, and had done foxhole duty with a few of them. "Hey, Burgin, do you remember..." they would ask. At first, he usually didn't. "Well, hell, you ought to. You were *there*," they would say. And gradually, and then faster, the memories returned. Soon he was talking freely, and reconnecting with everything he went through in the Pacific.

In 1991, at a reunion in Minneapolis, he decided to take part in a documentary project on the battle for Peleliu. The experience convinced him that the story should be remembered more widely. He feels to this day that history isn't taught anymore; how else to explain why a fight that took eighteen hundred American lives remains so obscure?

Mr. Burgin's effort to reverse that state of affairs led to his involvement in the HBO miniseries *The Pacific,* in which his story is told over the course of several episodes. The filmmakers changed some of the characters (and some history), but he says they got the big things right. The only mistake that bothers him is seeing the actor playing him wearing the wrong rank insignia on his shoulder. He's shown as a private first class. There's only one man in the world, of course, who can appreciate what he had to go through to get his corporal's second stripe.

He went through it the night he killed his first enemy soldier. On Cape Gloucester, he faced a banzai charge without a rifle. Since he was a mortarman, his main job was hauling around a heavy baseplate for the mortar. As a Japanese soldier rushed him, he pulled his .45 and caught him in the chest from ten strides away. Only one or two of the enemy escaped. "That attack broke me in right away," he said.

He went through it on another night, on Peleliu, when he heard scuffling a short distance away, a few men down the line. An enemy soldier had jumped on top of one of his teammates while he was sleeping. There was grunting, and then a drawn-out scream. The awakened Marine had reached up, gouged the eyes of the Japanese soldier, and as that soldier fell back, the Marine rose, grabbed him by the neck and seat of the pants, and flung him off a cliff. "I heard that Jap screaming all the way down, from the second his eyes were gouged till he hit bottom," Mr.

Burgin said. "I've never heard such a bloodcurdling sound in my life," he said.

He went through it again a few days later, while assaulting a cluster of craggy hillocks known as the Five Sisters. Mr. Burgin was sickened to find the bodies of a four-man Marine recon team wedged in among some rocks.

These were the things—among many—that pushed him up the ranks. And these were the things that closed up the years between us. When he told the Five Sisters story, I couldn't help but think of my teammates from Operation Redwing. He and I share much in common, including the experience of fighting in confined spaces and harsh terrain. Later on, the death of his skipper, Captain Andrew A. "Ack-Ack" Haldane, and his platoon leader, a popular, soft-spoken mustang first lieutenant named Edward A. "Hillbilly" Jones, hit home with me as well. In life-or-death situations, Mr. Burgin faced moments of moral compromise that I could relate to. Things you can't imagine happen to you under fire in the dark. I read about a few of them in his book, *Islands of the Damned*, and I didn't need him to explain the details. His war ran on amphibious tractors and DUKWs; mine ran on Black Hawks and Humvees. But the sensations, the shocks to the system, and the screams don't change. The big things never do. "It's impossible to imagine the look and smell of a battlefield if you've never been on one, and impossible to forget if you have," he said. Any soldier of any war knows this.

In San Antonio, in 2010, I joined R. V. Burgin in the proud company of his unit. I saw the continuous thread of gallantry that runs from his day to the present. The Fifth

Marines have a glittering battle history, and K Company's contribution to it was significant. In 1967, the K/3/5 was deployed to the Que Son Valley in Vietnam, thirty miles south of Da Nang. From April through September, they and other outfits from the Fifth Marines took on North Vietnamese Army forces holding fortified positions along a highway known as Route 534. In May, during the first Operation Union, they assaulted a well-defended hill and became pinned down by heavy fire. The gunnery sergeant was killed, and K Company's commanding officer, Lieutenant Robert O. Tilley, was badly wounded. A lance corporal attached as a forward air controller, Christopher K. Mosher, ran toward the front and put himself in an exposed position for five hours, directing air strikes. Finally wounded in the back by mortar shrapnel, he was evacuated, never to walk again. He was awarded the Navy Cross for his valor.

Three times during those brutal months, K Company took casualties bad enough to knock it off the line. Each time, it came back from combat-ineffective status. In Operation Adair, a five-day operation fought in June, it suffered nine KIA from just two platoons, which have about forty men apiece. The officer who replaced Lieutenant Tilley, Captain Joseph Tenney, was hit in the back of the head and evacuated. Declared combat-ineffective once again, the K/3/5 returned in September to take part in another major operation. Back in command, Captain Tenney earned a Silver Star.

By the end of those six months, the Marines in the valley, though outnumbered in every fight, had destroyed most of the NVA division facing them. Six members of the K/3/5 received Silver Stars. But the triumph came at a high price: from April to December of 1967, the North Vietnamese boasted of killing more Americans in the Que Son Valley than anywhere else. The Marines soon began calling Road 534 the Road of Ten Thousand Pains, a phrase taken from Homer's *Iliad*.

At the Rio Rio Cantina in San Antonio the night I met up with him and his unit, R. V. Burgin, the anchor of the Old Breed, held court and served as emcee. He had been the group's treasurer for twenty-one years, taking care of the funds that paid for Marine Corps monuments that stand today on Peleliu and Okinawa. Just as Mr. Burgin looked up to his senior enlisted leadership—hard veterans of Guadalcanal, such as his first sergeant, Mo Darsey, or his sergeant, Johnny Marmet—the Vietnam generation looked up to him. The Marines who enlisted to fight in Vietnam didn't need a history book to tell them what they're all about. They had the World War II generation to look back to—and they did. "We never qualified to carry these guys' mess gear," said Harvey Newton, who served in the K/3/5 as a nineteen-year-old lance corporal in Vietnam.

I don't endorse Mr. Newton's modesty, because the legacy of K Company's valor got a new chapter in Vietnam, and it's gotten one in our time as well. A Marine of my generation who served with the K/3/5, my friend Jeremiah Workman—a mortarman just like Mr. Burgin—received a Navy Cross for his actions during the Battle of Fallujah in December 2004. In April 2011, when Third Battalion returned from Helmand Province, Afghanistan, Jeremiah's company had taken record casualties for a Marine Corps unit its size on a single deployment in the modern era: twenty-five KIA and another 140 wounded, including more than a dozen amputees. In spite of that bloody record, its instances of post-traumatic stress have been almost nil, largely thanks to the way the families of the veterans have circled up and looked after each other back at Camp Pendleton.

It takes that kind of close brotherhood to get by. I'll never forget how the brotherhood circled around the Tumilson family in Rockford, Iowa. The SEAL family held close to them, ensuring JT isn't forgotten. At the funeral, the presiding pastor recited from Psalm 18:

> He made my feet like the feet of a deer and set me
>   secure on the heights.
> He trains my hands for war, so that my arms can bend
>   a bow of bronze.
> You have given me the shield of your salvation, and
>   your right hand supported me, and your gentleness
>   made me great.
> You gave a wide place for my steps under me, and my
>   feet did not slip.
> I pursued my enemies and overtook them, and did not
>   turn back till they were consumed.

This might be the Bible's most powerful call to military service. Those of us who are forged in that vision can relate to the way R. V. Burgin sums up his service: "What sticks with me now is not so much the pain and terror and sorrow of the war, though I remember that well enough. What really sticks with me is the honor I had of defending my country, and of serving in the company of these men."

I see it all as a single piece of fabric. Americans should never forget that the founders of this country, like all who have served her in uniform, were willing to die defending everything its flag represents. It's so easy to get lost in the controversies that divide us. But I believe, no matter what our race, religion, or beliefs may be, that Americans should be able to come together to keep our country rooted in what made it great: a land of opportunity, a place where people can make something of themselves, limited only by their imaginations and willingness to work hard; a country where we all can come together, whatever our differences, for the greater good; a country of hands up, not handouts, where we try to live by the meaning of the words "Love thy neighbor," and put as much effort into helping others as we do helping ourselves. By doing those things, we can continue to live up to the idea of *One nation, under God, indivisible, with liberty and justice for all.*

Epilogue

The Flaming Ferris Wheel Spins

Today, Boss is still working in a classified capacity on a team that will be bringing hell to terrorists worldwide. He recently got hold of the original drawings that JT had used as a model for the elaborate Oriental carp design he had on his right arm. As I write this, Boss is finishing the last installment of the painful, eighteen-hour process to inscribe this work of everlasting art into his left arm. "Art, life, and remembrance of living through pain and loss," Boss calls it. The ultimate tribute to a brother, fallen but not forgotten.

Prior to August 6, 2011, I was looking forward to nothing more than seeing Morgan return to Texas. His bags were just about packed in Virginia Beach as he finished his med boards. He was playing out time, waiting for his exit letter from the Navy. He was planning to shift gears, maybe go to graduate school, or even run for political office. He was also going to get busy working with me on the Lone Survivor Foundation.

But when JT, Matt Mills, Trey Vaughn, and all the others went down, Morgan had a change of heart. It was an immediate decision on his part, though he didn't tell me about it for a few weeks. He didn't want to give me any distractions as we prepared to celebrate JT's life in Iowa. Morgan knew right away what he needed to do: he was staying in the teams and going back for another deployment, in honor of his fallen brothers.

Morgan went to his command, pulled his retirement papers, and told them he wanted to become operational again. He's in the training cycle now and will be serving back in the Sandbox by the time this book is published. It will be his tenth combat tour. And he wasn't the only frog to walk that path after this latest tragedy hit our community.

The war in Afghanistan may end someday, as the war in Iraq officially has. We'll see headlines about the drawdown of conventional forces, leaving all the problems to the locals to deal with. For our special operations forces, however, employment opportunities downrange will continue to be plentiful—and more dangerous, after the Army and Marine Corps aren't around to secure the areas we operate in.

It's hard for me to express what all this means to me. Maybe words just can't say the things that come so deeply from the heart. It's a feeling that comes from experience, from blood, sweat, and mourning. There are many reasons why my military service has meant so much to me—and to those who have come before me and those who are yet to deploy. It isn't the danger by itself. It's the brotherhood, the bonds you form with people who, like you, are willing to give everything away for a greater good. The brotherhood carries on, and in this way, and in ways you'll never read about, the flaming Ferris wheel really does continue to spin.

The urge to serve something larger than myself drew me into the military, and serving for nine years has taught me a few things. But service in the military isn't the only way to go. Now that I'm out of uniform, I see that my deployments were only the beginning, a workup for whatever the rest of my years call me to do. You can serve your family, and put their needs in front of yours. You can do the same thing in your community, your town, and your city. I think all of us who serve—in any type of uniform—can arrive at this broader view of service faster than most other people, because of what we go through.

Service is selflessness—the opposite of the lifestyle that we see so much of in America today. The things that entertain us don't often lift us up, or show us as the people we can rise up to become. The people who appear in this book—and others who did things I can't talk about—are my role models. They quietly live out the idea expressed in the Bible (John 15:13): "Greater love has no man than this, that a man lay down his life for his friends."

But you don't have to be a Christian, or even particularly religious, to serve. You just have to be willing to understand your place and put yourself at the end of the line. Still, my faith has helped me toward a deeper understanding of what service really means. You do what's expected of you, and more. You look after others, and put their welfare ahead of your own. You don't worry about the big purpose of it all—it's beyond your pay grade. But if you do the small things right long enough, you might find yourself coming out the other side having done something important.

It's an evolution you follow, a tour on the great Ferris wheel, which doesn't have to burn. It never stops turning until the day you take your last breath. And you hope that by the time you leave this earth, it will be a better place than it was when you got here. The causes you've served in your life will have meant something. Someone will have picked up on your work, run with a legacy you left behind, and used it to put his or her own stamp on the world.

All I can really tell you after walking this particular path is that I'm proud to have served my country. I know that part of me will always bleed with the teams, and that my time in uniform, which at the moment seems so long, has been just a short chapter in a far longer book, and brief preparation for what the future holds.

Thank you, God, for all these days.

SEALs and Underwater Demolition Team Members Killed in Action, 1943–Present

Pirro, Carmon F.	December 30, 1943	Anzio
Donnell, John Gerald	January 30, 1944	Anzio
Olson, Richard Roderick	February 4, 1944	Unknown
Tascillo, Matteo	February 17, 1944	Marshall Islands
Abbott, George L.	June 6, 1944	Normandy
Alexander, Henry Richard	June 6, 1944	Normandy
Bussell, John Edward	June 6, 1944	Normandy
Cook, John William	June 6, 1944	Normandy
DeGregorio, Carmine	June 6, 1944	Normandy
Demmer, Peter Mathew	June 6, 1944	Normandy
Dillon, Thomas Justin	June 6, 1944	Normandy
Dombek, Walter Joseph	June 6, 1944	Normandy
Doran, William Robert	June 6, 1944	Normandy
Drew, Elmer Malcolm	June 6, 1944	Normandy
Duncan, Harold E.	June 6, 1944	Normandy
Fabich, Henry Samuel	June 6, 1944	Normandy
Fleming, Andrew Jackson	June 6, 1944	Normandy
Fuller, John Anthony Sr.	June 6, 1944	Normandy
Gouinlock, George Linzy	June 6, 1944	Normandy
Goulder, Preston Hardaway	June 6, 1944	Normandy
Greenfield, Edward Joseph	June 6, 1944	Normandy
Harang, Richard David	June 6, 1944	Normandy

Herring, Clifford Palmer	June 6, 1944	Normandy
Hickey, Arthur Burton	June 6, 1944	Normandy
Holtman, Orvid J.	June 6, 1944	Normandy
Hudson, Alton E.	June 6, 1944	Normandy
Jacobson, John A.	June 6, 1944	Normandy
Jarosz, Edward Anthony	June 6, 1944	Normandy
McDermott, John Daniel	June 6, 1944	Normandy
McGeary, Donald C.	June 6, 1944	Normandy
Millis, Conrad Clarence	June 6, 1944	Normandy
Mingledorff, Ozie Claud Jr.	June 6, 1944	Normandy
Olive, Jesse D.	June 6, 1944	Normandy
Perkins, Frank James	June 6, 1944	Normandy
Pienack, Raymond Rudolph	June 6, 1944	Normandy
Sullivan, Maurice Francis Jr.	June 6, 1944	Normandy
Vetter, Alvin Edward	June 6, 1944	Normandy
Weatherford, Milton Parker	June 6, 1944	Normandy
Weckman, Lawrence I.	June 6, 1944	Normandy
Weidner, Albert Garhardt	June 14, 1944	Saipan
Christensen, Robert V.	June 16, 1944	Saipan
Blowers, Ralph A.	July 15, 1944	Guam
Nixon, Thomas Dervus	July 21, 1944	Guam
Black, Robert Armstrong	August 14, 1944	Yap
MacMahon, John Churchill	September 2, 1944	Yap
Roeder, Howard Livingston	September 2, 1944	Yap
Audibert, Benoit Bernard	October 18, 1944	Leyte
Kasman, Brennan W.	October 18, 1944	Leyte
Lauderdale, Kenneth Broughton	October 19, 1944	Leyte
Tilton, Edward	October 19, 1944	Leyte
Blettel, David	January 12, 1945	USS *Belknap*
Castillo, Guadalupe	January 12, 1945	USS *Belknap*
Gamache, Wilfred Dolar	January 12, 1945	USS *Belknap*
Hopkins, Robert Lee	January 12, 1945	USS *Belknap*
Lewis, William Robert	January 12, 1945	USS *Belknap*

Malfeo, Marvin Antonio	January 12, 1945	USS *Belknap*
McKnight, Thomas Rex	January 12, 1945	USS *Belknap*
Rodriquez, James Lawrence	January 12, 1945	USS *Belknap*
Rossart, Joseph William	January 12, 1945	USS *Belknap*
Scoggins, F. P.	January 12, 1945	USS *Belknap*
Sugden, William Lloyd	January 12, 1945	USS *Belknap*
Anderson, Edward Wilson	February 17, 1945	Iwo Jima
Sumpter, Frank Warren	February 17, 1945	Iwo Jima
Yates, Lee Carlton	February 17, 1945	Iwo Jima
Allen, Kermit	February 18, 1945	USS *Blessman*
Beason, Edwin Albert	February 18, 1945	USS *Blessman*
Blackwood, Buress Lee	February 18, 1945	USS *Blessman*
Blanot, Harry Thomas	February 18, 1945	USS *Blessman*
Davis, Paul Harrison	February 18, 1945	USS *Blessman*
Dolan, Patrick Raymond	February 18, 1945	USS *Blessman*
Flemming, Joseph Leo	February 18, 1945	USS *Blessman*
Gordon, Paul Eugene	February 18, 1945	USS *Blessman*
Hilke, Earl Everett	February 18, 1945	USS *Blessman*
Kalman, Louis Emery	February 18, 1945	USS *Blessman*
Maki, Eugene Elmer	February 18, 1945	USS *Blessman*
Mecale, John	February 18, 1945	USS *Blessman*
Rodman, James Emerson	February 18, 1945	USS *Blessman*
Runnels, Adrian	February 18, 1945	USS *Blessman*
Szych, Chester	February 18, 1945	USS *Blessman*
Watkins, Thomas Jackson	February 18, 1945	USS *Blessman*
Willbanks, Herman Delmar	February 18, 1945	USS *Blessman*
Lynch, Francis Joseph	March 30, 1945	Okinawa
Bock, Leonard Joseph Jr.	April 9, 1945	USS *Hopping*
Masden, Charles F.	June 8, 1945	Balikpapan
Frey, Edward Ivan Jr.	January, 19, 1951	Korea
Satterfield, Paul Veston	January, 19, 1951	Korea
Fay, Robert Joseph	October 28, 1965	Vietnam
Gough, Marcell Rene	November 29, 1965	Vietnam

Machen, Billy Wayne	August 19, 1966	Vietnam
Boston, Donald Earl	April 7, 1967	Vietnam
Mann, Daniel McCarthy	April 7, 1967	Vietnam
Neal, Ronald Keith	April 21, 1967	Vietnam
Patrick, Donnie Lee	May 15, 1968	Vietnam
Funk, Leslie Harold Jr.	October 6, 1967	Vietnam
Antone, Frank George	December 23, 1967	Vietnam
Mahner, Lin Albert	May 25, 1969	Vietnam
Nicholas, David Lamprey	October 17, 1969	Vietnam
Wolfe, Richard Ogden	November 30, 1969	Vietnam
Ashton, Curtis Morris	December 27, 1969	Vietnam
Brewton, John Cooke	January 11, 1970	Vietnam
Donnelly, John Joseph III	June 23, 1970	Vietnam
Durlin, John Stewart	June 23, 1970	Vietnam
Gore, James Raymond	June 23, 1970	Vietnam
Solano, Richard John	June 23, 1970	Vietnam
Thomas, Toby Arthur	June 23, 1970	Vietnam
Palma, Luco William	September 18, 1970	Vietnam
Williams, Lawrence C. Jr.	September 18, 1970	Vietnam
Bomar, Frank Willis	December 20, 1970	Vietnam
Riter, James L. Gasman	December 20, 1970	Vietnam
Thames, James Franklin	January 19, 1971	Vietnam
Birky, Harold Edwin	January 30, 1971	Vietnam
Collins, Michael Raymond	March 4, 1971	Vietnam
Moe, Lester James	March 29, 1971	Vietnam
Dry, Melvin Spence	June 6, 1972	Vietnam
Schaufelberger, Albert Arthur III	May 25, 1983	El Salvador
Butcher, Kenneth John	October 23, 1983	Grenada
Morris, Stephen Leroy	October 23, 1983	Grenada
Lundberg, Kevin Erin	October 24, 1983	Grenada
Schamberger, Robert Rudolf	October 24, 1983	Grenada
Connors, John Patrick	December 20, 1989	Panama
McFaul, Donald Lewis	December 20, 1989	Panama

Rodriguez, Isaac Georgetti III	December 20, 1989	Panama
Tilghman, Christopher Chris	December 20, 1989	Panama
Burkhart, Chad Michael	November 24, 2000	Kosovo
Roberts, Neil Christopher	March 5, 2002	Afghanistan
Bourgeois, Matthew Joseph	March 28, 2002	Afghanistan
Retzer, Thomas Eugene	June 26, 2003	Afghanistan
Tapper, David Martin	August 20, 2003	Afghanistan
Ouellette, Brian Joseph	May 29, 2004	Afghanistan
Axelson, Matthew Gene	June 28, 2005	Afghanistan
Dietz, Danny Phillip Jr.	June 28, 2005	Afghanistan
Fontan, Jacques Jules	June 28, 2005	Afghanistan
Healy, Daniel Richard	June 28, 2005	Afghanistan
Kristensen, Erik Samuel	June 28, 2005	Afghanistan
Lucas, Jeffrey Alan	June 28, 2005	Afghanistan
McGreevy, Michael Martin Jr.	June 28, 2005	Afghanistan
Murphy, Michael Patrick	June 28, 2005	Afghanistan
Patton, Shane Eric	June 28, 2005	Afghanistan
Suh, James Erik	June 28, 2005	Afghanistan
Taylor, Jeffrey Scott	June 28, 2005	Afghanistan
Lee, Marc Alan	August 2, 2006	Iraq
Monsoor, Michael Anthony	September 29, 2006	Iraq
Schwedler, Joseph Clark	April 6, 2007	Iraq
Lewis, Jason Dale	July 6, 2007	Iraq
Carter, Mark Thomas	December 11, 2007	Iraq
Hardy, Nathan Hall	February 3, 2008	Iraq
Koch, Michael Eugene	February 4, 2008	Iraq
Harris, Joshua Thomas	August 30, 2008	Afghanistan
Freiwald, Jason Richard	September 11, 2008	Afghanistan
Marcum, John Wayne	September 11, 2008	Afghanistan
Job, Ryan	September 24, 2009	in surgery for wounds sustained in Iraq on August 2, 2006

Brown, Adam Lee	March 18, 2010	Afghanistan
Thomas, Collin Trent	August 18, 2010	Afghanistan
Looney, Brendan John	September 21, 2010	Afghanistan
Miranda, Denis C.	September 21, 2010	Afghanistan
Smith, Adam Olin	September 21, 2010	Afghanistan
Benson, Darrik Carlyle	August 6, 2011	Afghanistan
Bill, Brian Robert	August 6, 2011	Afghanistan
Campbell, Christopher George	August 6, 2011	Afghanistan
Faas, John Weston	August 6, 2011	Afghanistan
Houston, Kevin Arthur	August 6, 2011	Afghanistan
Kelsall, Jonas Benton	August 6, 2011	Afghanistan
Langlais, Louis James	August 6, 2011	Afghanistan
Mason, Matthew David	August 6, 2011	Afghanistan
Mills, Stephen Matthew	August 6, 2011	Afghanistan
Pittman, Jesse Daryl	August 6, 2011	Afghanistan
Ratzlaff, Thomas Arthur	August 6, 2011	Afghanistan
Reeves, Robert James	August 6, 2011	Afghanistan
Robinson, Heath Michael	August 6, 2011	Afghanistan
Spehar, Nicholas Patrick	August 6, 2011	Afghanistan
Tumilson, Jon Thomas	August 6, 2011	Afghanistan
Vaughn, Aaron Carson	August 6, 2011	Afghanistan
Workman, Jason Ray	August 6, 2011	Afghanistan
Nelson, Caleb Andrew	October 1, 2011	Afghanistan

Acknowledgments

Many thanks to my coauthor, Jim Hornfischer, for his tireless efforts while working with me to bring *Service* out of my mind and onto the page. I know it's been a crazy ride, my friend, but you handled it well. I can say without any hesitation that it has been an honor and a privilege not only to collaborate with you on this book, but to call you my friend.

To my teammates: It was the greatest honor to walk beside you both on and off the battlefield. To Task Unit Red Bull: Thanks for keeping me in the circle and trusting me enough to help carry the load—even to the very end, when I could barely carry myself. To the officers and chiefs of Naval Special Warfare: Thank you for allowing me to return to the line and get back some of what I lost in the mountains of Afghanistan in 2005. To the Air Force rescue squadron, the Army Rangers, the Green Berets, and everyone else who pulled me, Mikey, Danny, Axe, and the remains of Turbine 33 off the mountain. I will never forget you. Thank you for risking your own lives and for never giving up on us. May God bless you for all your days.

Many thanks to my Green brother Joe and Civil Affairs Major Clint Hanna for keeping watch over Gulab and setting up the reunion. Those days you gave me with him will hold a place deep in my heart always. Most important,

I would like to thank the Lord for giving me the strength to overcome all adversity and continue to do what I was born to do.

Finally, to my brother: Thank you for walking beside me through everything, and never once leaving my side. FTWTTT.

Bibliography

Bush, George W. *Decision Points*. New York: Crown, 2010.

Charlton, Colonel John. U.S. Department of Defense News Briefing, August 3, 2007. http://www.defense.gov/transcripts/transcript .aspx ?transcriptid=4019.

Couch, Dick. *The Sheriff of Ramadi: Navy SEALs and the Winning of al-Anbar*. Annapolis, Md.: Naval Institute Press, 2008.

Daly, Thomas P. *Rage Company: A Marine's Baptism by Fire*. New York: Wiley, 2010.

Doyle, William. *A Soldier's Dream: Captain Travis Patriquin and the Awakening of Iraq*. New York: NAL/Caliber, 2011.

Kyle, Chris. *American Sniper: The Autobiography of the Most Lethal Sniper in U.S. Military History*. New York: William Morrow, 2012.

Lubin, Andrew. "Ramadi from the Caliphate to Capitalism." *U.S. Naval Institute Proceedings,* April 2008.

MacPherson, Malcolm. *Roberts Ridge*. New York: Delacorte, 2005.

Mansoor, Peter R. *Baghdad at Sunrise: A Brigade Commander's War in Iraq*. New Haven: Yale University Press, 2008.

McWilliams, Timothy S., and Kurtis P. Wheeler, eds. *Al-Anbar Awakening, Volume 1: American Perspectives; U.S. Marines and Counterinsurgency in Iraq, 2004–2009*. Quantico, Va.: Marine Corps University Press, 2009.

Michaels, Jim. *A Chance in Hell: The Men Who Triumphed over Iraq's Deadliest City and Turned the Tide of War*. New York: St. Martin's, 2010.

Montgomery, Gary W., and Timothy S. McWilliams, eds. *Al-Anbar Awakening, Volume 2: Iraqi Perspectives; From Insurgency to Counterinsurgency in Iraq, 2004–2009.* Quantico, Va.: Marine Corps University Press, 2009.

Self, Nate. *Two Wars.* Carol Stream, Ill.: Tyndale, 2008.

Walker, J. B. *Nightcap at Dawn: Soldiers' Counterinsurgency in Iraq.* 2010. http://www.lulu.com/product/ebook/nightcap-at-dawn -soldiers -counterinsurgency/17364118.

Waring, Brett. *Sandy, Earned.* Unpublished manuscript.

About the Authors

Marcus Luttrell became a combat-trained Navy SEAL in 2002 and served in many dangerous Special Operations assignments around the world. He is the author of the #1 *New York Times* bestseller *Lone Survivor* and is a popular corporate and organizational speaker. He lives near Huntsville, Texas.

James D. Hornfischer is the author of the *New York Times* bestseller *Neptune's Inferno: The U.S. Navy at Guadalcanal,* as well as *Ship of Ghosts* and *The Last Stand of the Tin Can Sailors,* which won the Samuel Eliot Morison Award and was a Main Selection of the Book-of-the-Month Club. He lives in Austin, Texas.